CRITICAL INSIGHTS

Brave New World

CRITICAL INSIGHTS

Brave New World

Editor
M. Keith Booker
University of Arkansas in Fayetteville

SALEM PRESS
A Division of EBSCO Information Services, Inc.
Ipswich, Massachusetts

GREY HOUSE PUBLISHING

∞ The paper used in these volumes conforms to the American National Standard for Permanence of Paper for Printed Library Materials, Z39.48-1992 (R1997).

Library of Congress Cataloging-in-Publication Data

Brave new world / editor, M. Keith Booker, University of Arkansas in Fayetteville. -- [First edition].

pages ; cm. -- (Critical insights)

Includes bibliographical references and index.
ISBN: 978-1-61925-238-7

1. Huxley, Aldous, 1894-1963. Brave new world. 2. Huxley, Aldous, 1894-1963--Criticism and interpretation. 3. Dystopias in literature. I. Booker, M. Keith, editor of compilation. II. Series: Critical insights.

PR6015.U9 B653 2014
823/.912

First Printing

PRINTED IN THE UNITED STATES OF AMERICA

Contents ────────────────────────────────

────────────────────────────────

Postmodernism and the Cultural Logic of Dystopian Fiction:
Brave New World and M. T. Anderson's *Feed*,
M. Keith Booker   214

About This Volume

M. Keith Booker

Aldous Huxley's *Brave New World*, first published in 1932, is one of the founding texts of the modern genre of dystopian fiction and one of the most important novels of the twentieth century. *Critical Insights: Brave New World* offers a variety of critical approaches to Huxley's novel. Together, the essays in this volume seek to provide interpretations of the novel from a variety of different perspectives, while placing it within the context of Huxley's own world and tracing its importance and influence up to our own day.

The first section of this volume, "Critical Contexts," contains a number of basic essays that help to provide a fundamental introduction to possible ways of reading *Brave New World* and of understanding it within both its historical and its literary context. The first essay, by Richard Carr, provides an extensive discussion of the British political context of the early 1930s, in which *Brave New World* was produced. Carr demonstrates the extent to which many of the issues addressed in Huxley's text grow directly out of this specific context, as well as out of a concern for the broader and more general concerns in which the text is usually read. In particular, Carr shows the strong impact of Huxley's concern that the centralization of the British state in the quarter century prior to the publication of his book posed a genuine threat to individual liberties, thus making Huxley's attitude in the text appear more conservative than it has typically been perceived.

The next essay, by Gerardo Del Guercio, reviews the critical reception of *Brave New World*, focusing particularly on early responses and also on critical controversies concerning the novel. For example, Del Guercio notes the concerns of some that the novel, in its description of the Savage Reservation, represents Native Americans in stereotypical, even racist ways. Del Guercio also notes some of George Orwell's criticisms of Huxley's novel, including his suspicion that Huxley might have lifted many of his ideas from

Yevgeny Zamyatin's *We* (1924). Ultimately, Del Guercio concludes that some of these controversies are themselves quite instructive, offering insights into the way values, in general, change over time.

Thomas Horan's "Critical Lens" chapter looks at *Brave New World* from the perspective of feminist literary theory. Horan notes the many feminist criticisms of Huxley's novel, which sometimes seem blind to problematic attitudes toward gender in his future dystopian society, even though he provides sophisticated criticisms of other aspects of that society. Noting many of the apparent limitations in Huxley's vision with regard to gender, Horan concludes that considerable room remains for more critical work on Huxley's portrayal of women and other historically marginalized groups, including Jews.

In the "Comparative Analysis" chapter, Jackson Ayres notes the way *Brave New World* and George Orwell's *Nineteen Eighty-Four* (1949) have come to be widely thought of by both scholars and general readers as companion texts that outline terrifying dystopian futures. However, while Ayres notes that this linkage between the two texts is appropriate in many ways, it can sometimes obscure important differences between the two texts. Ayres notes that, apart from the particular targets of their critiques—Huxley is more concerned with the depravities of consumer capitalism, whereas Orwell focuses his attention on totalitarian tendencies in modern politics—the two novels are separated by the authors' ideas about human nature. *Brave New World*, on one hand, presumes an essential human nature that must be safeguarded from perversion and suppression, while, on the other hand, *Nineteen Eighty-Four* suggests that "humanity" itself is a cultural invention that, for better or worse, is largely determined by political structures and arrangements.

The bulk of this volume consists of a series of critical readings of *Brave New World*, beginning with Claeys' discussion of the novel within the context of Bolshevism. Even if *Brave New World* addresses itself primarily to the potential excesses of capitalist society, events in the Soviet Union provided a crucial part of the global political climate of the late 1920s and 1930s and thus were an important part of the background of Huxley's novel. This is especially true given that the project of building socialism in the Soviet Union was an overtly scientific utopian one, as was the fictional project that led to the conditions described in Huxley's novel.

In the next essay, Bradley W. Hart looks at what many perceive to be the most striking aspect of the dystopian society depicted in *Brave New World*: its scientifically-designed manufacture of human beings to fulfill specific roles in society. In particular, Hart places this motif within the context of the twentieth-century eugenics movement, which agitated for the biological improvement of society through selective reproduction—largely through the sterilization of individuals who were deemed "unfit" to reproduce and raise children. Hart notes that Huxley's treatment of the motif can be read largely as a satire of the eugenics movement, but also notes that Huxley's attitude toward the movement was actually quite complex, partly because his brother, Julian, was one of its leaders.

Huxley's treatment of the artificial production of human infants in *Brave New World* also provides the central starting point for the next essay, in which Nicole Fares looks at the rejection of motherhood and maternity in the dystopian society of the text, where the very concept of "mother" is considered embarrassing and obscene. Fares demonstrates that this vision of maternity can be usefully described via the ideas of Judith Butler on the social construction of maternity, with secondary support from Michel Foucault's explorations of the role played by normativity in Western societies. Moreover, while the rejection of maternity in Huxley's World State seems diametrically opposed to the traditional glorification of motherhood in Western societies, Fares argues that both visions are patriarchal constructions that limit the roles available to women.

Josephine A. McQuail follows with another essay that begins with the system of artificial reproduction in *Brave New World*, but uses this motif as an occasion to discuss the relationship of Huxley's text to more general issues related to science in general and biology in particular. Importantly, McQuail concludes that, while Huxley's novel can be read as a warning against the dehumanizing effects of an overly scientific worldview, neither he nor his book were fundamentally opposed to science. While science in *Brave New*

World can be a tool of oppression, science, used properly, can, for Huxley, be a key to liberation.

Katherine Toy Miller's essay, meanwhile, looks at Huxley's figuration of the Savage Reservation, which functions as the major alternative to the scientific society of the World State in *Brave New World.* Miller notes the problematic nature of Huxley's representation of many aspects of Native American culture, while demonstrating that many of his ideas about this culture were derived indirectly, especially via his friend D. H. Lawrence. While Huxley uses Native American culture symbolically, Miller reminds us that the culture he thereby misrepresents is a real one, making that misrepresentation highly problematic.

With the essay by Alexander Charles Oliver Hall, the collection moves into a focus on comparisons between *Brave New World* and more contemporary cultural productions. Hall's essay, in particular, looks at the two major made-for-television film adaptations of *Brave New World*, the three-hour 1980 adaptation, directed by Burt Brinckerhoff, which stays very close to its source in Huxley's novel, and the 1998 adaptation, directed by Leslie Libman and Larry Williams, which takes many more liberties with the source material, including the addition of several elements that do not appear in the original novel at all, although it is less than half as long as the 1980 version. Hall focuses on the utopian potential of Huxley's dystopian text and on the way this potential is reflected in the two adaptations. In particular, he notes the way the Libman and Williams adaptation adds new utopian energies through its reframing of Huxley's original narrative.

Robert Wilson addresses the global nature of *Brave New World*'s dystopian society within the context of the contemporary phenomenon of globalization. He notes that globalization in *Brave New World* is part of a homogenizing process that leads to an oppressive sameness, but also notes the ways various characters seek spaces of marginality from which to challenge this process. He argues that this aspect of the text contains important lessons for our own increasingly homogenized world.

Sean A. Witters continues this focus on contemporary issues by looking at *Brave New World* from the perspective of concerns about the growing level of surveillance, to which individuals are exposed in our contemporary world. While noting that surveillance is not in itself an overt concern of Huxley's text, Witters usefully reads *Brave New World* alongside Suzanne Collins' hugely popular *The Hunger Games* (2008), in which surveillance is very much a key concern. He concludes, in fact, that Huxley's novel anticipates the concerns of Collins' fiction in interesting ways.

Finally, M. Keith Booker's essay compares *Brave New World* to a much more contemporary dystopian novel, M. T. Anderson's *Feed* (2004). Anderson's novel is distinctive for the way its vision of a dystopian future is essentially an extension of the characteristics of our own postmodern world, as described by cultural theorists, such as Fredric Jameson. Booker, demonstrates, however, that Huxley's novel already anticipates many of these same characteristics, a phenomenon that he attributes to the fact that Huxley's novel itself grows so directly out of developments in the evolution of capitalism in the first decades of the twentieth century, developments that would ultimately lead to the historical phase that Jameson sees as "late capitalism," of which postmodernism is the "cultural logic."

Together, these essays provide readers with a useful introduction to the critical issues involved in reading *Brave New World*. They help to establish Huxley's novel as one of the founding texts of the genre of dystopian fiction, they indicate the way the novel responded directly to many contemporary concerns of Huxley's day, and they suggest some of the ways the novel continues to be relevant to our own world and contemporary culture.

THE BOOK
AND
AUTHOR

On *Brave New World*

M. Keith Booker

One of the key phenomena in Western literature of the late nineteenth century was the rise of utopian fictions that envisioned the coming of a better world, presumably fueled in one way or another by the fallout from the Enlightenment. Thus, a text such as Edward Bellamy's *Looking Backward* (1888), from the United States, responded directly to the recent Industrial Revolution with a confident sense that technological progress could ultimately solve both the material and the social problems of the era. Even an opposed text such as William Morris' *News from Nowhere* (1890), which responded directed to Bellamy with skepticism toward technology, still imagined a utopia, this time built on living in harmony with nature but still relying on individuals to behave rationally and in the best interests of themselves and others. The 1930s kicked off with a collapse of Western capitalist economies that triggered widespread economic depression, the confidence of such utopian thinkers had been shattered by a series of events, most notably World War I, which seriously called into question the notion that the rise of scientific rationalism and the concomitant spread of technological progress would necessarily lead to a better world.

Such events are reflected in the widespread sense of crisis that pervades early twentieth-century literature and that can be found, for example, in virtually every work of literary modernism. Meanwhile, by the 1930s, literary works had begun to appear that were built on visions of future societies based more on dystopian nightmares than on utopian dreams. As Tom Moylan puts it, noting that dystopian fiction is a very direct response to real-world events, "Dystopian narrative is largely the product of the terrors of the twentieth century … exploitation, repression, state violence, war, genocide, disease … and the steady depletion of humanity through the buying and selling of everyday life" (xi). This new dystopian literature not only suggested that the future might indeed be *worse* than the present, but also suggested that these baleful dystopian conditions might be triggered precisely by utopian attempts to solve the social and economic problems that were becoming more and more pressing through the first decades of the twentieth century. Early examples, such as E. M. Forster's story "The Machine Stops" (1919), began to set the tone for such dystopian visions, which were first fully realized in Yevgeny Zamyatin's *We* (1924), widely recognized as the first full-length dystopian novel, presenting a cautionary tale of the dangers involved should the utopian project of building socialism in the new Soviet Union go awry. Aldous Huxley then quickly followed, in 1932, with *Brave New World*, which expressed many of the same reservations about consumer capitalism.

We was actually originally published in English, and some (most notably George Orwell) would eventually remark on its possible influence on *Brave New World*, but Huxley had apparently not read it by the time he published his own dystopian masterpiece. By this time, of course, with the memory of the horrors of the war still vivid, the excesses of emergent consumer capitalism in the 1920s had led to depression at the beginning of the 1930s, so Huxley certainly had plenty to react to without recourse to Zamyatin's model. Eventually, the novels of Zamyatin and Huxley would be joined by Orwell's *Nineteen Eighty-Four* (1949) as the three major foundational texts of the modern genre of dystopian fiction, a mode that has become more and more characteristic of Western fiction in the ensuing years. Of the three, Zamyatin's dystopian vision is deeply rooted in a society that is now receding into the past, while Orwell's book is still the best known, largely because it was widely promoted during the Cold War as a warning against the evils of Stalinist communism (even though Orwell himself insisted that it was also a warning against anticommunist excess). But Huxley's novel, with its chilling vision of a hedonistic consumerist "paradise" run amok, leading to intellectual stagnation and emotional sterility, and is probably now the most relevant of these three crucial texts, at least to readers in the relatively affluent Western capitalist countries.

That Huxley's vision should remain so relevant is not surprising given that he was reacting directly to events of the first decades of the twentieth century, which saw an unprecedented, dramatic change in the texture of everyday life. Swept away was the primarily rural, agricultural lifestyle that had been dominant in the West for hundreds of years. Replacing it was an urban modernity, in which the majority lived in cities and began to enjoy the fruits of a consumerist explosion that saw the introduction of a wide array of new commercial products, which caused a revolution in the idea that life could be made better and easier by the mere consumption of products. Part of this new lifestyle was an increase in the time available for recreation, and one of the great innovations of the consumerist revolution of the first three decades of the twentieth century was the rise of an entirely new popular culture industry, designed to meet the needs of an increasingly urban population with growing amounts of leisure time. Of course, technological innovation was at work in this revolution as well, as entirely new entertainment media (first radio, then film) became popular during this period, while other media (such as phonograph records and even printed books) underwent technological improvements that made them much more commercially viable. Meanwhile, all of these material changes were accompanied by, or in some cases led to, substantial social changes as well. For one thing, all of the new innovations that accompanied the rise of consumer capitalism had more benefits for some than for others, deepening the class-based rift between the rich and the poor that had long been the most troubling aspect of capitalism in general. For another, First Wave feminism, combined with new scientific insights into sexuality on the part of such professional experts as Sigmund Freud and Havelock Ellis, had ushered in the new century with demands for the radical reconsideration of gender roles and of the role of sexuality in modern life.

Brave New World responds quite directly to all of these historical phenomena. For example, the specter of World War I clearly hovers over the book, which specifies that the World State came into being in response to a cataclysmic "Nine Year's War," in which horrific biological weapons (anthrax bombs) were used to produce massive casualties, clearly echoing the use of such technological innovations as poisonous gases and aerial bombing in World War I. This war, we are told, began in the year "A. F. 141" (35), with the "A. F." clearly standing for "Anno Ford," echoing the "Anno Domini" designation that Western societies had long used to date their calendars since the birth of Christ. With American industrialist Henry Ford worshipped like a god in this society, dates are measured from his birth (in 1863), which would place the beginning of the Nine Years' War in 2004. We also learn that this war, traumatic enough in itself, was followed by "the great Economic Collapse" (36), an event that clearly echoes the recent onset of economic depression in Western capitalist economies in Huxley's own world, which was marked especially in the U.S. by the stock market collapse of October 29, 1929 and which had spread throughout the Western capitalist world by 1932. The war and the Great Economic Collapse left the future world of Huxley's book with "a choice between World Control and destruction" (36). So the World State was initiated in order to save civilization, and its policies of enforced tranquility were designed to ensure that the kind of soaring passions, which had led to the war, could never again occur.

   Brave New World, of course, focuses on the dehumanizing consequences of this overall policy, suggesting that, by limiting human passions, and by particularly seeking to mute the human desire to explore new ground in areas, such as science and literature, the World State has achieved its objective of ongoing peace at the price of numbing the hearts and minds of its population. Numerous practices are in effect to ensure that no one is ever unhappy, but no one ever experiences joy, either, and much of the text is designed to explore the consequences of this situation. Of course, the text focuses primarily on characters—such as Bernard Marx and Humboldt Watson and, ultimately, John the Savage—who do not quite fit in with the conformist tendencies of this society, which tends to cast a critical light on it. At every step of the way, however, Huxley deftly creates tensions and leaves open the possibility of alternative interpretations. The World State may be clearly dystopian, but it contains strong utopian energies as well, and it has, in fact, solved many of the problems of Huxley's contemporary world. Every aspect of the text, then, must be looked at from both sides, as a dystopian critique of certain negative directions, in which Huxley saw his own society moving, and as a utopian vision of possible alternatives.

The recent historical phenomenon, to which Huxley most directly responds, is the recent rise of consumer capitalism, which, as William Leach has so convincingly outlined in *Land of Desire*, transformed the nature of day-to-day life in the Western world between the 1890s and 1930s. The economy of the World State depends heavily on consumerism, and individuals in this world are encouraged to spend freely. For example, one of the slogans that passes for education in this society is the mantra, "ending is better than mending" (37), which urges consumers to throw away any item that breaks and simply buy a new one. On the other hand, the Controllers who govern this highly administered society know all too well that consumerism is best based not on fear, but on desire. So they have learned, following the strategies of the new discourse of advertising that had grown up in Huxley's world as a crucial part of consumer capitalism, not to demand that consumers buy things, but simply to manipulate them so that they *want* to buy things.

Huxley does not seem to have been entirely aware (as few people were in 1932) that this kind of irresponsible consumption can lead to serious consequences for the natural environment, and concerns, such as pollution and global warming, are not a part of his dark vision of the future. Indeed, consumerism in the World State has a clear upside in that consumption does seem to provide a modicum of satisfaction; on the other hand, consumerist satisfaction must always be fleeting and incomplete, and the desire of consumers to acquire more and more must never be quenched, lest the economy stagnate. Meanwhile, what we see of the lives of individuals in the World State suggests that the economy is thriving and that individuals live in a relative state of affluence. Goods exist for them to consume, and they have the money to buy them. At the same time, we see very little of the lives of this intensely class-differentiated society, and it is safe to assume that the lowly epsilons and gammas have far less in the way of material wealth than the upper-class alphas and betas, who are the main characters of the book. Then again, those classes have been conditioned to have lower expectations and to remain happy with their lot, whatever it might be.

For many readers, the most striking aspect of *Brave New World* is the way in which individuals are literally manufactured in factories, using principles of Fordist assembly-line production. This aspect of the text directly addresses specific contemporary issues, such as the eugenics movement, which sought to use scientific principles to improve the genetic quality of the human race in a move that many found problematic, if not downright chilling. However, this aspect of *Brave New World* is also highly allegorical, suggesting among other things the general dehumanizing effects of modern industrial capitalism. After all, Karl Marx had suggested, nearly a century earlier, that one of the central consequences of capitalism was to turn people into things, and the synchronized factory production systems pioneered by Ford had only exacerbated this effect by forcing human workers to become little more than cogs in the factory machinery, a development that would be captured brilliantly on film only a few years after Huxley published *Brave New World* with the tribulations suffered by Charlie Chaplin's Tramp in *Modern Times* (1936). In this film, the Tramp must not only synchronize his actions with the factory machinery, but he literally gets caught in the gears of that machinery, passing through them very much like film passing through a projector.

Of course, that famous scene is indicative of the way in which *Modern Times* serves not only as a commentary on the dehumanizing consequences of modern industrial capitalism in general, but in particular on what Chaplin saw as the growing industrialization and commercialization of the filmmaking process. *Modern Times* was Chaplin's farewell to silent film and his acknowledgement that market forces were demanding that he move into sound, catching him up in the new technology, much as the Tramp is caught up in the gears of that factory machinery. Film, Chaplin seems to be saying, was becoming more of a business than an art, with box office receipts seen as more important than artistic success. Film, for Chaplin, had been swept up, like everything else, in the wave of consumerism

---

that flooded Western societies in the first decades of the twentieth century.

This notion of the complicity of film—and, by extension, popular culture as a whole—in consumerist conformism, is one of the central themes of *Brave New World*. Citizens of the World State are kept in a permanently pacified condition by a combination of what would come, in the 1960s, to be widely referred to as "sex, drugs, and rock and roll," seen by those who practiced them as countercultural activities that were inherently subversive because of the way they offended conventional bourgeois sensibilities. It might be noted, incidentally, that Huxley's later novel *Island* (1962), which seems to counsel the use of consciousness-altering drugs as a mode of mind expansion, was extremely popular with the counterculture of the 1960s. However, *Brave New World* is much more skeptical of the possibilities offered by soma, the drug of choice in its dystopian future. Soma has the advantage of having few unpleasant side effects, but rather than expanding consciousness, it would seem to narrow it, having an essentially numbing effect that helps the citizens of the World State enjoy their material comforts without asking too many questions. If, for Marx, religion was the opiate of the masses, encouraging them to blindly follow an authority that did not work to their advantage, the opiate of Huxley's essentially religion-free society is, well, an opiate that keeps the mind of individuals too befogged to be capable of critical thinking, though it must be said that it does keep them happy.

One might compare this concept to the original *Star Trek* episode "This Side of Paradise" (March 2, 1967), in which the *Enterprise* travels to the planet Omicron Ceti III with the expectation that deadly radiation has wiped out the human colony there. Instead, they find the colonists living in unnaturally perfect health amid what seems to be a utopian paradise of peace, plenty, and tranquility, a situation that turns out to be due to the effects of strange plants, whose spores give those exposed to them both perfect physical health and complete mental contentment. Even the normally stoic half-Vulcan Spock is affected, causing him to relax his usual logical exterior and even to fall in love. Eventually, the entire crew of the *Enterprise* (with the exception of Captain Kirk) is affected, until Kirk manages to intervene and end the effect. The crew returns to the ship, and the colonists agree to move to a new planet free of both deadly radiation and healing spores, so that they can resume their struggle to build a better new world rather than simply live in passive tranquility. For Kirk, after all, struggle and strife are central to the very definition of what it means to be human. Spock, on the other hand, is not quite so sure, pointing out that the situation on Omicron Ceti III was not entirely bad. "For the first time in my life," he notes, "I was happy."

The drug soma, so crucial to the functioning of the society of the World State in *Brave New World*, plays very much the same role as the spores of this *Star Trek* episode. While soma apparently has no physical healing effects, Huxley stipulates that the drug has no harmful physical side-effects, and it does seem to bring mental and emotional peace and happiness to those who take it. Granted, the drug removes a certain amount of ambition and creativity, but with all basic needs provided for, it is not unequivocally clear that ambition and creativity are really needed in this society. And, of course, that drug use would have a certain utopian dimension in *Brave New World* is perhaps not surprising, considering the positive figuration given to drugs in *Island* thirty years later. One thing that is clear in the earlier novel, however, is that popular culture also functions as a sort of drug and, this time, as one that substitutes for something that might potentially be much more fulfilling. Indeed, in many ways, the most one-sided critique embedded in *Brave New World* involves its treatment of popular culture, which is almost entirely negative. The popular culture of the World State is intentionally impoverished and debased; further, it is the *only* culture, with the kinds of artworks that were once considered "high" art (such as the plays of Shakespeare, to which this popular culture is frequently contrasted in *Brave New World*) now having been completely banned to the general public.

Huxley's book, of course, was written at a time when many were becoming concerned that the emergent film industry (often associated with immigrants and the working class) might have negative moral and intellectual consequences. For example, Huxley's book was written in the midst of a four-year study sponsored by the Payne Fund of New York City, beginning in the spring of 1929 and based on the assumption that movies have a powerful and probably negative impact on young audiences. Conducted by a large network of psychologists, sociologists, and educational specialists, the Payne studies produced a number of research reports as well as summaries intended for popular audiences. One of the latter was Henry James Forman's 1934 *Our Movie Made Children*, which concluded that movies have tremendous educational potential, but that this potential was not being effectively utilized for the public good. Indeed, Forman argues that the film industry as currently run (mostly by, he hints with what may be thinly disguised anti-Semitism, "questionable characters") was "extremely likely to create a haphazard, promiscuous and undesirable national consciousness" (140). Forman argues that the minds of young children are "unmarked slates" that can be written upon by movies for good or ill.

What is interesting about Forman's analysis is that he happily supports the notion of using films to indoctrinate children: he just doesn't feel that the film industry as currently constituted (i.e., dominated by Jews) is necessarily indoctrinating children with the right values. Huxley, in *Brave New World*, goes further, questioning the notion of using popular culture for indoctrination at all, while at the same time acknowledging the growing potential of popular culture for just that purpose, especially with ongoing improvements in technology. Forman and others were concerned precisely because such improvements were making film more and more attractive to young audiences and presumably more and more able to influence them. *Brave New World* was written in this same context, in the wake of the rapid rise of film as a new entertainment medium, including the then still-recent extension of film to include integrated sound, the technological development that so troubled Chaplin. Alfred Hitchcock's 1929 film *Blackmail*, for example, is widely regarded as the first British sound film, and Huxley merely projects this technological innovation to other senses with his vision of the "feelies," which extend the experience of film-viewing to *all* the senses. In so doing, of course, the new medium enfolds audiences completely, cutting them off from any external experience that might interfere with the intentionally numbing effect of the feelies themselves. Like the films of the time, these feelies are mostly experienced in theaters d0esigned for the purpose, which enhances the immersive experience. However, other technologies (echoing radio, which had really only become a common, everyday experience in the 1920s) are available to deliver a constant stream of mindless, but pleasing entertainment to all citizens, no matter where they might go. And, of course, this popular culture is supplemented by the "hypnopaedic conditioning," through which the official messages of this culture are drilled into the brains of individual citizens even as they sleep, assuring that there is no escape, even in sleep from the nonstop flow of official ideology. Education and entertainment are, in fact, merged, both designed to further the desire of the state to keep individuals content with the status quo.

Even personal relationships in this future dystopia are part of this same project, becoming just as thoroughly commodified as everything else in this ultimate consumerist society. On the plus side, the World State of the book has removed strict Victorian taboos against sexual activity, thus eliminating what Freud and others had identified, at the beginning of the twentieth century, as a key source of personal unhappiness in the modern world. Indeed, the policies of the Worlds State can, in many ways, be read virtually as a direct response to Freud's most important late work, *Civilization and Its Discontents*, first published in German in 1930, just two years before *Brave New World*. Here, Freud outlines a rather gloomy theory that civilization, in order to function, must force individuals to cooperate and thus must place restraints on the fulfillment of individual desire (sexual and otherwise), leading to a situation in which civilization, by its very nature, will tend to make people unhappy. By removing most restraints on the fulfillment of sexual desire, the World State would seem to be designed to overcome this difficulty, meanwhile using its extensive programs of genetic design and psychological conditioning to trick individuals into believing that there are no restraints on the fulfillment of their other desires as well. The World State seems almost custom-designed to overcome the difficulties noted by Freud, producing a genuinely happy population, not by repressing desire, but by managing it.

This aspect of Huxley's future world thus has a strong utopian dimension, producing an environment that is conducive to human happiness in ways that real-world societies have never been. On the other hand, the lifting of sexual repression in this society has a dark side as well, and one of its central motivations is the production of an unrestrained and officially endorsed heterosexual promiscuity that turns sexual relations into a recreational sport, though homosexual conduct seems to be absent altogether (a fact that can be explained either by the society's demands for conformity or by the simple fact that, in 1932, homosexuality was still quite often left out of discussions of new sexual morés). With sexual relations now entirely superficial, a matter of entertainment rather than emotion, marriage and the nuclear family have been swept away, for better or worse. But this conventional social unit has not really been replaced by anything better. The basic social unit is now the individual, and individuals are prevented in a variety of ways from developing loyalties or attachments to any group larger than themselves, with the exception of the entire World State itself, to which all are expected to show the ultimate loyalty. Meanwhile, that these superficial relationships are part and parcel of the consumerist mentality of this society can be seen by the fact that its central motto governing interpersonal relationships is "Every one belongs to every one else, after all," suggesting the way in which individuals are encouraged to view other individuals strictly as commodities (35).

Such advertising-style slogans permeate this society, promulgating its official ideology, while, at the same time (in a motif that is quite frequently found in dystopian fiction), leading to an impoverishment of language that makes it difficult to even formulate ideas outside of that ideology. Within the text, of course, a seeming alternative to the official policies of the World State is presented in the form of the plays of Shakespeare, which presumably involve a richness of language that stands in stark contrast to the advertising-speak of the World State, allowing, among other things, the expression of precisely the kind of strong emotions that the State seeks to prevent, while also revolving around deeply emotional attachments among the characters. Given this situation, it should come as no surprise that Shakespeare (and most other classic literature) has been banned from popular consumption in this future world, although the official authorities seem to recognize the value of Shakespeare's works in the way they have been privately preserved for consumption by elite individuals, such as World Controller Mustapha Mond.

Importantly, though, Huxley refuses to present Shakespeare (or the other great works of Western art and literature) as an automatic cure for the dehumanization of life in the World State. Thus, John the Savage, who has grown up with the works of Shakespeare, but reads them naïvely and uncritically, spouts the lines of the Bard in a way that makes them little different from the advertising-style slogans that dominate the culture of the World State. Indeed, John's use of Shakespeare, if anything, would seem to provide support for the ban on such works in the World State: far from providing solace, the words of Shakespeare seem to make John *more* unhappy and *less* able to cope with reality because he lacks the resources to interpret or apply them properly. Thus, while art and literature often stand as antidotes to dystopian repression (see, for example, the role of books in general in Ray Bradbury's 1953 dystopian classic *Fahrenheit 451*, or the role of poetry in Jean-Luc Godard's 1965 dystopian film *Alphaville*), Huxley shows a sophisticated awareness that this opposition is not simple and that the works of a writer, such as Shakespeare, do not automatically shatter consumerist mentalities—and would not automatically produce a preferable alternative even if they did shatter such mentalities.

The dumbing down of culture in the World State thus consists not merely in the elimination of great literature, but in the creation of a world in which that literature is no longer really relevant in the first place. In this sense, the text addresses very much the same concerns as T. S. Eliot's classic modernist poem *The Waste Land* ten years earlier. Many observers at the time were, in fact, concerned that the onward march of capitalist modernization was creating a cultural climate that was inimical to genuine literature, or even to genuine humanity. It should come as no surprise, then, that *Brave New World* has had such staying power and that a text so rooted in the issues of its contemporary world still seems so relevant more than eighty years after its initial publication. After all, these same basic concerns have only become more urgent in those intervening eighty years, and a whole body of dystopian literature—much of it directly influenced by *Brave New World*—has arisen during that period, making the vision of Huxley's text seem more and more familiar to us. Indeed, while the tribulations of the 1930s may have slowed the reception of Huxley's text—British dystopian fiction of the decade was dominated by anti-fascist dystopias, such as Katharine Burdekin's *Swastika Night* (1937), for example—the direction of global history after World War II has been very much in the direction Huxley warned against at the beginning of the 1930s.

Indeed, while it was Orwell's *Nineteen Eighty-Four* that did the most to make dystopian fiction a popular genre after World War II, *Brave New World* remained a major influence on other writers in the genre, and all of the major critical discussions of the dystopian genre that have arisen in the past few decades have identified *Brave New World* as a central text, further solidifying its position at the heart of the genre. Booker, in particular, has identified *Brave New World* as the founding text of the "bourgeois" dystopia that is aimed at a critique of capitalism, as opposed to Zamyatin's *We* as the founding "communist" dystopia.

Huxley himself helped to revive interest in *Brave New World* immediately after the war with the commentary contained in his foreword to a 1946 reprinting of the book. He then added an even more important commentary with his look back at many of the ideas of the original book in *Brave New World Revisited*, first published in 1958, then republished together with the original novel in a 1965 edition that has become the most often cited edition of the novel over the years. In particular, Huxley in the latter, with the benefit of more than a quarter century of hindsight, examines the accuracy of his vision of the future and concludes, with considerable regret, that the world is approaching his dystopian vision far more rapidly than he could have imagined it would. Now that more than an additional half century has passed, we can only say that the world continues to careen ever more rapidly toward Huxley's vision.

Works Cited

Booker, M. Keith. *The Dystopian Impulse in Modern Literature: Fiction as Social Criticism*. Westport, CT: Greenwood Press, 1994.

Forman, Henry James. *Our Movie Made Children*. New York: Macmillan, 1934.

Freud, Sigmund. *Civilization and Its Discontents*. Trans. James Strachey. New York: Norton, 1961.

Huxley, Thomas. *Brave New World*. 1932. *Brave New World & Brave New World Revisited*. New York: Harper Perennial, 1965.

Leach, William R. *Land of Desire: Merchants, Power, and the Rise of a New American Culture*. New York: Pantheon, 1993.

Moylan, Tom. *Scraps of the Untainted Sky: Science Fiction, Utopia, Dystopia*. Boulder, CO: Westview Press, 2000.

Biography of Aldous Huxley

M. Keith Booker

Born in Godalming, Surrey, England, on July 26, 1894, Aldous Leonard Huxley was a member of one of England's most prominent intellectual families. He also went on to become one of the most important English writers of the twentieth century, though he was also important as a social and philosophical commentator—and though he spent the last twenty-six years of his life living in the United States. Huxley's father, Leonard Huxley, was a successful writer and educator, while Aldous's mother, Julia née Arnold, was the niece of the great critic and poet Matthew Arnold, one of the towering figures of nineteenth-century British culture. Aldous's brother, Julian Huxley, and half-brother, Andrew Huxley, were prominent biologists; Julian was also a leading figure in the twentieth-century eugenics movement and achieved such success that he was eventually knighted by the queen. Finally, Aldous and Julian were the grandsons of well-known naturalist Thomas Henry Huxley, known as "Darwin's Bulldog" for his fierce advocacy of Charles Darwin's theory of evolution.

Aldous Huxley was himself interested in biology as a child and, for a time, considered a career in biology or medicine, though an illness in his teens temporarily led to a partial blindness that both curtailed his career plans in that area and kept him from military service in World War I. However, after attending the prestigious Eton College preparatory school, his eyesight recovered sufficiently for him to study English literature at Balliol College, Oxford, graduating with first-class honors. He would, nevertheless, be plagued with vision problems the remainder of his life, though the exact seriousness of these problems remains a matter of dispute.

Huxley published a minor volume of poetry in 1916, but pursued a variety of early career possibilities, including a time working as a teacher of French at Eton College, where one of his students was a young Eric Blair, who would go on to change his name to George

Orwell and become a writer whose work would be much associated with Huxley's. In particular, Orwell's *Nineteen Eighty-Four* (1949) would join Huxley's *Brave New World* as two of the most important founding texts of modern dystopian fiction. Huxley was reportedly ill suited to teaching, though, and seemed no better suited for the bureaucratic work he did at the British Air ministry in 1918. In 1919, he accepted a position on the staff of the distinguished *Athenaeum* literary magazine, which had been in publication since 1838, but was then being reorganized to try to reflect contemporary changes in the world of British letters. He remained on the staff there until 1921, when the publication was again reorganized, folded into its younger and now more successful competitor, *The Nation*. That same year, however, saw the publication of Huxley's first novel, *Crome Yellow* (1921), which launched the career that would make him arguably the most important figure in British literature in the 1920s.

Crome Yellow is a satire of the British upper-class lifestyle Huxley observed during World War I, when he was working as a farm laborer at Garsington Manor, home of Lady Ottoline Morrell. This work, performed in lieu of the military service for which he was deemed unfit due to his eye problems, helped (along with his own family connections) to put him into contact with some of England's leading intellectual figures, including Bertrand Russell and Clive Bell. *Crome Yellow* is a comedy of manners set during a house party at the Crome estate, clearly modeled on Garsington. While it is primarily concerned with satirizing the pretentious behavior of the members of England's upper classes, the novel also includes one character who prefigures *Brave New World* by describing his vision of a world of the future, in which sexuality will be freed of its reproductive function and will be taken over by a rationally designed system of incubators to produce new infants as needed by society.

Huxley and his wife, the former Maria Nys (a war refugee from Belgium whom he had met while at Garsington), spent a great deal of time during the 1920s in Italy, where Huxley frequently saw his friend D. H. Lawrence, perhaps his closest associate among other prominent British writers. The influence of Lawrence's eccentric, but largely right-wing political views on the generally more liberal-minded Huxley is not entirely clear. However, Lawrence had spent time in New Mexico, and his observations on the Native American cultures he observed there were clearly a major source for Huxley's representation of the Savage Reservation of *Brave New World,* Huxley himself not having visited America at that time. Lawrence died in 1930, and Huxley edited the collected edition of his friend's letters, which was published in 1933, including Huxley's defense of Lawrence's importance as a writer.

By this time, Huxley had published several more novels, as his literary reputation grew throughout the 1920s. *Antic Hay* (1923), set in London, again satirizes the English upper classes. Set in the years just following World War I, it includes an especially liberal sprinkling of characters from the cultural and intellectual elite. Their conversations constitute a comic version of many of the key debates of the day, while at the same time suggesting that these elite characters might not always have any idea what they are talking about.

Antic Hay was followed by the relatively minor novel *Those Barren Leaves* (1925), which again satirizes the pretentions of the cultural elite. Huxley's next novel, *Point Counter Point* (1928), is somewhat more serious and is regarded by many as the pinnacle of his achievement as a literary artist. A complex and elaborate work, this novel draws upon a much broader cross-section of English society, rather than simply focusing on the elite classes who had populated Huxley's earlier novels. It is notable, among other things, for its inclusion (and criticism) of the Brotherhood of British Freemen, a right-wing paramilitary group whose ideas have much in common with fascism.

Brave New World, which followed in 1932, is less elaborate in a literary sense than *Point Counter Point,* but it further extends Huxley's range, moving him, for the first time, outside the realm of contemporary British society, many aspects of which he had perhaps captured more accurately than any writer of the 1920s. However, though set more than 600 years in the future, *Brave New World,* in many ways, still represents essentially an extrapolation from contemporary British society, itself at that time caught up in the throes of an emergent consumer capitalism that had led to a catastrophic depression, resulting in widespread skepticism about whether capitalism was really the best basis for a modern society.

Brave New World would go on to become one of the most widely read novels of the twentieth century, and it is certainly the work on which Huxley's ongoing reputation as an important author most depends. Huxley's next novel, *Eyeless in Gaza* (1936), narrates in a complex, non-chronological fashion, the life story of British socialite Anthony Beavis, at the same time, providing a chronicle of British life in the first decades of the twentieth century. Shortly after its publication, Huxley and his family moved to the United States, where Huxley would reside until his death. His repeated applications for U.S. citizenship were, however, denied because— now a committed pacifist—he refused to pledge to take up arms to defend the United States if needed.

Settling in Southern California, Huxley pursued a career as a Hollywood screenwriter, but like many other prominent writers who flocked to Hollywood, achieved only very limited success. His attempt at writing a screen adaptation of *Brave New World*, for example, was never produced. The novels written in the U.S.— including *After Many a Summer* (1939), *Time Must Have a Stop* (1944), *Ape and Essence* (1948), *The Genius and the Goddess* (1955), and *Island* (1962)—were also generally less successful than his earlier ones and are, as a group, held in lower regard by literary scholars than is his earlier work. However, at least two of these later novels bear direct thematic comparison to *Brave New World*. *Ape and Essence*, for example, is another dystopian satire, this time aimed at militarization and warmongering. Though less effective than *Brave New World*, this work, which features a nuclear holocaust, was one of the first major works to envision the potential disastrous consequences of the Cold War nuclear arms race. A further speculative fiction novel, *Island* (1962), is a largely a utopian narrative, in which more successful and humane methods have been found to achieve the ideal social conditions that were a goal of the World State in *Brave New* World. These methods include Eastern mysticism, drug use, and sexuality as keys to enlightenment and discovery, characteristics that understandably made the novel a favorite of the 1960s counterculture that was still in its infancy at the time of the novel's publication.

The thematic emphasis of *Island* is indicative of Huxley's own personal interests during his years in the United States, including an enthusiastic endorsement of the use of psychedelic drugs (including peyote, mescaline, and LSD) that led him to ask, as his dying request, to be injected with LSD in his final moments of life. That request, incidentally, was granted. Meanwhile, his interest in such drugs was part and parcel of his devoted search for alternative modes of consciousness, a search that, in the latter years of his life, was particularly dominated by his extensive interest in Eastern mysticism—an interest that would also come to be reflected in the concerns of many involved in the 1960s counterculture. Indeed, by the time that counterculture began to rise, Huxley was already a famous figure for many of his ideas, some of which are expressed in a well-known 1958 television interview with journalist Mike Wallace.

Soon after his arrival in the United States, Huxley, who had already been introduced into the Upanishad-centered Eastern philosophy known as Vedanta, became friends with the prominent Indian-born mystic philosopher Jiddu Krishnamurti, whose teachings he greatly admired. Huxley also joined the circle of followers surrounding the Hindu Vedantist teacher Swami Prabhavananda. As Huxley's own philosophical ideas and interest in spiritualism began to mature, he wrote a highly popular text designed to introduce Western audiences to the teachings of renowned mystics around the world. This work, *The Perennial Philosophy* (1945), was essentially an anthology of brief passages from spiritualist thinkers of various kinds, accompanied by Huxley's own brief commentaries. It drew considerable attention and was, for many readers in the West, their first introduction to many of the thinkers included in the book. It also garnered largely positive reviews, though many reviewers were highly skeptical of its perceived gullibility in accepting the truth of various paranormal claims.

Much of Huxley's interest in such topics was nurtured by his extensive participation in Swami Prabhavananda's Vedanta Society of Southern California, which began in 1939 and continued until Huxley's death. Among other things, Huxley put his writing skills to use in the service of the society, as when he wrote the introduction to its edition of the *Bhagavad Gita* in 1944. Meanwhile, between 1941 and 1960, Huxley contributed nearly fifty articles to the society's journal, *Vedanta and the West*, also serving on the journal's editorial board.

During his career, Huxley also published a number of volumes of short stories. He was particularly important as an essayist, and over twenty volumes of his essays have been published. Huxley died on November 22, 1963, the same day as important British fantasy and science fiction writer C. S. Lewis, a coincidence that no doubt would have received more media attention had it not been for the fact that this attention was focused primarily on the assassination of U. S. President John F. Kennedy, which occurred on this same day.

CRITICAL
CONTEXTS

Huxley's Changing Homeland: Politics and the Planned Society in Britain, 1906–1931_____

Richard Carr

Brave New World is clearly, in many ways, a perspective on a future dystopia, but, as this chapter shows, it also reflected the changing nature of contemporary politics in Aldous Huxley's homeland of Great Britain. Whilst much attention understandably has been given to Huxley's view of both American capitalism and Soviet communism, the encroachment of the British state into areas unimaginable in the nineteenth century, along with the veneration politicians of left and right were enjoying, provided him with significant contemporary context for his output. Mussolini's Italy and Stalin's Russia were held in high regard by many mainstream British thinkers, and this worried a varied cast of anti-totalitarians, from the Austrian émigré economist F.A. Hayek to the many-time Conservative Prime Minister Stanley Baldwin. The fact that one of the leading 'pro-planning' politicians of the interwar period was Harold Macmillan—who walked many of the same educational paths as Huxley—lends a neat symmetry to considerations of Huxley and the British planners. Whilst Huxley, it must be said, sometimes denied following politics in any avid sense, this was something he conceded was only a half-truth. Writing to his brother shortly after leaving England for Italy in 1923, he argued that, "I try to disinterest myself from politics; but really, when things are in the state they are, one can't help feeling a little concerned about them" (Smith 222). It was this concern, the political context in which it was held, and how British politicians reacted to *Brave New World* that form the basis for this chapter.

Like many leading Britons of this—or any—era Huxley was schooled at Eton College in Windsor. A few months before the young Huxley travelled to Eton, a reforming new Liberal Government was swept to power in Westminster with a thumping majority of one hundred-twenty five seats. The 1906 Liberal government in Britain brought in several interventionist policies designed to alleviate the plight of the poor. These included labour exchanges to provide hubs of information for local jobs, compulsory health insurance for thirteen million low-paid workers, and unemployment insurance for professions where employment was largely seasonal. These reforms changed Britain for the better, and still are almost universally lauded across the political spectrum. But they also involved a degree of involvement by the state that was rather alien to the British tradition at the time. The New Liberalism stressed the use of wealth taxation to fund measures to alleviate working class struggle, whereas the same party fifty years earlier had been arguing for generally *lower* levels of taxation. A commission into Britain's Poor Laws—the previous rather ad hoc method of welfare dispersal—split into so-called 'minority' and 'majority' factions, with the former arguing that the state needed to do more and the latter contending that any action from the state would simply displace private sector activity and thereby lower wages, making things worse. What government could and should do was certainly a live issue in Huxley's youth.

The 1906 administration fundamentally changed the way British politics worked. In 1906, public spending as a percentage of GDP, i.e., total output, was around fifteen percent. By 1910, this more than tripled to 50.3 percent (to drop to 30.2 percent by the time Huxley emigrated in 1923). According to the website www.ukpublicspending.co.uk, public expenditure rose fourfold from £308.5 million in 1906 to almost £1.4 billion by the time *Brave New World* was published in 1932. This latter figure no doubt was exacerbated by Britain's war-debt payments to her former allies after 1918, but it also reflected a shift in attitudes of what a good government should do, and where this action should emanate from. Local government expenditure exceeded that of the central government for the last time in British history in 1914. Huxley was no doubt thinking wider than Whitehall-municipality relations, but he did touch on this broad phenomenon in the foreword to *Brave New World*: "unless we choose to decentralize…. We have only two alternatives to choose from: either a number of national, militarized totalitarianisms…or else one supranational totalitarianism" (xxi).

At Eton, Huxley first encountered Harold Macmillan, then a fellow pupil and subsequently Britain's Conservative Prime Minister between 1957 and 1963. Macmillan—later widely described/ derided as a stuffy old gentleman—appears, at first glance, quite the contrast from the meditating, drug using, and very much new wave Huxley. Yet the two had much in common. After Eton, both would go on to study at Balliol College, Oxford. And both would discuss issues of planning throughout the 1920s and 1930s—Macmillan from parliament, and Huxley through the written word. The one major difference would be their respective experiences of the First World War, with Macmillan performing active service and receiving three bullet wounds for his troubles, whilst Huxley was rendered unable to fight by his keratitis. Given his hatred of war, this was a blessing in disguise. And though he hadn't suffered Macmillan's fate of spending an entire day lying wounded in a slit trench, it is not so hard to envisage Huxley taking the similar decision to read the classical playwright Aeschylus in the original Greek to help numb the pain.

Whether at home or abroad during the conflict, however, one could hardly fail to notice British society again changing. Fighting a total, global war necessitated further expansion of state apparatus. The Defence of the Realm Act gave the state the power to requisition land or buildings needed for the war effort, to limit the opening hours permitted to pubs, and to allow breweries to water down beer. More seriously, it imposed state censorship, which allowed the imprisonment of anti-war protestors, such as Bertrand Russell— an associate of Huxley. The press, as World War I historian Adrian Gregory notes, provided a framework in which stories of German atrocities—some no doubt true, but vastly inflated—became *the* truth: "Most British people, by as early as the middle of September 1914, had no doubt in their minds that Germany bore responsibility for the war" (Gregory 68). Much of this emerged from bottom-up gossip rather than top-down imposition—with stories heard from "a friend of a friend" of crimes committed by the German army becoming accepted truths as many more nuanced accounts either fell victim to government censorship or were simply deemed unprintable. War began a culture where alternate narratives were hardly welcome.

It is not so hard to read the Pavlovian overtones of *Brave New World* from such an atmosphere. And certainly Huxley's later foreword to the book—and not, of course, to say his general pacifism—suggested that he did not approve of such jingoism:

> For the last thirty years there have been no conservatives; there have only been nationalistic radicals of the right and nationalistic radicals of the left. The last conservative statesman was the fifth Marquess of Lansdowne; and when he wrote a letter to *The Times*, suggesting that the First World War should be concluded with a compromise, as most of the wars of the eighteenth century had been, the editor of that once conservative journal refused to print it…with the consequences we all know…the ruin of Europe and all but universal famine (xlvi).

This view that the Great War was dysgenic to the British aristocracy sometimes is slightly dismissed by political historians, and exaggerated it no doubt can be. But it is worth outlining some recently analyzed statistics. One in five Etonians who fought in the Great War died (approaching double the national casualty rate of one in eight), with one in three winners of the Newcastle Prize for Classics also making the ultimate sacrifice (Seldon and Walsh 239). Huxley would not have been the only former Etonian to be affected by the loss of friends during the war, with future politicians like Alfred Duff Cooper and scientists such as J.B.S. Haldane in varying ways influenced by the loss of so many former classmates.

Tragedy apart, war also intensified the industrial process. Henry Ford's Model T had rolled off the production line in 1909—the same year Marconi received the Nobel Prize for his work in pioneering radio communication—but the technological advances seen in war and the collective labour required to produce them were both new phenomena. In many ways, the condition of the British working class was elevated by the war, with those previously deemed 'unemployable' being needed to fill jobs Britain's soldiers had left behind. But the incessant need to keep factories producing shell after shell, tank after tank, and gun after gun was no doubt grinding.

The fact that real wages remained ahead of production levels was doubtlessly of some comfort, but the type of Fordist production line mocked in Charlie Chaplin's 1936 film *Modern Times* was already present in the UK with all its de-humanising effects. And industry itself was heavily regulated. In a 1915 letter to his brother Julian, Huxley noted the introduction of:

> measures of a state socialistic kind, which will probably continue after the war and be extended to other trades besides the suppliers of war material…reduction of profits, fixation of wages and the like. And what will the Boches do afterwards? A republic I suppose…they can hardly tolerate Kronprinz…a sort of magnified Fabian society state, organised even further than at present…automatism as opposed to life (Smith 79).

Three years after this message, Britain and her allies proved triumphant. But the war unleashed a series of reactions across Europe, which split the continent between communist left and fascist right. Germany indeed became a republic as Huxley predicted, but it was not to be of a 'Fabian society state'—i.e., a reforming, centre-left democracy—for very long. To borrow the historian Mark Mazower's memorable description, Europe fast became a "dark continent," where democracy appeared to be a deserted temple, in which increasingly few had anything close to total faith in (Mazower 1998). Britain formed Europe's last major, non-totalitarian outpost by 1940, but several years earlier, and particularly in the 1920s, it was almost *de rigueur* to *praise* Mussolini and Stalin rather than denigrate them in English high society. Such sympathetic elements extended beyond politics into scientific practitioners like George Pitt-Rivers, but within Westminster circles, the British Conservative right welcomed Mussolini as ridding Italy of its potential to go Bolshevist—and if personal liberty was the price for that then, for many, it was probably worth paying (Hart 2015). Their reasons for doing so varied from directly pro-fascist types, such as Archibald Ramsay MP (imprisoned in 1940 as a potential enemy of the state) to more pragmatic elements who simply felt Mussolini's government was one they could do business with, but whatever the reason, the practical effect was more or less the same—totalitarianism of the right had been tacitly endorsed by the British government. Given this stance, it was somewhat ironic that the Conservative Party continued to bait their socialist Labour opponents as being sympathetic to the new Bolshevik regime in the Soviet Union. Some Tories— including Macmillan, who visited the Soviet Union in 1933—were more sympathetic to the collectivist aims of the Stalinist regime, but most used the connections between the Communist ideology and Labour's 1918 pledge to nationalize (i.e., bring under state ownership) "the means of production, distribution, and exchange" to portray that party as "un-British." In electoral terms, this clearly worked, as the Conservatives were in power nineteen of the twenty-one years between the two world wars, while Labour was in power for just two. However, it also meant that totalitarianism and the authoritarian state were constant reference points in British politics.

As Huxley was writing *Brave New World* in 1931, the Macmillan Committee (not referring to the aforementioned Harold) reported on the British banking sector. It recommended vastly expanded state interference in finance, with the creation of two new state-run banks to facilitate the movement of capital. This was a perfectly sensible policy, which was replicated in post-1945 Germany, Sweden, and other countries, but to one thinker, F.A. Hayek, this was the path to the destruction of free society. Hayek, later awarded the Presidential Medal of Freedom in 1991, was highly critical of the Committee's aims and wrote in his wartime tract, *The Road to Serfdom*, that this sort of policy was contrary the very notion of liberalism (Hayek 12).

Hayek's view was an extreme one, but, at the same time, fears regarding the increasingly centralized and planned economy were not his alone. As historian Richard Overy notes:

> planning…was far from a monopoly of the left. As a result of the slump, elements among the academic, political, and business community still favourable to the idea of economic individualism came to the conclusion that reliance on market forces or economic orthodoxy alone would not save capitalism from the consequences of its own deficiencies (Overy 80–81).

Even Huxley conceded in his foreword to *Brave New World* that "the people who govern the brave new world may not be sane (in what may be called the absolute sense of the word); but they are not madmen and their aim is not anarchy but social stability" (xlv). His fellow Etonian Harold Macmillan set out such a positive case for planning in 1938:

The fact is that we can only choose between muddling along from one disaster to another, or making the mental effort necessary to avoid those disasters. If we take the first course, we shall travel the now well beaten track of internal social conflict culminating in dictatorship and tyranny of one variety or another. If we take the second, our effort at intelligent direction will be rewarded not only with economic security but all the cultural opportunities that can be based upon it. The prize before us is nothing less than the saving of civilization. It is worth an effort (Macmillan 298–99).

But for Huxley, it was precisely through attempting to do good that democracy could go the way of the dictatorships. As he noted in a letter in 1940:

The precedents of Russia and Germany, where the middle classes were wiped out respectively by massacre and inflation, are not encouraging. It certainly looks as though an age of tyranny were before us; and indeed, quite apart from war, it seems that existing industrial techniques and financial organization must inevitably impose such tyranny—inasmuch as large scale organization produce problems too complex to solve except by bureaucratic planning, which always leads to more planning…which means more and more tyranny on the part of planners (however good their original intentions), more and more repression and regimentation in the desperate effort to simplify the problem and make the plan work (Smith 450).

And into this mixture, by 1944, he added the British Labour Party: "the Left-wing Intellectuals and the Labour Party are eager Totalitarians—because they're convinced that they can Do Good, that fatal illusion which justifies every form of wickedness, oppression, and tyranny" (Smith 503).

But such a message was so seductive because it had a key reference point—laissez-faire Britain was clearly not working. By January 1933, unemployment topped three million, and economic growth was sluggish. Huxley was not blind to the contemporary ills of unemployment and poverty, yet he remained profoundly pessimistic that they could be solved without greatly undesirable outcomes:

> What a world we live in. The human race fills me with a steadily growing dismay. I was staying in the Durham coal-fields this autumn, in the heart of English unemployment, and it was awful. If only one could believe that the remedies proposed for the awfulness (Communism, etc.) weren't even worse than the disease—in fact weren't the disease itself in another form, with superficially different symptoms (Smith 345).

A few months after the publication of *Brave New World*, Huxley was dismayed at this prospect, and noted that:

> I wish I could see clear into the economic problem. This system is bad, and on a large scale, seems not even to work. But at the same time without some private property, what is to become of individual liberty? Private property is the only guarantee possessed by individual against the tyranny of the State (Smith 300).

Oddly, this was a profoundly Conservative statement. Conservative Party politicians had made much play about enshrining a so-called 'property owning democracy' and bombarded a largely private and municipal-renting British nation with propaganda about the virtues of owning one's own house. Yet by the early 1930s, Britain had a shortage of one million homes, more even than at the end of the First World War (with the four lost years of construction it brought). Huxley acknowledged during his Durham visit in 1931 that he was only ever a 'tourist' in the lives of the poor—and his intellectualizing of the dangers of tyranny could often lie rather less high up the priority list of impoverished Britons than the need for a job or decent wages. In David Cannadine's study of *Class in*

Britain, Huxley's 'meritocratic, materialistic, Ford-worshipping order' is linked to the erosion of the class struggle in post-1918 England (Cannadine 128). Yet this always was more true in theory (and in the rhetoric of politicians, such as Baldwin) than in practice. Writing in the early 1930s, Labour Party leader George Lansbury noted that the "two nations" theorized by the nineteenth-century statesman Benjamin Disraeli—a supposedly mutually beneficial and sympathetic rich and poor—"no longer live together." This was because "the rich have settled their consciences over the question of poverty by going away where they cannot see it" (Lansbury 59). Though Huxley was no factory owner or financier, these ranks no doubt included him.

But for those in the corridors of power, such distance allowed a little more room for an intellectual debate over concepts of liberty. Seven years after the publication of *Brave New World*, the Conservative MP John Moore-Brabazon referenced Huxley in outlining his fear of a homogenized world:

> I feel that everywhere we are becoming more and more like the children in *Brave New World*. We are educated by the Press to think along the lines they want us to follow. Hon. Members will remember how the children in that book were taught not to like certain things by being given shocks when they were young. That is the sort of thing that is happening in Europe to-day. Our own Press, perhaps, is less blameworthy than the others, but you get things of a surprising type creeping in, like the case of the Duke of Windsor, which was not mentioned for a year, while the foreign Press was discussing it, and the case of Oswald Mosley, who, although he is the leader of a political party, is not mentioned at all. That must be because some form of arrangement and conspiracy exists within our Press. If that is so, we have not a free Press, and that state of affairs should be altered (Hansard, 15 February 1939, vol. 343, col. 1,832).

In referencing the press silence over the former King Edward VIII's relationship with American divorcee Wallis Simpson, and their unwillingness to cover the British fascist movement led by Mosley, Moore-Brabazon was again suggesting that paternalistic attempts to 'do good' would inexorably produce a tyrannical state devoid of freedom of speech. This had real Huxleyian overtones. As the Controller notes near the beginning of *Brave New World*, "stability [is] the primal and ultimate need. Hence all this" (36). But *all this*—Huxley implicitly argued—may be inherently destabilising, or at least stultifying, should it not allow freedom of discourse.

Parliamentary views on Huxley were far from universal—if MPs could buy his line on the free society, they did not necessarily agree with him all the time. Debating a bill on the censorship of religious satire, the Liberal MP Ernest Pickering cited Huxley as but one of a type who would eventually lead themselves beyond the pale of respectability:

> There is nothing so dangerous as reason allied with courtesy and wit, and the great enemies of orthodox Christianity to-day in this country are not the Red Schools, but educated men like Bernard Shaw, Aldous Huxley, Bertrand Russell, and Professor Gilbert Murray. It is they who are doing the greatest damage to orthodox Christianity, through reason, courtesy, and wit. Ridicule, scurrility, ribaldry are the weakest and most ineffective of weapons, and usually the people who seek to bring religion into contempt by such means end by making themselves contemptible (Hansard, 7 April 1933, vol. 276, col. 2,093).

But others, such as the Conservative MP Reginald Craddock, saw much danger in anti-religious propagandizing along the Huxley model:

> I have often heard quoted, from Lenin's article in the publication called "The Workers' Dreadnought," these two sentences: Give us the child for eight years, and it will be a Bolshevik forever. Hundreds of thousands of teachers constitute an apparatus that must push our work forward. It is no exaggeration to say that these two texts of Lenin are the inspiration of the anti-God campaigns which have, unfortunately, been introduced into this country. They are like the germs of some contagious disease, which may spread and destroy men's lives. They are germs which multiply, and, if unrestrained, may destroy men's minds and make them so perverse that they follow programmes

which, to the ordinary sober citizen, must seem to lead to nothing but destruction (Hansard, 7 April 1933, vol. 276, col. 2,071).

The notion that indoctrinating children was, in essence, indoctrinating society was certainly a Huxleyian position. Here, we may detect the words spoken to the young Lenina Crowe: "everyone works for everyone else. We can't do without anyone. Even Epsilons are useful. We couldn't do without Epsilons. Everyone works for everyone else. We can't do without anyone" (Huxley, *Brave New World* 64). These words, drummed in from an early age, shaped the ordered society, in which *The Brave New World* was set. Huxley's own views—at that time—was that no Valhalla was likely. As he noted in his *Texts and Pretexts*, also published in 1932:

Man is impelled to invent theories to account for what happens in the world. Unfortunately, he is not quite intelligent enough, in most cases, to find correct explanations. So that when he acts on his: theories, he behaves very often like a lunatic. Thus, no animal is clever enough, when there is a drought, to imagine that the rain is being withheld by evil spirits, or as punishment for its transgressions. Therefore you never see animals going through the absurd and often horrible fooleries of magic and religion. No horse, for example would kill one of its foals to make the wind change direction. Dogs do not ritually urinate in the hope of persuading heaven to do the same and send down rain. Asses do not bray a liturgy to cloudless skies. Nor do cats attempt, by abstinence from cat's meat, to wheedle the feline spirits into benevolence. Only man behaves with such gratuitous folly. It is the price he has to pay for being intelligent but not, as yet, intelligent enough (Huxley, *Texts and Pretexts* 270).

Later, his views subtly shifted. When Charlie Chaplin caught up with Huxley in the 1940s and 1950s, he noted that "at that time he was very much lulled in the cradle of mysticism. Frankly I liked him better as the cynical young man of the twenties" (Chaplin 428). But that cynical young man, as we have seen, was very much swimming against the tide of a significant proportion of mainstream opinion. Thinkers of left and right did indeed believe radical intervention *could* cure society of its various ills, such as unemployment and a lack of faith in government, and they were prepared to say as much.

The great point of *Brave New World*, Huxley later stressed, was not so much that tyranny existed. That, after all, was the general political climate of the 1930s. But there was something profound in the fact that people could grow to enjoy living in such an existence. In a 1962 talk, he argued that "all revolutions have changed the environment in order to change the individual…to get people to love their servitude—this is the ultimate in malevolent revolution" (Huxley 1962). As Henry rather chillingly observes in *Brave New World*, "fine to think we can go on being socially useful, even after we're dead" (63). And this, for Huxley, was a major difference between him and George Orwell, whom he had briefly tutored in French at Eton in 1919. Orwell's *Animal Farm* shows the dangers of a metaphorical and literal Napoleon—a leader who rules by fear rather than by consent. But Huxley maintained this was not the most invidious form of dictatorship—whilst Orwell had been obsessed with the 'terrorism' of Hitler and Stalin, Huxley pointed to the dangers of a highly suggestible population being duped, be it through soma or some other means, into providing their dictators with nominal consent and legitimacy. The next set of "dictators will become more interested in the kind of techniques that I described in *Brave New World*" he noted, pointing to television and other forms of mass media as the hook by which liberty may be snared (Huxley, "Ultimate Revolution").

Leadership was a key issue for Huxley. On the one hand, he abhorred the charismatic Mussolini type of dictator (not that it stopped Huxley from moving to Florence in 1923). But, precisely because the opportunity for the rise of the Mussolinis would occur on the back of such timidity, he also did not have much truck with democratic leaders who could not make an effective case for the continuance of their system. In the early 1920s, he complained that Britain was being "treated as a third-rate power. One determined [French Prime Minister] Poincaré can defeat and make life impossible for ten philosopher kings. And when in place of philosopher kings we have Baldwins—then it's all up" (Smith 222). Led by the 'boneless wonders' of Baldwin and Ramsay MacDonald (Labour Prime Minister turned Baldwin's ally after 1931), it indeed looked like it might all be up at one stage. In reference to the British fascist, Huxley remarked to his brother in 1933 that "let us hope we shall not have to scuttle when Tom [Sir Oswald] Mosley gets into power" (Smith 375).

Britain avoided such a *Brave New World*, but it did so, in part, by the major parties—the Conservatives and key elements of the Liberal and Labour Parties—forming a Coalition in 1931, whereby their policies became scarcely distinguishable. Huxley always stated that "if there are 20 percent of the population who can really be suggested into believing anything—and evidently they can be—then we must take extremely careful steps to curb demagogues" (Huxley, "Ultimate Revolution"). As Prime Minister Stanley Baldwin wrote to his friend, the future Foreign Secretary Lord Halifax in 1927, "democracy has arrived at a gallop in England, and I feel all the time that it is a race for life: can we educate them before the crash comes?" (Williamson 196). The electorate, in short, was viewed as a rather dangerous lot; it was wise not to trust them with too much power.

But the question *Brave New World* does not conclusively answer is where the *positive* platform for the status quo should come from. It ranges on many issues from eugenics to economics, but it is largely a warning from the future, rather than a solution for the here and now (Hart 301–325). It is, in many ways, a statement in favor of the philosopher Isaiah Berlin's concept of negative liberty (borrowed from Hegel)—the need to preserve the individuals' freedom of expression from external limitations. But Huxley clearly found it harder to square with the desire and need for some positive liberty—the freedom 'to do.' Writing to Berlin in 1997, just before the philosopher's death, none other a figure than three-term British Prime Minister Tony Blair attempted to enter the debate:

> The limitations of negative liberty are what have motivated generations of people to work for positive liberty, whatever its depradations [*sic*] in the Soviet model. That determination to go beyond *laissez-faire* continues to motivate people today. And it is in that context that I

would be interested in your views on the future of the Left. You seem to be saying that because traditional socialism no longer exists, there is no Left. But surely the Left over the last 200 years has been based on a value system, predating the Soviet model and living on beyond it. As you say, the origins of the Left lie in opposition to arbitrary authority, intolerance, and hierarchy. The values remain as strong as ever, but no longer have a readymade vehicle to take them forward. (Blair, "1997 Letter")

Blair's 'Third Way' was, in its initial phase, an attempt to marry the interests of positive and negative liberty: with a new national minimum wage to help reduce poverty on the one hand, but a continued emphasis on the privatization rhetoric of Margaret Thatcher on the other. Thatcher and Blair were indeed radicals of varying types.

In many ways, Huxley was more small 'c' conservative than that. Although we view him as a deeply inquisitive thinker, *Brave New World* can be read as a clarion call for a democratic state, albeit a more localized one. Whilst the centralizing of the British state after 1906 had many positive outcomes, for Huxley and like-minded thinkers, these were always contingent upon the preservation of individual liberty. In the Britain of 1932, this was by no means a racing certainty, and Huxley drew his conclusions accordingly.

Works Cited

Blair, Tony. Letter to Isaiah Berlin. 23 Oct. 1997. Web. 14 Jan. 2014. <http://berlin.wolf.ox.ac.uk/letterstoberlin.html>.

Cannadine, David. *Class in Britain*. London: Penguin, 1998.

Chaplin, Charles. *My Autobiography*. London: Penguin. 1964.

Gregory, Adrian. *Last Great War*. Cambridge, UK: Cambridge UP, 2008.

Hansard Parliamentary Debates. House of Commons, United Kingdom, n.d. Web. 24 Jan. 2014. <www.parliament.uk/business/publications/hansard/commons/>.

Hart, Bradley W. "Science, Politics and Prejudice: The Dynamics and Significance of British Anthropology's failure to confront Nazi Racial Ideology." *European History Quarterly*, 43.2 (2013): 301–325.

————. Biography of *George Pitt-Rivers*. Bloomsbury: London, 2015.

Huxley, Aldous. *Brave New World*. Vintage: London, 2007.

————. *Texts and Pretexts*. London: Chatto and Windus, 1932.

————."The Ultimate Revolution." Berkeley Language Center. Berkeley, California. 20 Mar. 1962. Web. 14 Jan. 2014. <http://www. informationclearinghouse.info/article24712.htm>. Lecture.

Lansbury, George. *My England*. London: Selwyn and Blount, 1934.

Macmillan, Harold. *The Middle Way*. London: Macmillan, 1938.

Mazower, Mark. *Dark Continent: Europe's Twentieth Century*, Penguin: London, 1998.

Overy, Richard. *The Morbid Age: Britain Between the Wars*, Penguin: London, 2009.

Seldon, Anthony and David Walsh. *Public Schools and the Great War*. London: Pen and Sword Books, 2013.

Smith, Grover. *Letters of Aldous Huxley*. London: Chatto and Windus, 1969.

von Hayek, Friedrich, *The Road to Serfdom*. London: Routledge, 2010.

Williamson, Philip. *Baldwin Papers: A Conservative Statesman, 1908–1947*. Cambridge, UK: Cambridge UP, 2004.

Huxley Meets the Critics: Commentaries on *Brave New World*

Gerardo Del Guercio

O, wonder!
How many goodly creatures are there here!
How beauteous mankind is!
O brave new world, that has such people in't!"

—William Shakespeare, *The Tempest*, 5.1.184–7

Aldous Huxley's *Brave New World* was a great success, "[s]elling thirteen thousand copies in 1932" and "ten thousand the following year" (Baker 11). The novel grew so popular that "it was eventually translated into nineteen languages and continues to sell at a substantial rate" (Baker 11). Despite its immense success, the novel "provoked a bewildered diversity of reactions—incomprehension, resentment, and hostility not the least among them ... [offending] the Australian censors" (Watt 15–6). H.G. Wells was, said Gerald Heard, moved "to write Huxley an angry letter charging treason to science" (Watt 16). Today, Huxley's novel is read for its refined use of allegory and the conflict between civilization versus savagery and its xenophobic representation of "Indians." This chapter will analyze the leading criticism on *Brave New World* from Rebecca West's review in the *Daily Telegraph* to Laura Frost's "Huxley's Feelies: Engineering Pleasure in *Brave New World*." Huxley's book made its impact because of its calamitous admonition on the future.

Chatto and Windus published *Brave New World* in 1932. In it, Huxley "turned his formidable intellect into something, which was in the air and which he feared and detested" (Stapleton 432) offering a "nightmare vision of the lengths to which physiological conditioning can be taken" (Stapleton 432). Other notable works by Huxley include: Antic *Hay* (1923), *Point Counter Point* (1928),

The Perennial Philosophy (1945), *The Doors of Perception* (1954), *Brave New World Revisited* (1958), and *Island* (1962).

The Title of Huxley's Novel

Brave New World took its title from Miranda's words to Prospero in William Shakespeare's *The Tempest*: "How beauteous mankind is! O brave new world, That has such people in't" (Shakespeare 5.1.182–183). The title proposed, like H. G. Wells suggested, the "idea of perfectible Man, achieved through communitarian ideals, technological enhancement, and an aggressive program of eugenics" (Nicol 44). In doing so, Huxley was permitted to bond his novel and Shakespeare's play together and emphasize the theme of that dictated both texts. Miranda's words also allowed Huxley's audience to draw correlations among personas like the animalistic Caliban in *The Tempest* and Huxley's John the Savage.

The Shakespeare reference placed John the Savage at the center of the novel's trajectory. The only texts available for John the Savage to learn from were Shakespeare's collected works, suggesting that John must remain obedient to white culture. Important to note is that John the Savage did not speak Shakespeare's words in consecutive lines like Miranda did in *The Tempest*. Instead, John the Savage broke the quote up in several parts during his dialogue with Bernard. Arguably, what was created in *Brave New World* when Huxley broke the Shakespearian quote into parts was a separation between Indians and whiteness. Huxley emphasised the Eurocentric lens he used to illustrate John when he referred to him as "[t]he other" (*Brave New World* 137). The xenophobia was reinforced further in the same line when John was described as having "nodded" (Huxley, *Brave New World* 137) in response to Bernard, signifying his subservience to white culture. The character's names are another important aspect of the novel. John was named "the savage" because not only was he depicted as being uncivilized, but for the reason that he was considered the stark opposite of the biblical figure, John the Baptist. Bernard Marx, who carried what is traditionally regarded a white-sounding name because of its association with Marxism and money, normalized the supremacy of the white race that *Brave*

New World advocated. Indeed, derogatory references to groups like Indians have led to debates on whether *Brave New World* should be banned from libraries and school curriculums, as in a recent case in Seattle, Washington (Walsh). Besides Miranda's words, Huxley used several other Shakespearian quotes throughout his novel to highlight the renaissance of the Eurocentric and revolutionary world he anticipated.

The Shakespearian allusion also added irony and tone of voice to Huxley's novel. In *The Tempest*, Miranda's statement was spoken in terror and delight at the hope of the new world and its potentials. Argued here is that John the Savage's knowledge of the new world was the opposite. While John the Savage began with a buoyant tone, he was nevertheless appalled and revolted by his new world. Huxley's combining of John the Savage's reaction with Miranda's made the feelings he intended to convey even more affecting.

Criticisms of the Novel (1932–2013)

The critical reception of *Brave New World* has ranged from "confused resentment, even outright hostility, to high acclaim" (Baker 11). Most critics were discontented or revolted with what they considered as unfounded alarmism. Completely affronted, H. G. Wells stated that "[a] writer of the standing of Aldous Huxley has no right to betray the future as he did in that book" (Reitt 121). Wells felt admonished, since many of his novels had motivated Huxley's works. Huxley told a friend in 1931 that he was "writing a novel about the future—on the horror of the Wellsian Utopia and a revolt against it" (Nicol 41). Scientist Joseph Needham provided one of the first positive reviews of Huxley's novel, arguing that "only biologists and philosophers will really appreciate the full force of Mr. Huxley's remarkable book" (Watt 204). Other reviewers suggested that the book was a badly thought-out story or a set of half-truths. Robert S. Baker has asserted that perhaps the book's negative reception stemmed from the inability or unwillingness "to comprehend the seriousness of Huxley's satire, and going so far as to speculate on whether he approved of his vision of a technocratic future" (Baker 11). Rebecca West's review in the February 5,

1932 *Daily Telegraph* praised Huxley's book as a work "of major importance" (Watt 197), noting that "the society which Mr. Huxley represents as being founded on this basis [generic engineering] is actually the kind of society that various living people, notably American and Russian, and in connection with the Bolshevist and Behaviorist movements, has expressed a desire to establish" (Watt 198). Later in her review, West stressed the significance of Huxley satire and its political implications as well as clearly exploring the dispute in chapter seventeen and "The Grand Inquisitor" section of Fyodor Dostoyevsky's *The Brothers Karamazov*. West was the first to praise Huxley's use of humanism. She defined it as a continuous assault on the materialism that had replaced religion and philosophy with a belief in technology. West ended her review stating that "[i]t is, indeed, almost certainly one of the half-dozen most important books that have been published since the war" (Watt 202). Notable is that reviews like West's have become the fundamental pieces in establishing criticism on Huxley's oeuvre because they are the texts scholars look to when trying to establish how the criticism on Huxley has evolved since the 1930s to the present day.

Joseph Needham, in his May 1932 review appearing in *Scrutiny*, strengthened Rebecca West's extremely positive appraisal of *Brave New World*. Needham was known worldwide as a scientists and leading biochemist. In his review, Needham stressed how, in the world at large, those persons, and there will be many, who do not approve of Huxley's "utopia", will say, we can't believe all this, the biology is all wrong, it couldn't happen. Unfortunately, what gives the biologist a sardonic smile as he reads it, is the fact that *the biology is perfectly right*, and Huxley has included nothing in his book but what might be regarded as legitimate exploitations from knowledge and power that we already have. Successful experiments are now being made in the cultivation of embryos of small mammals in vitro, and one of the most horrible of Huxley's predictions, the production of numerous low-grade workers of precisely identical genetic constriction from one egg, is perfectly possible" (Watt 204). Needham's assessment of Huxley's *Brave New World* is an important one that demonstrates technology's continuing impact on literature.

H.G. Wells is typically regarded as the innovator of twentieth-century science fiction. In his many novels, Wells forecasted tanks, airborne conflict, and the A-Bomb; as J. B. S. Haldane states, "the very mention of the future suggests him" (Nicol 41). While Wells' previous and most unforgettable writings spoke on the eviler potentials of technical development, in Huxley's peak of success Wells was composing utopias packed with technological gadgets that would revolutionize the world. In *The Road to Wigan Pier*, George Orwell referred to Wells' writing as "enlightened sunbathers" (Orwell 159). Snubbing Rousseau's dignified beast and the passionate utopias of Coleridge and Wordsworth, Wells saw the Industrial Revolution and contemporary science as continuing and principally optimistic growth in humanity's everlasting clash with merciless nature. His *Men Like Gods* narrates the tale of an assembly of modern Englishmen inadvertently brought into an alternate world of serene, passionless Utopians who are uncritically dedicated to logical rationalism and the self-negating collectivist state. As the book's name proposes, this was Wells' design of perfectible Man, achieved through communitarian ideals, technological enhancement, and a hostile program of eugenics. The Utopians divide their insight with the time-travelers, amplifying how they placed "the primordial fierce combativeness of the ancestral man-ape" (Wells 58) behind them. Just as humanity's basic belligerence had brought society to the edge of collapse, a great diviner saw hope. In "a dawn of new ideas" (Wells 61), a privileged group of researchers rearranged civilization until, ultimately obliterating the cause of strife, they attained a cooperative state with "no parliament, no politics, no private wealth, no business competition, no police nor prisons, no lunatics, no defectives nor cripples," (Wells 60) whose motto is "Our education is our government" (Wells 61). The link between Huxley and Wells is a significant one that portrays the preoccupation of the modern world with time and the possibility of how the world will develop in the future.

Prior to the publication of *Brave New World*, Russian author Yevgeny Zamyatin wrote *We* to depict a technological civilization, wherein its inhabitants are numbers ruled with complete power in a scheme where political and quantitative rules are melted into one. Having edited the Russian translations of Wells' novels, Zamyatin had initially backed the Bolshevik Revolution. Although he was pressured through the 1920s for critiquing the Soviet Union, Zamyatin's texts were barred, and he was eventually detained many times. He finally moved to Paris in 1931. Originally printed in England in 1924, "the Russian edition of *We* was released in 1988 as *glasnost*" (Nicol 43). Dissatisfied with *Brave New World*, George Orwell stated that the novel was a "brilliant caricature of the present" that "probably casts no light on the future" (Orwell 30). Orwell accused Huxley of lifting *We*, but ultimately concluded that Huxley had read *We* only after *Brave New World* was published. Arguably, the similarities between *Brave New World* and *We* simply showed the apprehension with world dominance that was present in the first part of the twentieth century.

The connection between Huxley and Orwell, however, did not begin and end with *Brave New World*. Huxley taught Orwell French at Eton College in 1917. In a letter written in Wrightwood, California and dated October 21, 1949, Huxley commented on the novel *Nineteen Eighty-Four*. Orwell's publisher mailed a copy of the book to Huxley upon its publication. Huxley, who was swamped with work and suffering from "poor sight" (Smith 604), did not read Orwell's novel for a several months. The letter starts as praise, but turns into a concise contrast of *Brave New World* and *Nineteen Eight-Four*. The penultimate section of Huxley's letter reads:

> Within the next generation I believe that the world's rulers will discover that infant conditioning and narco-hypnosis are more efficient, as instruments of government, than clubs and prisons, and that the lust for power can be just as completely satisfied by suggesting people into loving their servitude as by flogging and kicking them into obedience. In other words, I feel that the nightmare of *Nineteen Eighty-Four* is destined to modulate into the nightmare of a world having more resemblance to that which I imagined in *Brave New World*. The change will be brought about as a result of a felt need for increased efficiency. Meanwhile, of course, there may

be a large scale biological and atomic war—in which case we shall have nightmares of other and scarcely imaginable kinds (Smith 605).

The section cited is particularly important because it demonstrates, in a very clear way, Huxley's explanation as to why *Brave New World* presented a more rational forecast of the future than *Nineteen Eighty-Four*. Even though Huxley effectively used language to support his claim, the society *Brave New World* envisioned never came true because of the fall of Communism and the creation of a Global Village.

Brave New World and its political significance continued into the 1950s. Judith Shklar's *After Utopia: The Decline of Political Faith* contends that Huxley's novel "is not a picture of a totalitarian state" (Shklar 257). Baker supports Shklar's statement positing that Huxley "associate[d] technology with totalitarianism (although Huxley [made] no such connection) and fail[ed] to enter into a detailed political analysis" (Baker 14). Peter Frichow later advocated that, if politics can be correlated with "the behavior and organization of men into groups, especially large groups, such as cities or states," then "politics certainly played a very important role in *Brave New World*" (Frichow 303). Shklar's and Fichlow's comments are important ones that show how Huxley influenced politics in the second half of the twentieth-century.

British philosopher Bertrand Russell composed one of the most fascinating first reviews of *Brave New World*. In the March 11, 1932 *New Leader*, Russell stated that Huxley displayed "his usual masterly skill in producing his results upon the reader, for he has undertaken to make us sad by the contemplation of a world without sadness" (Watt 210). What impressed Russell were Huxley's brilliant analyses of freedom with respect to the present-day view of war. Russell seriously contemplated Huxley's idea of a threat created by "the technocratic ruling class described in *Brave New World*" (Baker 14) because he saw human progress the same way Huxley's antagonist Mustapha Mond did. Russell saw history as evidence of incessant brutality and absurdity. Fearing the destructive advancement of military expertise, Russell was scared that the world envisioned in *Brave New World* was unavoidable. In his review, Russell noticeably stated that:

> If you follow out this thought you will be led straight to Huxley's world as the only world that can be stable. At this stage most people will say: "Then let us have done with civilisation." But that is an abstract thought, not realizing in the concrete what such a choice would mean. Are you prepared that ninety-five per cent of the population should perish by poison gases and bacteriological bombs, and that the other five per cent should revert to savagery and live upon the raw fruits of the earth? For this is what will inevitably happen, probably within the next fifty years, unless there is a strong world government. And a strong world government, if brought about by force, will be tyrannical, caring nothing for liberty and aiming primarily at perpetuating its own power. I am afraid, therefore, that, while Mr. Huxley's prophecy is meant to be fantastic, it is all too likely to come true (Watt 212).

Russell seems correct in his assessment, given that the "strong world government" (Watt 212) was never established and that strict controls on poisonous weapons have been enforced since the publication of Huxley's book.

On February 17, 1932, Economist Henry Hazlitt ironically commented that "a little suffering, a little irrationality, a little division and chaos, are perhaps necessary ingredients of an ideal state, but there has probably never been a time when the world has not had an oversupply of them" (Watt 215). Charlotte Haldane wrote a sarcastic review for *Nature* on April 23, 1932, belligerently contending that Matthew Arnold, Huxley's great-uncle, had possessed his great-nephew, claiming that "biology is itself too surprising to be really amusing material for fiction" (Watt 208). Respected critic and novelist G. K. Chesterton also argued that Huxley's *Brave New World* was gloomily preposterous. Chesterton said that "[h]owever grimly he may enjoy the present, he already definitely hates the future. And I only differ from him in not believing that there is any such future to hate" (Watt 230). Afterwards in his review, Chesterton stated that "... People will call Mr. Huxley a pessimist; in the sense that he make the worst of it. To me he is that far more gloomy character; the man who makes the best of it" (Watt 230). Notable is that generally negative reviews, like the ones Hazlitt, Haldane, and Chesterton presented shortly after *Brave New World*'s publication, demonstrates that, although a novel might be considered flawed or unrealistic when first published, it later can be classified as a classic text that helped shape the canon. What critics discuss regarding a particular text also changes over from one generation to the next. In a contemporary framework, criticism on Huxley's novel are concerned more with whether Huxley wrote a utopia or a dystopia and how the novel's different characteristics make classifying it difficult.

On February 13, 1932, *Spectator* published a review by poet and novelist L.A.G. Strong. The critique makes clear Strong's feelings of disappointment for a talented writer's ridiculous recoil into a preposterous future. Strong wrote that:

> Mr. Huxley has been born too late. Seventy years ago, the great powers of his mind would have been anchored to some mighty certitude, or to some equally mighty scientific denial of a certitude. Today he searches heaven and earth for a Commandment, but searches in vain: and the lack of it reduces him, metaphorically speaking, to a man standing beside a midden, shuddering and holding his nose (Watt 206).

Strong pessimistically argued that the ideas advocated in *Brave New World* were ones that were irrelevant during the 1930s, because they were rooted too much in the nineteenth-century. Reviews like Strong's provide readers with a balanced example of how critical analysis sometimes portrays critics condemning works written by authors they consider talented.

Critics like Thomas Mann considered Huxley's novels "a splendid expression of the West European spirit" (Watt 17), although he was disturbed by what he regarded as Huxley's "hate of all fleshy life" (Watt 17). Essayist Gerald Bullett wrote a review of *Brave New World* that appeared in the March 1923 *Fortnightly Review*. Bullett noted that Huxley was guilty of "contempt [for] ordinary human nature" (Watt 213). Herman Hesse states in the *Die Neue*

Rundschau (May 1933) that he saw only "melancholy irony" (Watt 222) in *Brave New World*'s mechanical world of a utopia where "the humans being themselves have long since ceased to be human but are only 'standardized' machines" (Watt 221). Huxley's use of mechanical imagery suggested trepidation that machines would soon dominate the world. The anxiety Huxley advanced had been one that was evident since the Industrial Revolution.

Reviewing in the *Cambridge Review* of February 17, 1933, English writer C.P. Snow extolled Huxley for having composed a story that is a "response to the sensuous world which has been bred in every major novelist since Proust" (Watt 223). Snow further claimed that Huxley was "the most significant novelist of his day" (Watt 225) because of his "emotional sensitivity" (Watt 225). Snow's review elicited a letter in reply from Elizabeth Downs on February 24, 1933, stating that Huxley's writing was a "masterly and effective satire" (Watt 227) filled with "the art of exposure, not of creation" (Watt 227), because of his "brutal dislike and contempt of the very limited range of characters he presents" (Watt 227). Huxley's close friend D.H. Lawrence commented that Huxley's fiction was insidiously filled with "murder, suicide, and rape" (Ellis 447). Arguably, Aldous Huxley's use of emotions and genres are what made *Brave New World* a stylistically interesting novel. It is also important to note that Huxley's relationship with canonical novelists, like D.H. Lawrence, made his writing effective in tracing the correspondences that formulated the canon from the first half of the twentieth-century.

Aldous Huxley gave Mike Wallace a rare interview on May 18, 1958, during which he was asked about how the "enemies of freedom" were leading humans to the "brave new world" Huxley had predicted. Wallace ended by asking "what life in this brave new world would you fear so much, or what life might be like?" Huxley authoritatively answered "I think it will be very unlike the dictatorships which we've been familiar with in the immediate past." Huxley drew an analogy between his analysis of future dictatorships and the dictatorship Orwell presented in *Nineteen Eighty-Four*. Although, as stated earlier, Huxley and Orwell had different visions of what the future leadership might be like, Huxley nonetheless praised Orwell's book and its representation of tyranny after Hitler. The interview with Wallace demonstrates Huxley's prominence and how his notion of what the future will be like was one that drew great critical and popular attention.

Huxley later was interviewed in the Spring 1960 issue of *The Paris Review*. In their opening statement, interviewers Raymond Fraser and George Wickes introduced and praised Huxley's *Brave New World*: "[i]n the thirties [Huxley] wrote his most influential novel, *Brave New World*, combining satire and science fiction in the most successful of futuristic utopias." Later in the interview, Huxley very adamantly affirmed that there was no "resemblance between lysergic acid, or mescaline, and the 'soma'" in *Brave New World*, stating that "Soma is an imaginary drug, with three different effects— euphoric, hallucinant, or sedative—an impossible combination. Mescaline is the active principle of the peyote cactus, which has been used for a long time by the Indians of the Southwest in their religious rites" (Fraser and Wickes). Appearing in *The Paris Review* is, conceivably, an important indication of Huxley's popularity and the continuing influence speculative fiction was having on American letters.

In 1962, Cyril Connolly commented on Huxley's use of the Utopian, arguing that "to write a philosophical, even didactic novel about an imaginary Utopia is a most difficult thing. Too often the characters in Utopias are unreal while their opinions are cloaked in the dust of the lecture room. *Brave New World* is an exception because of the ferocious energy of the satire" (Watt 446). What energized Huxley's novels were the fierce satiric critiques against his generation's obsession with thinkers like Freud and Marx. Huxley also challenged scientific data of the 1930s, using a morose tone of voice to demonstrate the complexity of the human psyche and the apprehension that humans have always had with regards to the future. Arguably, Connolly's statement on *Brave New World* has helped shape our views on Utopian fiction and also to elucidate Huxley's place in the literary canon. Connolly's words were regarded as important ones because of his stature in the literary marketplace. From 1940–1949, Connolly was the editor of the popular magazine *Horizon*. In 1938, two years prior to his tenure at *Horizon*, Connolly authored the influential *Enemies of Promise*, a book that *Daily Mail*'s Michael Gove said, "explore[d] the ways in which the talented individuals of his time were prevented from achieving their full potential" ("Refuse to Surrender... "). Huxley's work was explored in Connolly's book for its use of the Mandarin style. Arguably, being included in the criticism of leading writers, like Connolly, demonstrated the authority Huxley had in literary scholarship.

The 2007 Vintage Publishing edition of *Brave New World* contains an introduction by Margaret Atwood that caused a debate among contemporary critics regarding genre in Huxley's novel. Atwood's claim is best encapsulated in the following passage:

> *Brave New World* is either a perfect-world utopia or its nasty opposite, a dystopia, depending on your point of view: its inhabitants are beautiful, secure and free from diseases and worries, though in a way we like to think we would find unacceptable. "Utopia" is sometimes said to mean "no place," from the Greek ou-topos; others derive it from eu, as in "eugenics," in which case it would mean "healthy place" or "good place." Sir Thomas More, in his own 16th-century Utopia, may have been punning: utopia is the good place that doesn't exist (Atwood vii-viii).

The citation details the Utopia formed as a genre from its Ancient Greek origins to the Renaissance. Atwood successfully explores what critics have debated since the 1930s—that it remains uncertain whether Huxley intended his novel to be a utopia or a dystopia. I consider Atwood's statement a well-balanced one that makes both arguments equally possible given that a lot of evidence exists to support both theories.

Laura Frost's essay "Huxley's Feelies: Engineered Pleasure in *Brave New World*" from her 2013 volume *The Problem With Pleasure: Modernism and Its Discontents* explored the correlation between sound in cinema and technology. "Huxley's cranky response to *The Jazz Singer*, a film that stood as both a technological landmark and a massive box-office success, is a key window onto a key moment in the history of cinema" (Frost 130–1) claimed Frost. Cinema was "perceived as revolutionary" (Frost 131) in Huxley's era, much like the future that was illustrated in *Brave New World*. Suggested in this essay is that Huxley wrote his novel to reflect on the technological developments that were emerging in the 1930s. Even if Huxley's vision of the future never came true, it still reveals the concern humans have about the future. We obviously cannot know for sure what will happen after the present time, given the possibility that the variables available to us today may change over time. What we do know for certain is that past and present actions could alter what will occur later.

Changes over Time

As this analysis has attempted to demonstrate, *Brave New World* remains at the core of the literary canon for its strong use of language and style. The critics, whose critical works I have detailed, each had a different interpretation of Huxley's novel. What the diverse scholarship on *Brave New World* demonstrates is that the values we use to judge works typically change over time. Values change because our perception between right and wrong become clearer or opaque. Argued here is that the futures on studies of *Brave New World* are strong and that novels like Huxley's can be used to demonstrate that xenophobic behavior ought to be contested and replaced with ideas that refute discrimination of all sorts.

Works Cited

Atwood, Margaret. "Introduction." *Brave New World*. Toronto: Vintage, 2007. i–xiv.

Baker, Robert S. "Critical Reception." *Brave New World: History, Science, and Dystopia*. Boston: Twyane Publishers, 1990. 11–18.

Bullet, Gerald. "Gerald Bullet, review in *Fortnightly Review.*" *Aldous Huxley: The Critical Heritage*. Ed. Donald Watt. London and Boston: Routledge & Kegan Paul, 1975. 213–14.

Chesterton, G.K. "G.K. Chesterton on Huxley: 1933." *Aldous Huxley: The Critical Heritage.* Ed. Donald Watt. London and Boston: Routledge & Kegan Paul, 1975. 228–231.

Connolly, Cyril. "Cyril Connolly, review in *Sunday Times.*" *Aldous Huxley: The Critical Heritage.* Ed. Donald Watt. London & Boston: Routledge & Kegan Paul, 1975. 446–49.

Downs, Elizabeth. "Letter in Reply from Elizabeth Downs." *Aldous Huxley: The Critical Heritage.* Ed. Donald Watt. London and Boston: Routledge & Kegan Paul, 1975. 226–27.

Ellis, David. "June-November 1928: The Search for Health." *D.H. Lawrence: Dying Game, 1922–1930.* Cambridge: Cambridge UP, 1996. 421–450.

Fraser, Raymond and George Wickes. "Aldous Huxley, The Art of Fiction No. 24." *The Paris Review.* 23 (Spring 1960). Web. 8 Nov. 2013. <http://www.theparisreview.org/interviews/4698/the-art-of-fiction-no-24-aldous-huxley>.

Frichow, Peter. "Science and Conscience in Huxley's *Brave New World.*" *Contemporary Literature.* 16.3 (Summer 1975): 301–316.

Frost, Laura. "Huxlies Feelies: Engineered Pleasure in *Brave New World.*" *The Problem with Pleasure: Modernism and Its Discontents.* New Work: Columbia UP, 2013. 130–161.

Gove, Michael. "I Refuse to Surrender to the Marxist Teachers Hell-Bent on Destroying Our Schools: Education Secretary Berates 'the new enemies of promise' for Opposing His Plan." *Daily Mail.* Mail Online. 23 Mar. 2013 Web. 1 Dec. 2013. <http://www.dailymail.co.uk/debate/article-2298146/I-refuse-surrender-Marxist-teachers-hell-bent-destroying-schools-Education-Secretary-berates-new-enemies-promise-opposing-plans.html>.

Haldane, Charlotte. "Charlotte Haldane, review in *Nature.*" *Aldous Huxley: The Critical Heritage.* Ed. Donald Watt. London and Boston: Routledge & Kegan Paul, 1975. 207–9.

Hazlitt, Henry. "Henry Hazlitt: review in *Nation* (New York)." *Aldous Huxley: The Critical Heritage.* Ed. Donald Watt. London and Boston: Routledge & Kegan Paul, 1975. 215–17.

Hesse, Herman. "Herman Hesse, review in *Die Neue Rundschau* (Berlin)." *Aldous Huxley: The Critical Heritage.* Ed. Donald Watt. London & Boston: Routledge & Kegan Paul, 1975. 221–22.

Huxley, Aldous. *Brave New World.* 1932. New York: Perennial Classics, 1998.

———. "Interview with Mike Wallace." *The Mike Wallace Interview.* ABC, New York & Los Angeles. 18 May 1958.

Needham, Joseph. "Joseph Needham, review in *Scrutiny.*" *Aldous Huxley: The Critical Heritage.* Ed. Donald Watt. London & Boston: Routledge & Kegan Paul, 1975. 202–5.

Nicol, Caitrin. "*Brave New World at 75.*" *The New Atlantis: A Journal of Technology & Society.* Spring 2007: 41–54.

Orwell, George. *The Road to Wigan Pier.* 1937. London and New York: Penguin Classics, 2001.

———. "Prophecies of Fascism." *The Collected Essays, Journalism, and Letter of George Orwell: My Country Right or Left, 1940–1943.* Vol. 2. Eds. Sonia Orwell and Ian Angus. Boston: David R. Godine Publisher, 2000. 30–2.

———. *Nineteen Eighty-Four.* 1949. London and New York: Penguin Classics, 1989.

Reitt, Raychel Haugard. *Aldous Huxley: Brave New World (Writers and Their Works).* Salt Lake City, UT: Benchmark Books, 2009.

Russell, Bertrand. "Bertrand Russell, review in *New Leader.*" *Aldous Huxley: The Critical Heritage.* London and Boston: Routledge & Kegan Paul, 1975. 210–2.

Shakespeare, William. "The Tempest." *The Norton Anthology of Shakespeare.* Ed. Stephen Greenblatt, et.al. New York: W.W. Norton & Company, 1997. 3055–3107.

Shklar, Judith. *After Utopia: The Decline of Political Faith.* Princeton, NJ: Princeton UP, 1957.

Smith, Grover, ed. *Letters of Aldous Huxley.* London: Chatto & Windus, 1969.

Snow, C.P. "C.P. Snow, "The Case of Aldous Huxley." *Aldous Huxley: The Critical Heritage.* Ed. Donald Watt. London and Boston: Routledge & Kegan Paul, 1975. 222–26.

Stapleton, Michael. "Huxley, Aldous (Leonard)." *The Cambridge Guide to English Literature: Including the Literatures of Great Britain, the United States, Canada, Australia, the Caribbean, and Africa.* Cambridge: Newnes, 1984. 431–32.

Strong, L.A.G. "L.A.G. Strong, review in *Spectator.*" *Aldous Huxley: The Critical Heritage.* Ed. Donald Watt. London and Boston: Routledge & Kegan Paul, 1975. 206–7.

Walsh, Sean Collins. "Seattle School Board Postpones Decision on Pulling 'Brave New World.'" *The Seattle Times.* 17 Nov. 2010. Web. 19 Nov. 2013. <http://seattletimes.com/html/localnews/2013460397_braveworld18m.html>.

Watt, Donald. "Introduction." *Aldous Huxley: The Critical Heritage.* Ed. Donald Watt. London and Boston: Routledge & Paul Kegan, 1975. 1–36.

Wells, H.G. *Men Like Gods.* 1923. New York: Ferris Printing Company, 2009.

West, Rebecca. "Rebecca West, review in *Daily Telegraph.*" *Aldous Huxley: The Critical Heritage.* Ed. Donald Watt. London & Boston: Routledge & Kegan Paul, 1975. 197–202.

Reading *Brave New World* through the Lens of Feminism_____

Thomas Horan

Dystopian fiction of the early-to-mid-twentieth century has provoked a range of feminist critiques. Much of this speculative literature was produced by male authors at a time when traditional gender roles were questioned less frequently and women faced substantially more discrimination than they do now. Some of these chauvinistic tendencies—such as a juvenile attitude toward the female body, a reliance on sexist stereotypes, and, occasionally, a troubling link between lust for and violence toward women—are fairly evident to contemporary readers. But these texts also contain subtler kinds of bias, of which even their authors were not always aware. Speaking generally about the writers of classic dystopian fiction (including Aldous Huxley), Deanna Madden sees such prejudice as a combination of cultural and personal misogyny: "They project into their visions of a future the patriarchal power structure and gender inequities of their own times as well as their own prejudices" (Madden 289). But other critics, such as June Deery, identify some progressive trends in this literature, specifically in *Brave New World*: "In some instances, Huxley both recognizes the bias in the system and explicitly condemns it, but in other instances it is a function of his own perspective, and he is oblivious to the inequalities his illustration introduces" (Deery 260). We cannot always be sure whether each instance of sexism in *Brave New World* is deliberate or inadvertent. Huxley's treatment of gender issues is nearly as nuanced as it is problematic. Moreover, since *Brave New World* is a satire, it is sometimes difficult to know which aspects of the possible future depicted in the novel are intended by the author to be viewed with scorn, derision, or horror. It is due to this ambiguity that Deery proves more reluctant than others to conclude that Huxley is willfully misogynistic: "In the area of female rights, one might say that Huxley sins more by omission than intention" (Deery 271). This chapter will provide a survey of feminist readings of *Brave New World*, as well as some thoughts on the issues that these analyses address.

As Christie March points out, gender equality is, at least superficially, a priority in Huxley's World State: "The genders appear equal within the social order; both men and women work at the same jobs, have equal choice in sexual partners, and participate in the same leisure pursuits" (March 53). However, by giving us an outsider's perspective on the World State, initially through the eyes of Bernard Marx and ultimately through those of John the Savage, Huxley positions the reader to recognize that inequities remain:

> Beneath the surface of this seeming equality are hints that the same old inequities of a patriarchy persist. The typical boss is still a male and his secretary female.... A male in charge patronizingly "pats" a female underling, who in turn gives him a "deferential smile".... The heroes revered by this society are male—Ford and Freud—and the positions of power are held by men, like the Director of Hatcheries and Conditioning and Mustapha Mond, the Resident Controller for Western Europe (Madden 291).

While the handsomeness of certain men, Helmholtz Watson for example, attracts the attention of and even invites pursuit by female characters (March 53), Madden makes clear that in the World State, physical appearance determines how female characters are valued by others and, more importantly, how they value themselves. As Deery observes, even the not-explicitly-gendered, third-person narrator seems primarily interested in women's secondary sexual characteristics: "The anonymous narrator is not explicitly gendered. Indeed, Huxley's desire to create a sense of lifeless uniformity means the language he employs is often less gendered than one might expect in a text of this period. Yet our first view of a woman is undoubtedly through male eyes, and the first comment is on her sexual attractiveness" (Deery 261). This bias within the narrative voice suggests that even when Huxley endeavors to be neutral his subconscious prejudices emerge.

The relative dearth of female historical and literary figures among the characters' names also suggests that women are undervalued by the author. Jerome Meckier notes that "The World State likes to name females after puissant males. Except for Calvin Stopes, no brave new worlder has a famous female surname" ("Onomastic Satire" 168). It may be that Huxley wants us to think that the World State's failure to commemorate women in this way is one of the society's dystopian characteristics, but the fact that he recycles famous names for comedic and ironic purposes that depend on the cultural significance of these figures indicates that he thinks individual women have made few, if any substantive contributions to human development. Furthermore, the names with which female characters are saddled carry troubling implications: Bernard's sexual partner at the Solidarity Service is named Morgana Rothschild. Morgana is an Alpha, but the reader's attention is directed to her unattractive unibrow (62) rather than her intellect, placing her within the unflattering stereotype of the "bluestocking." Meckier observes that her name combines the Rothschild bankers with Henry Morgan, the ruthless privateer, and Morgan Le Fay, the nefarious witch of Arthurian legend:

> Perhaps the brave new world has not sought to strengthen Alpha women by giving them masculine names; instead, it announces the elimination of trouble-makers, having feminized them unappealingly. Money-lending, once the mainstay of capitalism but actually a combination of piracy and sorcery, survives in brave new world only in Morgana Rothschild's names ("Onomastic Satire" 169).

Miss Keate, also an Alpha and the headmistress at Eton College, is another example of a woman delegitimized by her name. As Meckier notes, her name is derived from that of "John Keate (1773–1852), an actual Eton headmaster notorious for administering severe canings" ("Onomastic Satire" 189). Even though Miss Keate holds a prestigious position unavailable to women in Huxley's day, her name fits within the same disturbing paradigm that Morgana's does: names that recall unappealing or villainous characters go predominantly to women. Focusing on the appellation "Miss," Deery questions whether Miss Keate's femininity is compromised: "'Miss' Keate, [is] surely an anachronistic form of address in a society where there is no marriage. Perhaps Huxley has forgotten this in his desire to recreate the stereotype of the spinsterish headmistress, the woman who achieves position only by forfeiting her 'true femininity'" (Meckier 262). As with Morgana, the specter of the spinsterish bluestocking compromises the impression made by this female character.

Deery convincingly argues that the derogatory labeling of women actually is encoded in the World State's labels, symbols, and icons. For example, as we find at times even today, male adults are regarded as men, but grown women are referred to as girls. Deery thus notes that "as opposed to the 'Girls' Dressing Room'… the men emerge from the upper-class 'Alpha Changing Rooms,'" though he also notes that the text gives us little basis on which to judge "whether the bias is the dystopians' or Huxley's" (Deery 262). Deery identifies a similar disparity in the technical signs for men and women:

> The association of technology with masculinity is reinforced by the fact that the sign for males in this society happens to be identical to the divine symbol of Fordian technology, the T…. Fertile women, on the other hand, are represented by a circle, which, apart from its obvious genital associations, suggests zero, nothingness, hollow space, and passivity…. Moreover, if we see it as our own symbol of women (♀Venus) minus the Christian cross, then, as men have gained divinity, women have had it taken from them (Deery 263).

While it is unclear if Huxley chose these signifiers to provoke the reader's satirical scrutiny, they do elevate men through an association with technological innovation, while devaluing women through a visual representation of their genitals. The semiotic implications are even more troubling for women, who were sterilized at birth:

> Other women who have been sterilized are designated by a question mark, as though suspicious or doubtful, and certainly something to

snigger at. These 'freemartins' do not constitute a third gender. They are still heterosexual and feminine, though, incidentally, since the latter comes from the root 'to suckle,' none of these childless women are in fact strictly 'feminine' (Deery 263).

Arguably, the question mark tends to undermine not just the femininity but the full humanity of the freemartins, indicating that both a woman's worth and her identity depend upon her sexual and reproductive fitness. Deery concedes that it is unclear whether Huxley "acknowledges a bias in the labelling of any of these categories" (Deery 263), but she reminds the reader that only women are sterilized: "In *Brave New World* 70 percent of females are sterilized and the remaining 30 percent are drilled on how to use the pill; yet men's natural processes are not modified in any way, an imbalance which is not remarked upon in the text" (Deery 265). Thus, while men are left to their own devices, some women bear sole responsibility for administering birth control and the rest are rendered sterile. Again, it remains unclear whether Huxley deliberately presents this as a dystopian feature of the novel, but the fact that it receives minimal narrative consideration suggests that he does not.

The genetic engineering of babies may be a predicative rather than a cautionary feature of Huxley's dystopia. The women of the World State—at least under typical circumstances—are free of the individual obligations of pregnancy, birth, and child rearing. However, we must consider both whether this is a good or a bad thing and how the author appears to feel about it. Deery views the elimination of maternity as a negative development, with which Huxley was entirely comfortable, noting that: "Huxley also found the intimacy of natural motherhood to be repugnant and even dangerous, especially for the child…though again female disempowerment is not his explicit focus (Deery 264–65). Deery perceives the decanting of babies as a troublingly foreseeable extension of the medical appropriation of midwifery and other natural childbirth practices that arose in the latter part of the nineteenth century. March is more ambivalent about this development, but also has well-justified qualms, noting that the freeing of women from procreation also leads to their devaluation within the society at large (March 54–55). Since the androcentric state now has absolute societal authority, women—despite the putative freedom to be a variety of things other than daughters, wives, and mothers—are now valued only as "meat" for the physical gratification they can impart to men. Whether or not he is fully aware of it, Huxley illustrates how women can be liberated without being truly free. For Madden, separating reproduction from the female body facilitates an unnatural male appropriation of science that is such a hallmark of this perverse society that it is manifest even in the urban landscape: "The setting of *Brave New World*, a future London of phallic skyscrapers, is a world, in which the male principle of science has subjugated and nearly eradicated the female principle of nature…. In this world…science has usurped the female's ability to reproduce" (Madden 289–90). March, Deery, and Madden agree that the losses incurred by women through this putative liberation from reproduction and the attendant domestic sphere far outweigh the meager gains. March asks why Huxley feels compelled to present the liberated women either unflatteringly or as a mere sex object: "A more complex discussion involves questioning the roles of women when divorced from reproductive imperatives—why does Huxley see this as threatening?" (March 55).

Given the extent to which women are socially and physically disempowered in Huxley's vision of the future, it is not immediately clear whether they have sufficient agency to rebel or whether insurgency is another area within the exclusive domain of male characters. Madden believes that Huxley portrays the female citizens of the World State as far more compliant than their male counterparts, implying that Huxley imbues only men with the ability to question the status quo: "The women seem more naturally promiscuous than their male counterparts, and only men appear to have reservations about engaging in promiscuity" (March 291). Sanjukta Dasgupta reaches the same conclusion: "women in *Brave New World* experience complete satiation or feel deprived if they are denied access to technology-generated creature comforts" (Dasgupta 210). But the reluctance of Lenina Crowne—the most fully realized female character in the novel—to stop exclusively dating Henry Foster undercuts these dubious generalizations. When queried by her friend Fanny, Lenina has this to say: "'it's only about four months now since I've been having Henry…. No, there hasn't been any one else,' she answered almost truculently. 'And I jolly well don't see why there should have been'" (29). Here, Lenina seems defiantly resistant to the social and legal obligation to live promiscuously.

In his analysis of Lenina, David Leon Higdon wonders if Huxley's sexism precluded the realization that women could have the necessary independence of thought to rebel: "Either Lenina is as self-consciously a rebel against her benevolently totalitarian world as are the men, but left undeveloped because Huxley could not conceive of a woman rebel, or Huxley allowed gross inconsistencies onto his pages that threaten the integrity of his closed system and the themes of his work" (Higdon 81). But in Huxley's defense, Mustapha Mond, while discussing Bernard's fate with Helmholtz and John, does reveal that both men *and women* have been sent to islands for subversive behavior: "'He's being sent to an island… to a place where he'll meet the most interesting set of men and women to be found anywhere in the world. All the people who, for one reason or another, have got too self-consciously individual to fit into community life'" (*Brave New World* 174). Although the novel focuses primarily on male characters, Huxley clearly saw women as capable of radical thought and action, which is why some critics are puzzled by his apparent failure to count Lenina among the novel's insurgents and exploit her destabilizing tendencies.

Not everyone finds insurrectionary potential or, for that matter, depth of any kind in Lenina. Meckier suspects that her surname signals her foolish nature: "Fanny and Lenina Crowne provide another example of a joke at a character's expense that grows steadily more complicated. The surname they share stems from John Crowne (1641–1712), a largely forgotten Restoration playwright. Perhaps Huxley was thinking of Crowne's song 'The Foolish Maid' from *The Married Beau*" ("Onomastic Satire" 160). Worse than her being simply foolish, C.S. Ferns thinks that Lenina is a repository of every conditioned behavior and prefabricated banality of the World State; he finds her bereft of any individuality:

> Lenina is... the product of conditioning rather than a person in her own right. Yet by her very vacuousness she helps to expose what a great deal of romantic love is all about—the projection onto someone else of a private fantasy, rather than a genuine attempt to *know* them. Lenina shows up this element of projection so clearly because she is, so to speak, a blank screen (Ferns 111).

To Ferns' thinking, John has fallen in love with a persona of his own making that he unwittingly projects onto Lenina's nubile body; she is a tabula rasa beneath the wafer-thin personality conferred on her by the state and John's subsequent idealization. Milton Birnbaum concurs, deeming Lenina to be interested only in sex and too shallow to be capable of reciprocal love:

> Most of...[Huxley's] female characters...seem to be completely insensitive to the more delicate nuances of love or the cravings in their lovers for emotional as well as physical satiety. Lenina Crowne... symbolizes this preoccupation with the physical side of love when she cannot understand why the Savage and Bernard Marx are so hesitant in making love to her, especially in view of the many testimonials of other men to her "pneumatic" quality (Birnbaum 287).

March provides a similar assessment of Lenina, whom she describes as "vacuous" (March 53) and regards as a cautionary specimen of what genetic and social engineering produce, facilitating "Huxley's warnings about the impact of mass consumerism and sexual liberty—she acts out the familiar 'dumb blonde' stereotype" (March 54). For March, Lenina goes "speedily back to the comforts of *soma* and promiscuity" following her "awkward encounters" with John the Savage (March 54). This reductive interpretation of Lenina misrepresents her response to John's rebukes. Lenina does not, as March asserts, revert to *soma* and promiscuity following her "awkward encounters" with John. Instead, as Peter Edgerly Firchow points out, she exhibits genuine frustration with her life in World State, finding *soma* and casual sex for the first time insufficient. Remarkably, Lenina begins to fall progressively deeper in love with John, a process that Firchow deftly catalogs:

> There is the scene following Lenina's and the Savage's return from the feelies when the Savage sends her off in the taxicopter just as she is getting ready to seduce him. There is the touching moment when Lenina, who had once been terrified of pausing with Bernard to look at the sea and the moon over the Channel, now lingers "for a moment to look at the moon," before being summoned by the irritated and uncomprehending Arch-Songster. There is Lenina's increasing impatience with the obtuseness of Henry Foster and his blundering solicitousness. There are the fond murmurings to herself of the Savage's name. There is the conference with Fanny as to what she should do about the Savage's strange coldness toward her. There is the blunt rejection of Fanny's advice to seek consolation with one of the millions of other men (Firchow 147–48).

Lenina's innate ability to love arguably differentiates her from every other citizen of the World State, including Bernard, Helmholtz, and Mustapha Mond. These other characters *may* be capable of falling in love, but Lenina is the only one who actually does. Krishan Kumar persuasively argues that she demonstrates emotional depth (through her relationship with Foster and her friendship with Bernard) even before meeting John:

> Thus it is not really surprising that she should fall for the Savage. But her feeling for him develops well beyond anything she has ever experienced before.... She actually falls *in love*—an extraordinary and utterly reprehensible thing in *Brave New World*; ... and any further progression in her attachment could very well lead to trouble and even exile for her. Such demonstrations of feeling for one person are in the highest degree subversive. She is saved from this fate by the Savage's own violent repudiation of her and his subsequent self-seclusion and suicide (Kumar 287).

The fact that Huxley endows a woman with the ability to feel and return love in a loveless dystopian world implies that he is less sexist than critics such as March and Madden claim. Unlike John's ludicrous attempt to "free the slaves" by throwing *soma* rations out of a window, Lenina's expression of love for John presents a genuine threat to the status quo.

Bradley W. Buchanan explains why romantically loving only one person is such a volatile taboo in *Brave New World*: "An 'only love' is an incestuous love, in Huxley's futuristic world, because it tends to work against the social solidarity, which is the key to peaceful life" ("Oedipus Against Freud" 29). Lenina's love for John threatens the principles of "community, identity, stability" (Huxley, *Brave New World* 1) on which the World State depends, especially since she acts on her feelings by engaging in monogamous behavior, initially with Henry Foster and, ultimately, when she pines after John. Even Theodor Adorno, who, in my opinion, inaccurately describes Lenina as a character "determined to preserve her incomprehension intact" (Adorno 101), concedes that she is capable of analytical reasoning; she questions the artistic merit of the feelies as much as John does and without his prompting:

> Lenina's overzealous defensiveness betrays insecurity, the suspicion that her kind of happiness is distorted by contradictions, that it is not happiness even by its own definition. No pharisaical recollection of Shakespeare is necessary to become aware of the fatuousness of the feelies and of the 'objective despair' of the audience which participates in it (Adorno 111).

Firchow notes that Lenina moves beyond critical thought to decisive action "in defiance of what she knows to be the properly promiscuous code of sexual behavior" (Firchow 147). Sean A. Witters asserts that, through Lenina, Huxley suggests that the inclination to be monogamous is instinctive and so deeply ingrained that it resists both genetic manipulation and relentless conditioning:

> In Huxley's schema, this is a way of naturalizing monogamy, or rather, indulging the notion that the desire for long-term individual

commitment is innate. For Lenina, it seems an instinctual behavior that emerges against her will. It denies her conditioning and the state's power to undo what nature has built (Witters 82).

Witters makes clear that Lenina's monogamous ways are not simply shocking but a challenge to state authority.

In light of Lenina's destabilizing potential as a revolutionary, it is revealing that Huxley does not appear to regard her as a bona fide threat to the social order. Higdon attributes Huxley's failure to do so to his misogyny:

> A careful consideration of Lenina's attitudes, decisions, and actions shows that the overlay of misogyny careened Huxley into contradicting his ideas, into failing to see that Lenina is more heroic in her resistance to the Fordian world than are the men his narrative praises.... Lenina's resistance goes unnoticed in the novel because of the novel's misogyny, but it can go unnoticed no longer, given feminism's attention to such marginalized characters (Higdon 79).

For Higdon, Lenina resists conformity on multiple levels. Apart from embracing monogamy, she also defies the color coding, on which the World State's rigid caste system depends. Despite belonging to a privileged class, Lenina frequently wears the green color of a laborer, which:

> clearly places Lenina outside the color codes of the caste system, the only character, other than the outsider John, who is allowed this violation.... Lenina is not construed by Huxley as a rebel for wearing green even though her green wardrobe clearly marks her as being unorthodox. Lenina is, after all, either an Alpha (most likely) or a Beta and should be wearing gray or maroon.... Lenina's wardrobe of green, white (other than her at-work uniform), and pink directly interrogates the text in which it appears (Higdon 80–81).

Higdon argues that the potential ramifications of Lenina's challenge to the dress code are as serious as her sexual deviance, but more readily visible. Huxley's seeming inability to recognize the significance of Lenina's transgressions signals a profound inconsistency within the text. While focusing on the unsuccessful resistance of Bernard, Helmholtz, and John, Huxley has inadvertently made an instinctive rebel out of Lenina, demonstrating to the reader how misogyny and other prejudices diminish the ability to see clearly.

Higdon points out that, though Huxley reconsidered *Brave New World* and assessed some of its shortcomings in both his 1946 foreword to a reprint of the novel and in *Brave New World Revisited* in 1958, the author does not discuss the novel's problematic treatment of "Lenina or women" in either work (Higdon 82). Yet there is evidence that Huxley ultimately acknowledged Lenina's importance. Laura Frost claims that, in a planned musical adaptation of the novel from 1952, Huxley transforms Lenina into a free-thinking radical, who ultimately becomes John's willing accomplice:

> The most striking change is the character of Lenina, who is less sexually aggressive and much more intelligent than she is in the novel. She joins John in reading *The Complete Works of Shakespeare*, and in the conclusion of the musical—where Huxley takes the "third alternative" he mentions in his 1946 foreword to *Brave New World*— Lenina and John depart to join a community of like-minded exiles in Tahiti (Frost 465).

Had the completed script for this musical been produced, critical appreciation for Lenina might be more widespread and Huxley might be less susceptible to accusations of chauvinism.

Other critics have noted that Lenina brings an element of tragedy to an otherwise comedic satire of a Wellsian utopia. John Coughlin argues that by approaching the Savage with a look of yearning, outstretched arms, and tears in her eyes in the novel's penultimate scene, Lenina shows not only love but pathos: "The fact that Lenina had the emotion of pathos was her greatest assertion of individual humanity and compassion, with compassion heretofore an unknown element" (Coughlin 93). While tragedy usually entails the death of the hero, Firchow maintains that Lenina's survival, as opposed to John's suicide, is what makes the story of their love so tragic:

For him, the end is swift and tragic. For Lenina, however, there is no end; her tragedy—and for all the comedy and irony in which her love for the Savage is immersed, the word *tragedy* is not entirely inappropriate—her tragedy is that she has felt an emotion that she can never express or communicate or realize again (Firchow 148).

Kim Kirkpatrick stretches this motif even further, emphasizing Lenina's heroic quality by providing a Nietzschean reading of the text that casts her as the Dionysian sacrifice. Falling beneath the whip of the Apollonian John among chanting revelers, who become a de facto chorus:

> Lenina emerges as a far more necessary character within Huxley's novel than has been discussed previously. In fact, she is cast as the Dionysian god figure and, therefore, is the hero of the tragedy, with the expectation that she will be sacrificed at the conclusion of the drama so that the community can prosper and become artistically fertile (Kirkpatrick 107).

While Kirkpatrick's interpretation, which is premised on the unverifiable assertion that John kills Lenina, is a bit farfetched, it does lend credence to the idea that Lenina is potentially a richer, deeper, more complex character than Huxley realized.

The case can be made that John's mother, Linda, is similarly undervalued by the novelist and many critics of his work. Buchanan dismisses her as an unsympathetic parody of Frieda Lawrence: "Frieda exasperated Huxley by her unreliability, indolence, and stubbornness and may have provided a model for Linda" (Buchanan, "Oedipus in Dystopia" 88). Nonetheless, Linda is a survivor, who successfully adapts to harsh circumstances, raises and loves the child she could have abandoned, and, through her attachment to Popé, is as unconventionally monogamous as Lenina. Indeed, Meckier sees Linda and Lenina as two versions of the same person, noting the mirroring that occurs when they initially meet at Malpais:

> Spying Lenina, Linda, who is all "flabbiness" and "wrinkles" with "sagging cheeks" and "purplish blotches"… confronts her former self.

Part of a contrast in miniature between Malpais and Fordian London. Linda personifies the primitive past that John will be compelled to embrace in the novel's climatic debate. No brighter than Linda but shuddering with disgust at the sight of her. Lenina represents Mond's antiseptic alternative (Meckier, "Huxley's Americanization..." 441).

The validity of this revealing connection is buttressed by Huxley's alterations to the typescript of the novel, which show that Linda's name was originally supposed to be Nina, but was later changed to avoid confusion due to the excessive similarity between "Lenina" and "Nina" (Meckier, "Huxley's Americanization..." 440–41). Although she has received less critical attention, probably because of her physical unattractiveness, one could argue that Linda is as heroic and remarkable as Lenina. At the very least, a comprehensive understanding of Lenina is impossible without a comparative analysis of Linda.

Because Huxley's focus lay elsewhere, an examination of the treatment of gender in *Brave New World* provides intriguing insights to the author's personal views, biases, and blind spots. In contrast to the overtly satirical facets of the novel, the portions that deal with gender emerge from an unguarded narrative perspective. As Deery notes, the lower position of women relative to men in this society does not seem to be a concern of its dystopian critique: "there are many unattractive features of this society, but women's lack of position is not foregrounded as one of them" (Deery 262–63). Huxley's relative lack of sensitivity to gender issues leads us to question how other prejudices arise in *Brave New World*. Deery, for example, discusses the intersection of classism and sexism in the novel, noting the power imbalance of Alpha men pursuing Beta women (Deery 261–62). We might also identify traces of anti-Semitism in Huxley's depiction of Morgana Rothschild. In short, room remains for more critical work on Huxley's portrayal of women and other historically marginalized groups.

Works Cited

Adorno, Theodor W. "Aldous Huxley and Utopia." *Prisms*. 1967. Trans. Samuel and Shierry Weber. Cambridge, MA: MIT Press, 1983.

Birnbaum, Milton. "Aldous Huxley's Animadversions Upon Sexual Love." *Texas Studies in Literature and Language* 8.2 (Summer 1966): 285–296.

Buchanan, Bradley W. "Oedipus Against Freud: Humanism and the Problem of Desire in *Brave New World.*" *Huxley's Brave New World: Essays.* Eds. David Garrett Izzo and Kim Kirkpatrick. Jefferson, NC: McFarland, 2008. 26–45.

_____. "Oedipus in Dystopia: Freud and Lawrence in Aldous Huxley's *Brave New World.*" *Journal of Modern Literature* 25. 3–4 (Summer 2002): 75–89.

Coughlin, John. "*Brave New World* and Ralph Ellison's *Invisible Man.*" *Huxley's Brave New World: Essays.* Eds. David Garrett Izzo and Kim Kirkpatrick. Jefferson, NC: McFarland, 2008. 88–95.

Dasgupta, Sanjukta. "Geographies and Gender: Ideological Shifts in *Brave New World* and *Island.*" *Aldous Huxley Annual* 8 (2008): 207–219.

Deery, June. "Technology and Gender in Aldous Huxley's Alternative (?) Worlds." *Extrapolation: A Journal of Science Fiction and Fantasy* 33.3 (1992): 258–273.

Ferns, C.S. "Using Fantasy to Criticize Reality." *Readings on Brave New World.* Ed. Katie de Koster. San Diego, CA: Greenhaven Press, 1999. 106–113.

Firchow, Peter Edgerly. "Huxley's Characters Are Appropriate for the Novel." *Readings on Brave New World.* Ed. Katie de Koster. San Diego, CA: Greenhaven Press, 1999. 139–149.

Frost, Laura. "Huxley's Feelies: The Cinema of Sensation in *Brave New World.*" *Twentieth-Century Literature* 52.4 (Winter 2006): 443–473.

Higdon, David Leon. "The Provocations of Lenina in Huxley's *Brave New World.*" *International Fiction Review* 29.1–2 (2002): 78–83.

Huxley, Aldous. *Brave New World.* 1932. New York: Harper & Row, 1965.

Kirkpatrick, Kim. "*The Birth of Tragedy* and the Dionysian Principle in *Brave New World.*" *Huxley's Brave New World: Essays.* Eds. David Garrett Izzo and Kim Kirkpatrick. Jefferson, NC: McFarland, 2008. 107–115.

Kumar, Krishan. *Utopia & Anti-Utopia in Modern Times.* New York: Blackwell, 1987.

Madden, Deanna. "Women in Dystopia: Misogyny in *Brave New World, 1984,* and *A Clockwork Orange.*" *Misogyny in Literature: An*

Essay Collection. Ed. Katherine Anne Ackley. New York: Garland Publishing, 1992. 289–311.

March, Christie. "A Dystopic View of Gender in Aldous Huxley's Brave New World (1932)." *Women in Literature: Reading Through the Lens of Gender*. Eds. Jerilyn Fisher & Ellen S. Silber. Westport, CT: Greenwood Press, 2003. 53–55.

Meckier, Jerome. "Huxley's Americanization of the *Brave New World* Typescript." *Twentieth-Century Literature* 48.4 (Winter 2002): 427–460.

Meckier, Jerome. "Onomastic Satire: Names and Naming in *Brave New World*." *Aldous Huxley Annual*. 3 (2003): 155–198.

Witters, Sean A. "Words Have to Mean Something More: Folkloric Reading in *Brave New World*." *Huxley's Brave New World: Essays*. Eds. David Garrett Izzo and Kim Kirkpatrick. Jefferson, NC: McFarland, 2008. 73–87.

Portraits, not Prophesies: Huxley's and Orwell's Dystopian Visions

Jackson Ayres

Few twentieth-century British novels can boast legacies as powerful and pervasive, not to mention intertwined, as those of Aldous Huxley's *Brave New World* (1932) and George Orwell's *Nineteen Eighty-Four* (1949). Despite or because of their grim pessimism, Huxley's and Orwell's bleak dystopian narratives remain enduringly popular and have helped shape the postwar political and cultural landscapes. Indeed, Malcolm Bradbury, in *The Modern British Novel* (2001), notes that in "1997 Waterstone's bookshop and Channel Four television polled 25,000 British readers on the hundred most important books of the century...Orwell's *Nineteen Eighty-Four* [was ranked] at number two, [and] Aldous Huxley's *Brave New World* at fifteen" (Bradbury 505). Unsurprisingly, then, these two novels are consistently mentioned together in the same breath by literary critics and historians. Jesse Matz, for example, expresses a critical commonplace when he asserts that "*Brave New World* is an earlier attempt to do what Orwell would do fifteen years later: combine the experimental outlook with social responsibility" (Matz 93). To an extent, Matz is correct, for both texts are satirical dystopian novels intended to serve as sharp social and political commentaries. As such, the novels do invite comparison: Huxley and Orwell comparably project nightmarish visions of oppressive totalitarian societies, in which centralized power, extreme political and cultural organization, and state propaganda are portrayed as destructive of freedom and individuality. Yet, despite their shared anxieties, thematic overlaps, and similarly despairing tones, the two dystopian visions crucially differ when it comes to fundamental assumptions underlying their politico-cultural diagnoses.

Apart from the particular targets of their critiques—Huxley is more concerned with the depravities of consumer capitalism, whereas Orwell focuses his attention on totalitarian tendencies in modern politics—the two novels are separated by the authors' ideas about human nature, especially with regard to sex and sexuality. *Brave New World*, on one hand, presumes an essential human nature that must be safeguarded from perversion and suppression, while, on the other hand, *Nineteen Eighty-Four* suggests that "humanity" itself is a cultural invention that, for better or worse, is largely determined by political structures and arrangements. This disagreement on the nature of the human marks a critical—if often ignored or de-emphasized—line of separation between the two novels. Such fundamental differences between the novels, however, are frequently passed over in favor of somewhat superficial comparisons of the relative exactitude with which their authors "predicted" the future. Therefore, before pursuing the contending senses of the human in the two novels, this chapter will briefly outline the longstanding tendency to compare—and evaluate—*Brave New World* and *Nineteen Eighty-Four* on the basis of the apparent accuracy in their portrayals of the future and also suggest why this practice is problematic.

Getting the Future "Right"

Notably, Huxley and Orwell themselves seemed equally insistent that one novel's portrayal of a degraded future is more perceptive, and therefore, by extension, more probable than the other. Orwell, in 1940, wrote that *Brave New World* "was a good caricature of the hedonistic Utopia, the kind of thing that seemed possible and even imminent before Hitler appeared, but it had no relation to the actual future" (Orwell, *My Country...* 17). He repeated this estimation in a short essay on dystopian fiction that he wrote later that same year: "But though *Brave New World* was a brilliant caricature of the present (the present of 1930), it probably casts no light on the future. No society of that kind would last more than a couple of generations, because a ruling class which thought principally in terms of a 'good time' would soon lose its vitality" (Orwell, *My Country...* 31). Orwell's references to Hitler and class suggest that he believes Huxley's novel betrays its author's unsophisticated political consciousness—an implication that Orwell would make explicit in his 1946 review of Yevgeny Zamyatin's influential dystopian novel *We* (1923). In Orwell's view, *"Brave New World* must be partly derived from [*We*]...though Huxley's book shows less political awareness and is more influenced by recent biological and psychological theories" (Orwell, *In Front . . .*73). *Brave New World*'s grounding in contemporary science, according to Orwell's review, also mitigates its political incisiveness, in that it relies too heavily on a poorly conceived hyper-rationality: "It is [Zamyatin's] intuitive grasp of the irrational side of totalitarianism—human sacrifice, cruelty as an end in itself, the worship of a Leader who is credited with divine attributes—that makes Zamyatin's book superior to Huxley's" (Orwell, *In Front . . .*75). Though Orwell never outright disparages *Brave New World*, as he would Huxley's later work, he repeatedly indicates that Huxley's most famous novel, due largely to its political deficiencies, had become outmoded within ten years of its initial publication.

For his part, Huxley likewise staked a claim to greater insight and relevance. In *Brave New World Revisited* (1958), a treatise published nearly thirty years after *Brave New World*, Huxley reassessed his own novel with an eye toward proving his book's far-sightedness and emphasizing its urgent significance. Huxley justifies this claim, in part, by comparing his book to *Nineteen Eighty-Four:*

> George Orwell's *1984* was a magnified projection into the future of a present that contained Stalinism and an immediate past that had witnessed the flowering of Nazism.... In the context of 1948, *1984* seemed dreadfully convincing. But tyrants, after all, are mortal and circumstances change. Recent developments in Russia and recent advances in science and technology have robbed Orwell's book of some of its gruesome verisimilitude.... But...we can say that it now looks as though the odds were more in favor of something like *Brave New World* than of something like *1984*. (Huxley, *Brave New World Revisited* 2)

For a time, Huxley suggests, *Nineteen Eighty-Four* was—or at least appeared to be—the keener and more pertinent dystopian vision. However, if we take critical judgments to be marathons not sprints, Huxley seems to say, his novel surpasses the briefly intense, but soon exhausted, *Nineteen Eighty-Four. Brave New World Revisited* proceeds to systematically explain how *Brave New World* has grown increasingly germane, with occasional contrasts to the allegedly dated vision of *Nineteen Eighty-Four.*

Critics who have sought to differentiate *Brave New World* and *Nineteen Eighty-Four* have often taken similar approaches as Huxley and Orwell, in that they base their discernments on which of the two authors was "more right" in his depiction of the future. Michael Walzer, for example, recognizes that though "many of [*Nineteen Eighty-Four*'s] major themes had been anticipated ... in earlier anti-utopian novels, like Zamyatin's *We* and Huxley's *Brave New World*," Orwell's novel was the true "forerunner," for it is "as if *1984* released the flood" of "major theoretical works on totalitarianism as a political regime" (Walzer 103), which appeared immediately after Orwell's novel. In other words, Walzer suggests *Nineteen Eighty-Four* is partly responsible for the dominant political frameworks and debates of the late twentieth-century. Dominic Head similarly writes, "At the level of prophecy, it is true, the repudiation of the corrupt mechanics of the communist state implicit in...*Nineteen Eighty-Four* chimes with the Cold War mood, which is dominant in Western society through into the 1980s" (Head 13). By contrast, Bradbury implies that the remarkable accuracy of Huxley's novel was quickly apparent, melancholily noting that Huxley lived his final years watching "a good many of his bleaker predictions and prophesies come true in the age of science and mechanization" (Bradbury 189). Moreover, the conservative legal scholar Richard Posner argues that, while he finds *Nineteen Eighty-Four* to be a superior novel, *Brave New World* is the more foretelling cultural commentary: "The important point is that there is no contradiction in asserting that the novel which (though written earlier) predicted our current situation more accurately is the lesser work of literature" (Posner 211). Now, without question, critical comparisons of *Nineteen Eighty-Four* and *Brave New World* are wide-ranging and diverse, but the above assessments are nonetheless representative of the widespread tendency to evaluate the two novels in light of their apparent prophetic precision.

Such evaluations of accuracy in Huxley's and Orwell's respective visions, however, need to be properly contextualized. Reed Way Dasenbrock points to the forceful sway that context has upon evaluations of the two novels: "One's stance on this issue depends on one's location in space and time: life in Western Europe or the United States today feels more like *Brave New World*, while residents of dictatorships might consider *1984* closer to home" (Dasenbrock 247). Dasenbrock's claim here is driven home by Czesław Miłosz's assertion, in *The Captive Mind* (1953), that Orwell fascinated Eastern European anti-communist dissidents by virtue of "his insight into details they know well" (Miłosz 42). More recently, in 2011, a digital infographic, titled "Orwell versus Huxley"—which was created by the Column Five visual media group and which quickly went viral—avers that *Nineteen Eighty-Four* resonates with attempts of repressive non-Western regimes (specifically Egypt, Iran, and Turkey) to censor Internet access, while *Brave New World* speaks to the vapid consumer culture of the contemporary West: "In Orwell's world, communication would be limited between people to prevent conspiring against the government.... In the Huxlean future, governments encourage mass distribution of entertainment, as it pacifies the people and diverts attention away from political issues." The relative purchase *Nineteen Eighty-Four* or *Brave New World* has on the present moment, then, is in constant flux, a fact that mitigates any attempt to declare that one author "got it more right" than the other.

Indeed, the profound interpretive influence of the contexts within which readings of *Brave New World* and *Nineteen Eighty-Four* are made complicates the seemingly irrepressible tendency to read Huxley and Orwell as oracles rather than novelists. But, both *Brave New World* and *Nineteen Eighty-Four* are, above all else, novels. As *dystopian* novels, though, they are specifically fictions that draw upon past events, magnify current circumstances, and extrapolate from ongoing cultural trends. In this way, they are anatomies of the present, not prophecies for the future. Indeed, M. Keith Booker's conception of the subgenre, found in *The Dystopian Impulse in Modern Literature* (1994), "underscore[s] the role of dystopian fiction as social criticism" (Booker 18). Booker goes on to argue "that the modern turn to dystopian fiction is largely attributable to perceived inadequacies in existing social and political systems" (Booker 20). The presence of the word "existing" in Booker's explanation of the dystopian turn calls attention to the fact that, while such novels inescapably comment on the past and have implications for the future, their function as social criticism is distinctly oriented toward the present.

Curiously, taking such fictions as analyses of the contemporary casts a new light on the habit of *praising* dystopian novels that do in fact resemble their authors' futures. After all, if buried within (or explicitly stated by) the dystopian novel's social critique is a warning, then that, which is taken by later audiences to be perspicacity, can instead be seen as confirmation that the novel's critique went unheeded—the dystopian novelist as Cassandra. Orwell's Winston Smith recognizes this conundrum, lamenting, as he sets out to write in his journal, "How could you communicate with the future? Either the future would resemble the present in which case it would not listen to him, or it would be different from it, and his predicament would be meaningless" (Orwell, *Nineteen Eighty-Four* 10). Dystopian novelists, in a sense, aim to create future readerships who will find their renderings of the future to be incomprehensible, not to ring true. Given this paradoxical mission of the dystopian novel, Booker's analysis of the tradition helps explain why Huxley's novel is more recognizable to readers living in contemporary America and the West generally, while Orwell's novel resonates with the repressive dictatorial regimes of the twenty-first century. According to Booker, *Brave New World* is primarily "a warning against runaway capitalism and [is] an anticipation of coming developments in Western consumer society" while *Nineteen Eighty-Four* is best understood "as a commentary on Stalinism (and to some extent fascism)" (Booker 20). *Brave New World* and *Nineteen Eighty-Four* thus target the two social and political structures dominant at the time of their compositions: "bourgeois capitalism (exemplified by the United States) and Communism (exemplified by the Soviet Union)" (Booker 20). The two novels, it should be noted, do not comprehend these two political poles in strictly antithetical terms: Huxley is critical of authoritarianism, and his World State reflects anxieties over communitarian and internationalist political projects; likewise, the "immediate resonance" of *Nineteen Eighty-Four* "was dependent upon the [British] post-war experience of austerity, where shortages, rationing, and government control and bureaucracy made (in particular) the confinement of 'Airstrip One,' Orwell's depiction of London in *Nineteen Eighty-Four*, seem a faintly plausible extension of reality" (Head 13), a claim that ironically reverses Orwell's diminishing statement that *Brave New World* was "was a brilliant caricature of the present" (Orwell, *My Country...* 31). Nevertheless, taken together, Huxley and Orwell show how seemingly liberated and blatantly authoritarian political systems can alike oppress the individual. Yet, the actual nature of the individual, outside and within such nightmarish systems, constitutes a key point of disagreement for the novelists, which serves as the basis for the contrast to which this chapter now turns. Huxley's assumption of an essential human nature and Orwell's contrary view that humanity is a cultural invention can be detected in the novelists' contending depictions of sex.

Sex and Human Nature in Huxley's World State

Sex and sexuality, as represented by Huxley and Orwell, stand out as prominent points of contrast for the two novels—the ways that sex figures into Huxley's and Orwell's respective totalitarian societies are emblematic of their different social critiques. In *Nineteen Eighty-Four,* sexuality is repressed and sex is divorced from pleasure, while in *Brave New World*, sexuality is publicly expressed and sex is reduced to nothing but pleasure. Both renderings were likely affected by the authors' own attitudes toward sex. Margaret Drabble indicates Orwell's sexual anxieties, remarking that Orwell "was a prisoner of the brutal sexual politics of his day, and *Nineteen Eight-Four* was to show no sign of liberation from them" (Drabble 41). Moreover, Drabble notes that, during his lifetime, Orwell was subject to "accusations of sadism and flagellation fantasies" (Drabble 42), and that he frequently expressed discomfort over the trend, throughout the 1930s, for sexually explicit passages in fiction. On the other hand, Huxley's lifelong interest in alternative lifestyles and countercultures often brought him into the realms of sexual liberation and experimentation, though he also expressed a rather conventional discomfort over perceived increases in promiscuity and licentiousness. Huxley and Orwell's views on sexuality, understandably, reflect their conceptions of human nature, which means that their novels' depictions of sex can help clarify how the authors define "humanity."

Unlike *Nineteen Eighty-Four*'s totalitarian state, Oceania—in which sexual activity is meant exclusively for reproduction—sex in *Brave New World*'s World State has been made independent of reproduction. State-run laboratories (called hatcheries) and conditioning centers fertilize eggs and "decant" children, using various genetic engineering techniques. Procedures in these centers, such as the Bokanovsky's Process, which allows one egg to yield scores of children, represent "the principle of mass production at last applied to biology" (Huxley, *Brave New World* 4). Prenatal genetic manipulation leads to the creation of five distinct castes, from Alphas at top to Epsilons at bottom, with correspondingly descending levels of intellectual ability, physical attractiveness, social prestige, and civil rights. Women still capable of giving birth wear Malthusian Belts, popular fashion accessories resembling cartridge belts, which enable them to easily maintain a birth control regimen. The World State's elimination of natural childbirth carries with it cultural changes: pregnancy, childbirth, and parenthood are considered obscene, as words as well as concepts. When Mustapha Mond, Resident World Controller of Western Europe, encounters a group of students, he asks them, "'Try to realize what it was like to have a viviparous mother'" (Huxley, *Brave New World* 23). Apart from the titillation that comes from hearing "[t]hat smutty word again" (Huxley, *Brave New World* 23), Mond's challenge is met "without the smallest success" (Huxley, *Brave New World* 23) from the students. Separating sex from reproduction, as well as the conventional affiliations associated with reproductive sex (parent, child, sibling, and so on) is meant to promote social stability. This process is in fact two-fold: one, genetic engineering and "test tube babies" produce a rigidly stratified class system, in which citizens are conditioned, literally from before birth, to accept their position within the hierarchy, and two, the social expectation to engage in sexual activity without physical or emotional consequences pacifies the citizenry.

In *Brave New World*, Huxley decries the decoupling of sex from emotional commitment and reproduction as the degradation and destruction of naturally human responses and behaviors. Huxley's "savage" character, John, indicates the feelings of love and exclusivity that, in Huxley's view, "naturally" accompany human sexual attraction. John—who was born of English parents after an accidental pregnancy, but raised in a Native American "Savage Reservation" and, therefore, shielded from the World State's values and policies—is meant to represent an authentically primal or essential humanity. Even John's overriding "civilized" influence, the plays of Shakespeare (from which his mother taught him how to read), are naively positioned by Huxley as representative of the "authentic" human emotions and values that Shakespeare depicts—a suggestion curiously echoed by Orwell when Winston awakens from his dreaming reverie "with the word 'Shakespeare' on his lips" (Orwell, *Nineteen Eighty-Four* 29). The community in which John was raised, called Malpais and located in New Mexico, is ultimately cast not so much in an alternate civilization, but as civilization's antithesis. When two Londoners, Bernard Marx, an Alpha Plus with an inferiority complex that makes him something of an outcast, and his occasional lover, Lenina Crowne, a Beta hatchery worker who is fully integrated into and acclimated to World State society, take a plane to visit Malpais "they were crossing the frontier that separated civilization from savagery" (Huxley, *Brave New World* 70). John, then, has matured in a zone and community that constitute, as closely as possible, a true state of nature. His values and behaviors, therefore, are not portrayed by Huxley as the result of different ideological and social conditioning, but rather as the attitudes and actions of an unconditioned, or natural, human being.

For Huxley, a human in its essential form, in this case embodied by John, will experience feelings of affection and attachment concomitant with instinctual sexual desires and activities. Senses of affiliation, both tender and possessive, are presented in *Brave New World* as naturally coinciding with sexual urges and acts. For example, John's mother Linda, who stayed at the Malpais reservation to raise him among its natives, continued to have sexual encounters with various partners purely for pleasure, as she would have done in the World State. But, this behavior has severe social consequences in Malpais, as she explains to a horrified Bernard and Lenina: "'Well, here ... nobody's supposed to belong to more than one person. And if you have people in the ordinary way, the others think you're wicked and anti-social. They hate and despise you. Once a lot of women came and made a scene because their men came to see me. Well, why not? And then they rushed at me.... No, it was too awful. I can't tell you about it'" (Huxley, *Brave New World* 81). Another form of the sexual jealousy and resentment of the native women, directed at Linda for her refusal to maintain a monogamous relationship, is felt and expressed by John, who, as Linda puts it, "did get so upset whenever a man..." (Huxley, *Brave New World* 82). John's possessiveness toward his mother, which in that case is filial and protective, also manifests in his sexual anxieties over Lenina. After John tells Lenina that he loves her, she immediately disrobes and propositions him, which only serves to repulse John and ignite his temper: "he caught her by the shoulders and shook her. 'Whore!' he shouted. 'Whore! Impudent strumpet!'" (Huxley, *Brave New World* 132). This violent, angry outburst is in part motivated by John's belief that a person, throughout the entirety of his or her lifetime, remain the exclusive sexual partner for only one other person.

Of course, the notion of sexual fidelity is itself a component as well as product of cultural conditioning. Huxley points to this cultural element when he has John rationalize his rage at Lenina by referring to the marriage practices at Malpais and John's fascination with Shakespeare. Indeed, Linda herself claims that John, to his detriment, has been affected by his interactions with the natives.

When Linda tells Bernard and Lenina of John's hostility toward her multiple lovers, she laments, "'Because I never *could* make him understand that that was what civilized people ought to do. Being mad's infectious, I believe. Anyhow, John seems to have caught it from the Indians. Because, of course, he was with them a lot. Even though they always were so beastly to him and wouldn't let him do all the things the other boys did. Which was a good thing in a way, because it made it easier for me to condition him a little'" (Huxley, *Brave New World* 82). However, Huxley undermines the possibility that John's insistent monogamy is nothing more than the mirror image of the World State's enforced promiscuity. John's notions about sex may be culturally supported, but in Huxley's rendering, the norms and customs of Malpais encode and reinforce its citizens' natural predispositions and proclivities. Interestingly, Huxley seems to acknowledge that much of what constitutes human nature—brutishness, selfishness, and tendency toward superstition, among other attributes—is unsavory and atavistic, but it is authentic humanity nonetheless.

The authenticity of John's jealousies, relative to the attitudes of Lenina and others from the World State, is inadvertently affirmed by Linda even as she complains of the natives' influence upon John. Despite her disgust and embarrassment over her impregnation— "'And I *was* so ashamed. Just think of it: me, a Beta—having a baby: put yourself in my place.' (The mere suggestion made Lenina shudder.)" (Huxley, *Brave New World* 80)—Linda also acknowledges, "And yet John *was* a great comfort to me. I don't know what I should have done without him" (Huxley, *Brave New World* 82). Along these lines, Linda recalls an incident in the past in which John attacked one of her sexual partners. After the scuffle, John assumed that his mother would beat him: "But she didn't hit him. After a little time, he opened his eyes again and saw that she was looking at him. He tried to smile at her. Suddenly she put her arms round him and kissed him again and again" (Huxley, *Brave New World* 85). Even with her lifetime of cultural programming, Linda too is susceptible to the loving attachments of maternity; the only way to eliminate such bonds, Huxley suggests, is to eliminate parenthood altogether. Linda's love for her son, despite her revulsion at motherhood and the existence of cultural practices of Malpais, which again represents the state of nature, illustrate the assumption in *Brave New World* that humans are inclined to form emotional ties and affiliations as a result of sexual activity. Severing these bonds, by Huxley's logic, is an abrogation of inborn humanity. The World State, then, is unnatural and inhuman in the strictest senses of those terms.

Sex and Human Nature in Orwell's Oceania

In terms of sex, *Nineteen Eighty-Four* is an inversion of *Brave New World*: whereas the logic of the World State places extraordinary purpose in non-procreative sex, Orwell's ruling Party seeks to remove from sex any value other than reproduction. Under Party doctrine, the "only recognized purpose of marriage was to beget children for the service of the Party" (Orwell, *Nineteen Eighty-Four* 57). Familial allegiances and relationships, as in Huxley's World State, are also seen as threats to Party solidarity; however, since in Oceania the "family could not actually be abolished" (Orwell, *Nineteen Eighty-Four* 111), marriages are instead turned over to bureaucratic approval, in order to make personal relationships inextricable from the State. In fact, Party members "were encouraged to be fond of their children in almost the old-fashioned way" (Orwell, *Nineteen Eighty-Four* 111), but only because "children, on the other hand, were systematically turned against their parents and taught to spy on them and report their deviations. The family had become in effect an extension of the Thought Police" (Orwell, *Nineteen Eighty-Four* 111). The bourgeois conception of family has not, in *Nineteen Eighty-Four,* been destroyed as it has in *Brave New World*; rather, it has been transformed and repurposed in order to best suit the Party's ideological needs.

While the regulation of all relationships, including marriage, is one component of the Party's agenda, the underlying reason for its transformation of marriage into an institution meant solely for procreation is a wider and strategic campaign to denigrate sex: "Its real, undeclared purpose was to remove all pleasure from the sexual act.... The Party was trying to kill the sex instinct, or, if it could not be killed, then to distort it and dirty it" (Orwell, *Nineteen Eighty-Four* 57). Crucially, Orwell makes sure to clarify the exact target of the Party, noting that "[m]ere debauchery did not matter very much, so long as it was furtive and joyless, and only involved the women of a submerged and despised class" and that "[n]ot love so much as eroticism was the enemy, inside marriage as well as outside it" (Orwell, *Nineteen Eighty-Four* 57). The Party is not endangered by love or debauchery, but by the sexual drive itself, which is why, in Oceania, "[desire] is thoughtcrime" (Orwell, *Nineteen Eighty-Four* 59). Unlike *Brave New World*, where sex is detached from reproduction and the attainment of sexual satisfaction is an end of itself, in *Nineteen Eighty-Four* sex is only for reproduction and the pursuit, let alone attainment, of sexual pleasure is a subversive threat. Huxley positions sexual gratification divorced from consequence or commitment as a form of distraction and pacification. Orwell, by contrast, sees sexual abstinence as coterminous with doctrinaire political ideology. Winston's fellow dissident and lover, Julia, intuitively understands Party rationale more clearly than he does:

> Unlike Winston, she had grasped the inner meaning of the Party's sexual Puritanism. It was not merely that the sex instinct created a world of its own which was outside the Party's control and which therefore had to be destroyed if possible. What was more important was that sexual privation induced hysteria, which was desirable because it could be transformed into war fever and leader worship (Orwell, *Nineteen Eighty-Four* 110).

Upon hearing Julia's analysis, Winston concurs: "There was a direct, intimate connection between chastity and political orthodoxy" (Orwell, *Nineteen Eighty-Four* 111). Sexual promiscuity among Party members, then, is patently insurrectionist. Orwell's politicization of sex, a reversal of sex's role in Huxley's novel, points the way toward the authors' differing notions of human nature.

Winston and Julia's sexual relationship does indeed bring with it feelings of loyalty and love, but Orwell casts those commitments as utterly and entirely political. Their sexual encounters, far from being sentimental or even erotic, have little to do with mutual attraction, biological compulsions, or even the fulfillment of instinctual sexual desires. Winston describes his sexual liaisons with Julia and their significance: "Their embrace had been a battle, the climax a victory. It was a blow struck against the Party. It was a political act" (Orwell, *Nineteen Eighty-Four* 105). In other words, rather than sensuous and meant only for pleasure their sex is decidedly political. The force that Winston insists will bring down the Party, "simple undifferentiated desire" (Orwell, *Nineteen Eighty-Four* 105), does not actually exist, for as Winston himself recognizes, "you could not have pure love or pure lust nowadays. No emotion was pure, because everything was mixed up with fear and hatred" (Orwell, *Nineteen Eighty-Four* 105). Winston's claim that "[d]esire was thought crime" (Orwell, *Nineteen Eighty-Four* 59) must therefore be amended. Desire itself is not subversive, since a desire to fervently serve the Party is mandated. On the other hand, sexual desire is forbidden, not because it opposes ideological passion, but because it drains or redirects it. Sexual urges and activities, Orwell ultimately implies, are inextricable from the social and political conditions, in which they occur—not simply in how they are expressed, but in the very way they are conceptualized.

Sex in *Nineteen Eighty-Four* is neither an expression of love nor an outlet for uncontrollable instincts, but instead a gauge to measure a citizen's conformity to Party dogma and mission. As Elaine Hoffman Baruch argues, "In [Oceania], sexual rebellion, if it ever occurs, constitutes separation from authority figures, the mythic journey to adulthood, growth of consciousness, and total individuation. The more severe the prohibition overturned, the greater the heroism. ... Sexual freedom in *1984* is a political act" (Baruch 51–53). In contrast to the sexual revolutionaries, Winston and Julia, is Winston's estranged wife, Katherine. Winston's memories of Katherine revolve around the wedge driven into their marriage by sex: "To embrace her was like embracing a jointed wooded image.... The rigidity of her muscles managed to convey that impression. She would lie there with eyes shut, neither resisting nor cooperating, but *submitting*. It was extraordinarily embarrassing and, after a while, horrible" (Orwell, *Nineteen Eighty-Four* 58). Katherine refused to remain celibate, however, because following strict Party mandates, "[t]hey must, she said, produce a child if they could.... She had two names for it. One was 'making a baby,' and the other was 'our duty to the Party'" (Orwell, *Nineteen Eighty-Four* 58). Sexual desire, for Orwell, is not an *a priori* facet of human nature. Winston, Julia, and Katherine demonstrate that sexual urges can in fact be fully sublimated into political energies, whether orthodox or subversive.

This portrayal of sex as a creation of political circumstances comports with Orwell's broader notion of the human as rendered in *Nineteen Eighty-Four*. Orwell's novel, argues Irving Howe, "appals [sic] us because its terror, far from being inherent in the 'human condition,' is particular to our century" (Howe 236). Moreover, according to Howe, "The whole idea of the self as something precious and inviolable is a *cultural* idea, and as we understand it, a product of the liberal era" (Howe 237). *Nineteen Eighty-Four* depicts a world, in which that cultural conception of selfhood, of humanity—including its relation to sex—has been radically altered. This transformation's occurrence means that sexual identity and feelings are determined by the political and cultural structures, within which they emerge, which thereby destabilizes the notion of an immutable or essential human nature.

Absolute Destruction or Radical Transformation

In short, the difference between *Brave New World* and *Nineteen Eighty-Four* articulated in this chapter hinges on Huxley's and Orwell's opposing conceptions of human nature, which are refracted, in part, through the ways that sex and sexuality figure into their dystopian narratives. Both novels warn of totalitarianism's oppressive, indeed dehumanizing, effects upon the individual. But, Huxley's portrait of a primal sexuality suggests that his critique can be read as a warning against the possible *eradication* of authentic humanity by scientific excess, rampant consumerism, and extreme social organization, while Orwell's picture of a culturally-determined sexuality necessarily entangled with politics implies that his critique can be interpreted as a warning against the deleterious *redefinition* of the liberal idea of humanity by authoritarian totalitarian ideology.

This dispute over the human reflects a division between the novels that provides a more substantive and sustaining point of contrast than the misguided debate over which book made a better "prediction" of the future.

Works Cited

Baruch, Elaine Hoffman. "'The Golden Country': Sex and Love in *1984*." *1984 Revisited: Totalitarianism in Our Century*. Ed. Irving Howe. New York: Perennial, 1983. 47–56.

Booker, M. Keith. *The Dystopian Impulse in Modern Literature: Fiction as Social Criticism*. Westport, CT: Greenwood, 1994.

Bradbury, Malcolm. *The Modern British Novel, 1878–2001*. Rev. ed. New York: Penguin, 2001.

Dasenbrock, Reed Way. "An Absurd Century: Varieties of Satire." *The Cambridge Companion to the Twentieth-Century English Novel*. Ed. Robert L. Caserio. Cambridge, UK: Cambridge UP, 2009. 238–250.

Drabble, Margaret. "Of Beasts and Men: Orwell on Beastliness." *On Nineteen Eighty-Four: Orwell and Our Future*. Eds. Abbott Gleason, Jack Goldsmith, & Martha C. Nussbaum. Princeton, NJ: Princeton UP, 2005. 38–48.

Head, Dominic. *The Cambridge Introduction to Modern British Fiction, 1950–2000*. Cambridge, UK: Cambridge UP, 2002.

Howe, Irving. *Politics and the Novel*. 1957. Chicago: Ivan R. Dee, 2002.

Huxley, Aldous. *Brave New World*. 1932. New York: Bantam, 1946.

_____. *Brave New World Revisited*. New York: Bantam, 1960.

Matz, Jesse. *The Modern Novel: A Short Introduction*. Malden, MA: Blackwell, 2004.

Miłosz, Czesłław. *The Captive Mind*. Trans. Jane Zielonko. New York: Vintage, 1953.

Orwell, George. *Collected Essays, Journalism and Letters*. Vol. 2 *My Country Right or Left: 1940–1943*. 1968. Eds. Sonia Orwell and Ian Angus. Boston: Nonpareil Books, 2000.

_____. *Collected Essays, Journalism and Letters*. Vol. 4 *In Front of Your Nose: 1946-1950*. 1968. Eds. Sonia Orwell and Ian Angus. Boston: Nonpareil Books, 2000.

_____. *Nineteen Eighty-Four*. 1949. New York: Plume, 1983.

Posner, Richard A. "Orwell versus Huxley: Economics, Technology, Privacy, and Satire." *On* Nineteen Eighty-Four: *Orwell and Our Future*. Eds. Abbott Gleason, Jack Goldsmith, & Martha C. Nussbaum. Princeton, NJ: Princeton UP, 2005. 183–211.

Spencer, Neil. "#killswitch Infographic: Orwell vs. Huxley." *Visual News*. 23 Jun. 2011. Web. 14 Jan. 2014. <http://www.visualnews. com/2011/06/23/killswitch-infographic-orwell-vs-huxley/>.

Walzer, Michael. "On 'Failed Totalitarianism.'" 1984 *Revisited: Totalitarianism in Our Century*. Ed. Irving Howe. New York: Perennial, 1983. 103–121.

CRITICAL
READINGS

Bolshevism and *Brave New World*_____

Gregory Claeys

Many aims have been associated with Huxley's greatest work. The author himself said that the "theme of *Brave New World* is not the advancement of science as such, it is the advancement of science as it affects human individuals" (Huxley, *Brave New World* 9). Critics have also seen as its targets: contemporary America; the vulgarity of modern culture; "progress" in general and the cult of hedonism in particular, or a "bourgeois dystopia" (Booker 45), as well as utopia as such, and especially "the horror of the Wellsian utopia" (Huxley, *Letters* 353, 348); "the modern worship of science" (Morris and Kross 145); "the misuse by totalitarian government of science and technology, that is, scientism" (Trahair 47); and the growth of totalitarianism generally. Huxley himself called the book a depiction of a "utopia" in the 1946 foreword to the text, using the term in the sense of any imaginary projected vision of society, but clearly also where specific trends thought to bring positive results have the opposite effect (*Brave New World* 14). Though Judith Shklar pointedly described Huxley's key work as "not a political novel" and offering "no insights into totalitarian systems" (156), *Brave New World* has also been sometimes understood as an (admittedly quirky) anti-totalitarian work (Morris and Kross 46). Few, however, have seen Huxley chiefly as attacking *Bolshevik* totalitarianism. This essay examines the question of how far *Brave New World* can be read as a satire on Bolshevism, and the degree to which this was wedded to a critique of scientism, a mechanical world-view and modernity more generally. Clearly, *Brave New World* took as its target certain strands, which Huxley regarded as inherent in modernity as such, especially the scientific application of the psychology of propaganda, or indoctrination. This perspective, however, grew in part out of Huxley's understanding of Bolshevism. This essay's concentration, then, is mostly only on the period up to 1932, with a few comments on developments thereafter.

As David Bradshaw reminds us, Huxley had flirted with socialism since joining the Oxford Fabians in 1916 (Bradshaw viii–ix). Yet he regarded as "repulsive" the fact that Bolshevism was "a serious possibility" in November 1918 (Huxley, *Letters* 169). Huxley was not, as such, however, a political animal. But by 1932, he had acquired relatively sophisticated political instincts, and he had certainly given plenty of thought to the ultimate prospects of a world-state, especially in Wellsian guise. H.G. Wells; Vilfredo Pareto; H. L. Mencken; Mencken's master, Nietzsche; and eugenics had all reinforced a near-inherited sense of the value of an intellectual aristocracy in such schemes. With the sense of the inevitability of a small governing elite, or "ruling aristocracy of mind," probably determined by eugenic criteria, came the realization of the need for some new, or at least superior, religion, to serve "the cause of humanitarianism" (Huxley, *Complete Essays* 2: 225). Joined to this was the acceptance of the bankruptcy of the liberal mantra of the natural equality of mankind and of the herd-like nature of mass behavior, dominated as it was by "the newspaper-reading, advertisement-believing, propaganda-swallowing, demagogue-led man—the man who makes modern democracy the farce it is" (Huxley, *Complete Essays* 2:205–6). Huxley had long been contemptuous of parliamentary democracies, in which propaganda by manipulative elites successfully guided the ignorant masses. He clearly had a sense of the advantages of planned economies, writing in 1931 that, "I do feel more and more certain that unless the rest of the world adopts something on the lines of the Five Year Plan, it will break down. Modern industry is too huge and complicated to be left to individualistic enterprise" (Huxley, *Letters* 351). He was thus an opponent of the chaos of "planless individualism," as he described it in 1932. That year, Huxley was also quite prepared to "perfectly believe that a lot of people are happy in Russia—because happiness . . . is a by-product of something else and they've got a Cause ... the working for which gives them happiness . . . but it is always as history demonstrates, in the nature of a temporary intoxication". "In Russia", he added, "where propaganda is more efficient, it may last a bit longer," but would probably evaporate whether the "Plan" failed or succeeded (Bedford 2:262; Huxley, *Letters* 361–62). Some of the early novels also hint at skepticism about the recent Bolshevik revolution, as well as about the Wellsian utopia; in *Antic Hay* (1923) the "Red Guards" patrol the streets testing the class origins of people's accents—not an approach Huxley could warm to. Yet he remained curious, planning a trip to the USSR in 1931 with his brother Julian, although this trip was eventually aborted (Huxley, *Letters* 348–9).

In 1932, the year *Brave New World* appeared, Hitler had not yet come to power, though Mussolini had been Prime Minister of Italy for ten years and Huxley followed Oswald Mosley's early reform proposals with interest. Stalin had begun widespread collectivization and the implementation of the Five-Year Plan command economy in 1928 and was clearly master of the Soviet Union. The worst purges were yet to come, as was the massive and systematic extension of the GULAG slave labor camp system. Terror and large-scale killing, however, had been the order of the day since 1917. The potential excesses of Bolshevism had been satirized quite acutely in Zamyatin's *We*, but Huxley denied ever having read the book, and this supports the view that his anti-utopia was much less anti-Bolshevik than Orwell's. Huxley himself would later write that

> George Orwell's *1984* was a magnified projection into the future of a present that contained Stalinism and an immediate past that had witnessed the flowering of Nazism. *Brave New World* was written before the rise of Hitler to supreme power in Germany and when the Russian tyrant had not yet got into his stride…. But tyrants, after all, are mortal and circumstances change. Recent developments in Russia and recent advances in science and technology have robbed Orwell's book of some of its gruesome verisimilitude…. it now looks as though the odds were more in favor of something like *Brave New World* than of something like *1984* (Huxley, *Brave New World Revisited* 2).

How far, then, did an engagement with Bolshevism find its way into *Brave New World*? Huxley clearly understood Bolshevism as part of a wider series of modern developments, particularly respecting individual and collective identity. As early as 1930, he wrote, in respect to the modern decline of the family, that :

> The Russians…have frankly avowed their intention of suppressing individualism in the interests of society. They are hardly less merciful to the family, because of its tendency to create an *imperium in imperio*. The State-paid professional educator is to take the place of the parents. There is an obvious tendency, all over the western world, to follow the lead of Russia - not through any desire to imitate the Soviets but because circumstances are rendering it increasingly necessary for all States to guard against the dangers, of insurgent individualism. Human standardisation will become a political necessity (Bradshaw 49).

This is hardly an "anti-Bolshevik" starting-point, then, and seems to indicate sympathy for the view that benevolent dictatorship might plausibly restrain "insurgent individualism."

In a similar vein, Huxley wrote in September 1931, specifically advocating what Bradshaw has described as "*Soviet-style* planning", that:

> We may either persist in our present course, which is disastrous, or we must abandon democracy and allow ourselves to be ruled dictatorially by men who will compel us to do and suffer what a rational foresight demands.

> Or, if we preserve the democratic forms, we must invent some psychological technique for inducing the electorate to act before the crash rather than after; we must provide voters with bad emotional reasons for behaving with rational foresight.

> Or, finally, we may employ both these last methods together - compel and at the same time use propaganda to make the compulsion appear acceptable.

> This is the present Russian method. Refined and improved, it has a good chance of becoming universal (Bradshaw xviii).

Huxley wrote elsewhere in May 1931 that, if the Russian Five-Year Plan succeeded, the Soviets would be "in a position to convert the whole world to her way of thinking" (Bradshaw 62–63). And only a week before *Brave New World* appeared, he stated that "[a] ny form of order is better than chaos. Our civilisation is menaced with total collapse. Dictatorship and scientific propaganda may provide the only means for saving humanity from the miseries of anarchy" (Bradshaw xix). The scheme described in late 1931, then, seems broadly to be that adopted in *Brave New World*, where overt coercion plays a negligible role and benevolent dictatorship has evidently triumphed. *Music at Night*, also published in 1931, echoed the thought that "Scientific psychology may succeed where Christianity and the political religions have failed. Let us hope so. In a world where most people had been taught to love their fellows there would be no difficulty in reconciling the claims of Grace with those of Justice, of universality with favouritism" (Huxley, *Music at Night* 97). But here, Huxley also asserted that in "the egalitarian state of the future all excessive accumulations of property will be abolished. But this implies, apparently, the abolition of all excessive enjoyment of liberty", leaving everyone with the freedoms of "the contemporary confidential clerk" (*Music at Night* 121–22). Yet science and technology meant that these, too, would be sumptuous by contemporary standards. These, despite Huxley's worries about the law of diminishing returns (leaving the "eugenicists" to answer this), would include the "theatres in which the egalitarians will enjoy the talkies, tasties, smellies, and feelies, the Corner Houses where they will eat their synthetic poached eggs on toast-substitute and drink their surrogates of coffee" and would be "prodigiously much vaster and more splendid than anything we know to-day." This was clearly an exact anticipation of *Brave New World*'s amusements, though Huxley had already expressed skepticism about the value of modern leisure society as early as *Antic Hay* (1923).

Music at Night also gives us the clearest indication that linking a mechanical world-view and machine-worship to Bolshevism would be a dominant theme in *Brave New World*:

To the Bolshevik ... Individuals must be organized out of existence; the Communist state requires not men but cogs and ratchets in the huge "collective mechanism." To the Bolshevik idealist, Utopia is indistinguishable from one of Mr. Henry Ford's factories. It is not enough, in their eyes, that men should spend only eight hours a day under the workshop discipline. Life outside the factory must be exactly like life inside (Huxley, *Music at Night* 212–13).

In *Brave New World*, Huxley seeks to provide an account of how an ideal system of manipulation of this sort would function. For more than anything else, *Brave New World* is a vision of a world driven by propaganda. Huxley tell us that:

The love of servitude cannot be established except as the result of a deep, personal revolution in human minds and bodies. To bring about that revolution we require ... First, a greatly improved technique of suggestion - through infant conditioning and, later, with the aid of drugs, such as scopolamine. Second, a fully developed science of human differences, enabling government managers to assign any given individual to his or her proper place in the social and economic hierarchy. ... Third (since reality, however Utopian, is something from which people feel the need of taking pretty frequent holidays), a substitute for alcohol and the other narcotics, something at once less harmful and more pleasure-giving than gin or heroin. And fourth (but this would be a long-term project, which would take generations of totalitarian control to bring to a successful conclusion), a foolproof system of eugenics, designed to standardize the human product and so to facilitate the task of the managers. In *Brave New World* this standardization of the human product has been pushed to fantastic, though not perhaps impossible, extremes (*Brave New World* 13).

The net result of this scheme is to make everyone satisfied with their existing condition. This is the key to minimizing coercion in the new regime. "Everybody's happy nowadays", boasts Lenina, incanting the phrase rehearsed a hundred and fifty times per night for twelve years during sleep indoctrination, and observing that Epsilons, Betas and Alphas were all satisfied with their existing position (Huxley, *Brave New World* 67). Allied to this was a system of what Huxley called "the conscription of consumption", which required every person to consume so much in a year, epitomised in the phrases, "Ending is better than mending. The more stitches, the less riches". All this proved the superiority of conditioning over fear: "Government's an affair of sitting, not hitting. You rule with the brains and the buttocks, never with the fists" (Huxley, *Brave New World* 49). In a vital passage, Huxley revealed his assessment of the limits of Bolshevik terror as a lasting form of rule: "'In the end,' said Mustapha Mond, 'the Controllers realized that force was no good. The slower but infinitely surer methods of ectogenesis, neo-Pavlovian conditioning, and hypnopaedia'" had proven much more successful (Huxley, *Brave New World* 50). As the Controller expresses it, the world was "stable now": "People are happy; they get what they want, and they never want what they can't get ... they're so conditioned that they practically can't help behaving as they ought to behave. And if anything should go wrong, there's *soma*" (Huxley, *Brave New World* 173).

We know that Huxley's defense of this position was that, as *Brave New World Revisited* (1958) put it, specifically in contrast to Orwell, the odds were much more likely that:

> control through the punishment of undesirable behavior is less effective, in the long run, than control through the reinforcement of desirable behavior by rewards, and that government through terror works on the whole less well than government through the non-violent manipulation of the environment and of the thoughts and feelings of individual men, women and children (Huxley, *Brave New World Revisited* 2).

"In the immediate future," Huxley notes, "there is some reason to believe that the punitive methods of *1984* will give place to the reinforcements and manipulations of *Brave New World*" (Huxley, *Brave New World Revisited* 26).

This, then, is the most distinctive attribute of *Brave New World* as a dystopia (and indeed challenges the application of the term to the text). Dystopias are typically dominated by fear. But this emotion is virtually lacking in Huxley's tale, along with cruelty, pain, mass murder, even slave labor of the traditional type. Huxley well recognized the role of fear in everyday life in the modern world, terming it indeed "the very basis and foundation of modern life" (Huxley, *Ape and Essence* 37). But in *Brave New World* only once monthly is the "Violent Passion Surrogate" induced by flooding "the whole system with adrenalin. It's the complete physiological equivalent of fear and rage" (Huxley, *Brave New World* 187). This is a world, otherwise, in which stability, evidently our most heartfelt need, has finally been attained, along with the chief value of modernity, happiness. As Orwell wrote in 1940, in *Brave New World* "the hedonistic principle is pushed to its utmost, the whole world has turned into a Riviera hotel" (Orwell, *Collected Essays* 2: 32). Huxley in turn later wrote that the "society described in *1984* is a society controlled almost exclusively by punishment and the fear of punishment. In the imaginary world of my own fable punishment is infrequent and generally mild" (Huxley, *Complete Essays* 6: 224). In *Brave New World Revisited* he added that "Societies will continue to be controlled post-natally–by punishment, as in the past, and to an ever-increasing extent by the more effective methods of reward and scientific manipulation" (Huxley, *Brave New World Revisited* 5–6). Huxley also wrote Orwell that he believed that his own vision was much more likely to evolve out of current historical trends than Orwell's much more violent description (Huxley, *Letters* 604–5). What "Utopia" meant to Huxley in 1932 was thus the scientific and technological manipulation of humanity through officially organized hedonism.

In early 1932, in a BBC radio talk on "Science and Civilization," Huxley outlined most of the scheme shortly to appear as *Brave New World*. Here it is abundantly clear that he regarded the application of psychology to propaganda as the key to understanding the future. "Rulers", he stressed, had "only to devise some scheme for laying their hands on new-born babies to be able to impose on their people almost any behavior pattern they like." With "a little systematic conditioning of infant reflexes – it will have the fate of its future subjects in its hands ... This will make the overt use of force quite unnecessary.... When every member of the community has been conditioned from earliest childhood to think as his rulers desire him to think, dictatorship can be abandoned (Bradshaw 109–10).

Interestingly, too, Huxley here demonstrated that his target in *Brave New World* was less the eugenic engineers than the economists whose ideas dominated the debate about ending the Great Depression. Humanists, he thought "would see in eugenics an instrument for giving to an ever-widening circle of men and women those heritable qualities of mind and body which are, by his highest standards, the most desirable." But:

> what of the economist-ruler? Would he necessarily be anxious to improve the race? By no means necessarily. He might actually wish to deteriorate it. His ideal, we must remember, is not the perfect all-round human being, but the perfect mass-producer and mass-consumer.... a society composed in the main of stupid people is more likely to be stable than one with a high proportion of intelligent people. The economist-ruler would therefore be tempted to use the knowledge of genetics, not for eugenic, but for dysgenic purposes - for the deliberate lowering of the average mental standard (Bradshaw 112–13).

Eugenics, then, is not essentially portrayed negatively in *Brave New World*. This again indicates that Huxley's target is not "science" or the "scientific world-view" as such, but a particular application thereof. How then should we position Huxley as a critic of totalitarianism? The world of the novel is indeed totalitarian insofar as a world-state monopolizing power is the government. But its rule rests not upon coercion but on ensuring universal happiness through eugenic regulation, extremely manipulative propaganda, and mass enforced hedonism. We tend today to associate only the propaganda component of this scheme with Bolshevism, and might otherwise infer that it is a post-Soviet form of totalitarianism which Huxley was satirizing. Did Huxley himself take this view?

In utopia, happiness was for Huxley chiefly construed in terms of stability. In his 1946 foreword, he wrote that:

The people who govern the Brave New World may not be sane (in what may be called the absolute sense of that word); but they are not madmen and their aim is not anarchy but social stability. It is in order to achieve stability that they carry out, by scientific means, the ultimate, personal, really revolutionary revolution (Huxley, *Brave New World* 10).

In the first instance, this stability was to be attained through greater centralization and the creation of totalitarian governments, which Huxley believed would inevitably emerge on a large scale in the near future. The "immediate future," he thought, was:

likely to resemble the immediate past, and in the immediate past rapid technological changes, taking place in a mass-producing economy and among a population predominantly propertyless, have always tended to produce economic and social confusion. To deal with confusion, power has been centralized and government control increased. It is probable that all the world's governments will be more or less completely totalitarian even before the harnessing of atomic energy; that they will be totalitarian during and after the harnessing seems almost certain. Only a large-scale popular movement toward decentralization and self-help can arrest the present tendency toward statism (Huxley, *Brave New World* 11–12).

Yet what was really central to the vision of *Brave New World* was that the system rested upon the satisfaction of its supposed beneficiaries. "A really efficient totalitarian state" was:

one in which the all-powerful executive of political bosses and their army of managers control a population of slaves who do not have to be coerced, because they love their servitude. To make them love it is the task assigned, in present-day totalitarian states, to ministries of propaganda, newspaper editors, and schoolteachers (Huxley, *Brave New World* 12).

Their methods, however, were "still crude and unscientific" (Huxley, *Brave New World* 12). *Brave New World* showed satirically how these crude methods might be perfected. Orwell would later pick up on some of these themes, in describing the life of the proles in *Nineteen Eighty-Four* as dominated by the pleasures of football, the gutter press, and cheap beer. Orwell's proles do not love their servitude, but they are distracted from it. Because they do not love it, however, coercion is still required to keep them in place. Huxley's pleasures are much more refined, and his manipulation much more thorough. Happiness trumps fear completely throughout all the castes of society. Respecting these themes, then, Huxley's is, centrally, a critique of the hedonistic utopia, or a modern hedonistic anti-utopia, rather than a classical modern dystopia, or satire upon Bolshevik totalitarianism. It assails the utopia of modernity, the notion of progress defined as ever greater happiness, taking this idea to its logical consequences. And yet of course buried within this is also a critique of the ultimate aspirations of all forms of totalitarianism, however muted this may now seem by contrast to Orwell's great work. For Huxley's treatment of the art of propaganda is in some respects much more sophisticated than Orwell's, and much more all-encompassing. Huxley's disagreement with Orwell over the predominant use of fear in totalitarian regimes is thus a controversial aspect of their intellectual engagement. Orwell, then, would go on to satirize Bolshevism as it evolved into Stalinism. Huxley's target was a development several stages beyond that, the "really efficient" stage. We usually assume, then, that Orwell's is the more successful critique of Bolshevism because it recognizes fear to be central to Stalinism. Ubiquitous pleasure-seeking seems worlds away from Winston Smith's daily drudgery. And despite the presence of the telescreen, scientific optimism is at best only a minor target for Orwell, though Orwell too rejected mechanistic conceptions of humanity. But he did not think that Huxley's dystopia could last "more than a couple of generations, because a ruling class which thought principally in terms of a 'good time' would soon lose its vitality. A ruling class has got to have a strict morality, a quasi-religious belief in itself, a mystique" (Watt 333).

How did Huxley reach these conclusions? We know that there was one key source for his knowledge of Bolshevism, René Fülöp-Miller, whose *The Mind and Face of Bolshevism*, Huxley wrote in

December 1927, had very much confirmed "my leanings towards aristocracy" (Huxley, *Letters* 293; Huxley, *Music at Night* 214). Miller impressed upon Huxley the view that Bolshevism epitomised a "mighty and powerful organism" in which "the impersonal mass," or "mass man," was now "lord of Russia" (Fülöp-Miller 1, 3). Miller quotes a Soviet historian, Pokrovski, who suggested that "personality is only the instrument with which history works. Perhaps a time will come when these instruments will be artificially constructed, as today we make our electric accumulators. But we have not yet progressed so far; for the moment, these instruments through which history comes into being, these accumulators of the social process, are still begotten and born in an entirely elemental way" (Fülöp-Miller 7.) Here, then, as in Wells's writings, we may see the seeds of the eugenics project upon which *Brave New World* was to be based. Huxley would have perceived Miller's explorations of communist festivals devoted to "the visible God," the machine, and the linkage of the "mechanical interpretation" of life to opposition to the idea that individual personality had any value. He would have appreciated Miller's description of a communist future in which "the last human remnants of everything organic will be sloughed off and replaced by mechanism [and] finally transformed into the mechanical component parts of a gigantic productive automaton which will function reliably, and thereby will be realized the ideal collective man, for whom the Bolsheviks are striving" (Fülöp-Miller 13). He would have paused reflectively at the observation that "even Ford would certainly reject as a crazy scheme the ideal that this mechanization should be artificially extended from the factory to life itself" (Fülöp-Miller 20). He would have shared the conclusion that it was "a perversity to see an ideal aim in automatization; the salvation of humanity lies rather in those remnants of the life of the soul which can never be entirely mechanized or standardized" (Fülöp-Miller 21). Machine-worship loomed large in Miller's description of Bolshevism. This was not, in 1932, anything Huxley associated with Hitler, and *Brave New World* is not in this sense a critique of totalitarianism, but specifically of Bolshevik modernity and its implications.

It was the Bolshevik "machine cult," then, and not science as such, that caused Huxley to see freedom as the greatest casualty of this strand of modern revolutionism. Yet to Miller, Bolshevism, and Lenin in particular, also epitomized the appeal to violence, and here Huxley would depart from Miller's account. Miller also indicated how far America remained a bright ideal to the early Bolsheviks, and how far "superamericanism" became synonymous with "mechanical civilization" in general (Fülöp-Miller 215–16, 272, 278). Miller's identification of Bolshevism and the United States is thus much closer than is suggested in most of the literature on totalitarianism produced during the Cold War, and is mirrored in Huxley's ambiguous description of a world indebted to leading trends in both societies. It is also notable that Miller saw Bolshevism as "merely a change in the direction of the tyranny" of the old regime, the means of oppression being "exactly the same", the *Katorga* or system of Czarist punishment and exile having been merely replaced by its Chekist and then OGPU and NKVD counterparts. These were however even more malevolent than that of the Okhrana in being utterly free of judicial control, thus producing "an arbitrary rule unknown in the rest of the world for centuries" (Fülöp-Miller 268). None of this appears in *Brave New World*.

In summary, then, Huxley saw Bolshevism through the Fülöp-Miller lens as a nefarious example of machine-worship, not as the broader totalitarian political dictatorship familiar to us from Orwell and the later Cold War literature. The wider trend, however, or Fordism run riot, characterized modernity in general, and constituted a threat elsewhere as well. Thus "science" as such is not Huxley's great target. His achievement here was to warn that the underlying psychology of manipulation might prove as devastating in societies in which near-compulsory pleasure was widespread as those in which fear underpinned dictatorial power. There was, then, some ambiguity in Huxley's position in 1932. What Bradshaw has described as a "sea change" in Huxley's attitudes towards authoritarianism only occurred after *Brave New World* appeared (Bradshaw 1994, xxi). But 1932 appears to have been the peak of Huxley's ambiguities about the potential benefits of dictatorships. As late as 1934, in reviewing the Federation of Progressive Societies and Individuals' *Manifesto*, Huxley continued to see Communist party members, "trained up in habits of austere self-discipline", as functioning like Wells's Samurai in *A Modern Utopia*, and reflected that "There is even a great deal to be said for the creation of a caste of Brahmins above the Samurai. Their immediate, political, propagandist value would be less than that of the more active Samurai; but ultimately, it seems to me, society can derive nothing but benefit from the existence of such a caste" (Henderson 196). By late 1935, however, he asserted that any form of dictatorship was "intrinsically bad", and while his enthusiasm for enhancing the elite never waned, its combination with dictatorship was never again part of his political agenda. Huxley continued, of course, to be fascinated with the idea of a "science of propaganda." He remained certain that a narrow, nationalistic propaganda produced by totalitarian states would possibly achieve short-term success, but then fail in the long-term owing to the "impossibility of reducing a huge, educated population to the spiritual homogeneity of a savage tribe" (Huxley, *Complete Essays* 4: 18). In this area he greatly admired the work of the Italian engineer and sociologist Vilfredo Pareto, in particular. "In [Pareto's] monumental *Sociologia Generale*, Huxley wrote, "I discovered many of my own still vague and inchoate notions methodically set down and learnedly documented, together with a host of new ideas and relevant facts. I have borrowed freely from this almost inexhaustible store" (Huxley, *Complete Essays* 2: 149).

Huxley continued to be plagued by doubts about the incompatibility of industrial society with humanist aspirations. He deplored both the relations between man and machine and those between worker and boss, and moved steadily towards the co-operative, decentralist principles, which would dominate his later social thought (e.g., Huxley, *Complete Essays* 4: 153). He was, by 1937, a solid critic of the ruthless violence practiced by the Soviet regime on an unprecedented scale (Huxley, *Complete Essays* 4: 174). His concerns grew as to the potential uses of controlled television, press and other media as sources of propaganda (e.g., Huxley, *Complete Essays* 4: 288). His fascination with advertising was undiminished. He had by this period also begun to identify with an ideal of small-scale communitarianism "composed of carefully selected individuals, united in a common belief and by fidelity to a shared ideal," with "property and income ... held in common," and where "every member should assume unlimited liability for all other members" (Huxley, *Complete Essays* 4: 174). This ideal of self-sufficiency Huxley called "Jeffersonian democracy" as early as 1939, expressing a preference for American over Soviet collectivism of any type (Huxley, *After Many A Summer* 132). A growing flirtation with Eastern philosophies in the late 1930s, resulting in Huxley's immersion in a personal search for Vedantist enlightenment and the "Perennial Philosophy," produced the vision described in *Island* (1962). By 1948, Huxley had little good to say about the Russian Revolution, which he characterized as "two and a half times the population of London exterminated, in order that political power might be taken from one set of ruffians and given to another set; in order that a process of industrialization might be made a little more rapid and a great deal more ruthless than it otherwise would have been" (Huxley, *Ape and Essence* 190). In 1949, he worried that the revolution which would bring each individual's "body, his mind, his whole private life directly under the control of the ruling oligarchy" was not likely to occur in five or six centuries, as *Brave New World* imagined, but much sooner, following Orwell, indeed, within thirty-five years (Huxley, *Complete Essays* 5: 109). Ruling oligarchies, both capitalist and totalitarian, were gaining in power through the application of science to propaganda, and the preservation of liberty under law seemed unlikely (Huxley, *Complete Essays* 5: 256, 260). Huxley continued to advocate for:

> the division and dispersal of power, the de-institutionalizing of politics and economics and the substitution, wherever possible, of regional co-operative self-help for centralized mass production and mass distribution, and of regional, co-operative self-government for state intervention and state control (Huxley, *Complete Essays* 5: 272).

But there seemed ever less success of achieving these goals. And with Huxley's description of how a growing world population (then about 2.7 billion) would continue to support totalitarian tendencies, and "the ravaging of his planet, the destruction of civilization, and the degradation of his species", we see the very contemporary application of his ideas (*Complete Essays* 5: 132). For Huxley, despotism driven by overpopulation was the face of the future. Unless the tide could be turned, the struggle for resources would ultimately trump all other considerations, and, as the struggle intensified, the advanced countries would probably develop totalitarian institutions in order to exploit the less fortunate (Huxley, *Complete Essays* 6: 229). The early years of Chinese communism seemed a halfway house between *Nineteen Eighty-Four* and *Brave New World* (Huxley, *Complete Essays* 6: 261–62).

Brave New World, then, was not a critique of totalitarianism, but an exercise in what can only be described as post- or "perfected" totalitarian analysis. In it, the ideals of totalitarian social efficiency had indeed been achieved in "the completely controlled, collectivized industrial society" of *Brave New World* (Huxley, *Complete Essays* 5: 313). But they were maintained by a much more psychologically sophisticated system than anything that was evident in Huxley's life. This essentially benevolent global dictatorship Huxley later acknowledged had been a false prediction, but again, because the pressure of population made oppressive dictatorships more likely (Huxley, *Complete Essays* 6:189). As *Brave New World Revisited* stressed, he did not think he was wrong about the progress of conditioning and behavioral manipulation, and he upheld this warning to the end of his life.

Works Cited

Atkins, John. *Aldous Huxley: A Literary Study*. London: John Calder, 1956.

Bedford, Sybille. *Aldous Huxley: A Biography*. 2 vols. London: Chatto & Windus, 1964.

Booker, M. Keith. *The Dystopian Impulse in Modern Literature: Fiction as Social Criticism*. Westport, CT: Greenwood, 1994.

Bradshaw, David, ed. *The Hidden Huxley: Contempt and Compassion for the Masses, 1920–36*. London: Faber & Faber, 1994.

Claeys, Gregory. "News from Somewhere: Enhanced Sociability and the Composite Definition of Utopia and Dystopia." *History* 98 (2013): 145–73.

Firchow, Peter. *The End of Utopia: A Study of Aldous Huxley's Brave New World.* Lewisburg, PA: Bucknell UP, 1984.

Fülöp-Miller, Rene. *The Mind and Face of Bolshevism.* New York: G.P. Putnam's Sons, 1927.

Henderson, Alexander. *Aldous Huxley.* London: Chatto & Windus, 1935.

Huxley, Aldous. *After Many A Summer.* London: Chatto & Windus, 1939.

———. *Ape and Essence.* London: Chatto & Windus, 1949.

———. *Brave New World.* 1932. London: Flamingo, 1977.

———. *Brave New World Revisited.* New York: Harper & Row, 1965.

———. *Complete Essays*, 6 vols. London: Ivan R. Dee, 2002.

———. *Letters of Aldous Huxley.* Ed. Grover Smith. London: Chatto & Windus, 1969.

———. *Music at Night.* London: Chatto & Windus, 1931.

———. *Time Must Have a Stop.* London: Chatto & Windus, 1948.

Morris, James and Andrea L. Kross, eds. *Historical Dictionary of Utopianism.* Lanham, MD: Scarecrow Press, 2004.

Orwell, George. *The Collected Essays, Journalism and Letters of George Orwell.* London: Secker & Warburg, 1968.

Shklar, Judith. *After Utopia: The Decline of Political Faith.* Princeton, NJ: Princeton UP, 1957.

Trahair, Richard C.S. *Utopias and Utopians: An Historical Dictionary.* Chicago: Fitzroy Dearborn, 1999.

Watt, Donald, ed. *Aldous Huxley: The Critical Heritage.* London: Routledge & Kegan Paul, 1975.

Aldous Huxley and the Twentieth-Century Eugenics Movement

Bradley W. Hart

The first chapter of Aldous Huxley's *Brave New World* begins with a journey through a building grandiosely labeled the "Central London Hatchery and Conditioning Centre." Placing the reader among a group of "very young, pink and callow" students desperately taking notes as the Director of Hatcheries and Conditioning pontificates, it quickly becomes clear that this facility is not dedicated to animal husbandry or genetic engineering, as might initially be assumed, but the production of human beings. The language of the scene is cold, clinical and scientific—as becomes clear, there is no place for emotion in the Fertilizing Rooms of Central London. Huxley leaves even the Director's age ambiguous ("Old, young? Thirty? Fifty? Fifty-Five?") in this dehumanizing environment of pure scientific achievement: "anyhow, the question [of his age] didn't arise; in this year of stability... it didn't occur to you to ask it" (Huxley, *Brave New World* 4).

As the Director soon explains to the students and the reader, there are, in actuality, two related activities that take place in the facility. The first of these revolves around the physical production of human beings: as the Director describes it, human ova and sperm are extracted, placed in test tubes and eventually mixed to produce embryos—a process that would today be referred to as a form of *in vitro* fertilization. Following the fertilization process, embryos from the top two classes of society, the Alphas and Betas, are allowed to develop "normally." However, the three lower classes, the Gammas, Deltas, and Epsilons, are subjected to an additional treatment known as "Bokanovsky's Process." This procedure causes each fertilized egg to "bud" into dozens of embryos that will all develop into individual, identical humans. "Ninety-six seemed to be the limit; seventy-two a good average," with a facility record of more than sixteen thousand offspring from a single ovary (Huxley, *Brave New*

World 8). In essence, Bokanovsky's Process allows the biological managers of Huxley's dystopia to produce an unlimited supply of labor.

It is the second function of the facility, however, that is, in many ways, even more significant. Following the application of Bokanovsky's Process, Gammas, Deltas, and Epsilons are subjected to additional treatment, this time designed, as the Director puts it, to "predestine and condition" (Huxley, *Brave New World* 13). Thus, the "lower" embryos are deliberately deprived of oxygen to stunt their growth and mental development, while being subjected to environmental influences seen as important to their future professions: toleration to high levels of lead and tar (Huxley, *Brave New World* 17). In contrast, Alphas and Betas are given different conditioning (and sleep learning) suitable to their eventual station in society.

The goal of this biological hierarchy is described by Huxley's Director in a single phrase: social stability (Huxley, *Brave New World* 7). By conditioning Alphas and Betas to be intellectuals, managers, and leaders, Huxley's society could expect a constant stream of intelligent and well-prepared technocrats to take the reins of the state in the future. The three lower castes, in contrast, would provide the raw labor and technical expertise to keep the state functioning at a more basic level. With deliberately limited intelligence, powerful social conditioning, and the physical kinship of being identical to everyone else in their Bokanovsky group, Gammas, Deltas, and Epsilons would remain happy in their condition. With everything in society perfectly managed, there would be no opportunity for unrest, instability, or unpredictability. Even human emotion itself could be dulled with regular doses of narcotics (*soma*) and state-mandated, consequence-free sexual promiscuity intended to not only provide an unlimited source of carnal pleasure, but also undermine the possibility of family units emerging organically, beyond the reach of the state's influence.

The idea of social stability through biological progress thus lies at the heart of the dystopian society Huxley describes. This notion may, at first glance, seem to be purely science fiction to many twenty-first-century readers: after all, there are few, if any, mainstream voices calling for the state to directly regulate human reproduction to achieve political or social ends, and bioethicists would rightly raise serious concerns about such proposals. In Huxley's own time, however, a prominent and well-organized lobby of scientific experts, medical practitioners, political figures and non-expert activists proposed a set of ideas not entirely disconnected from Huxley's vision. Known as the eugenics movement, adherents to the idea of biologically improving the citizenry (and thus the state) gained significant influence in a number of countries. By the mid-1920s, eugenicists in the United States had secured laws in dozens of states providing for the voluntary or involuntary sexual sterilization of individuals deemed "unfit" to reproduce, and in the early 1930s, at precisely the time Huxley penned *Brave New World,* the London-based Eugenics Society was in the early stages of lobbying parliament for a voluntary sterilization bill. Huxley's connection to the Eugenics Society was significant: his brother Julian, one of the best-known public intellectuals of the time and a popular commentator on scientific issues, was a long-time member and leader in the organization. Along with Carlos Paton Blacker, a close friend and the Eugenics Society's leader through the 1930s, Julian Huxley used his prominent position in British society to frequently advocate eugenic ideas and legislation.

This chapter considers the similarities between Aldous Huxley's dystopian society, as presented in *Brave New World,* and the ideas and politics advocated by the British eugenics movement of the early twentieth century. In the first section, the intellectual underpinnings of eugenics are examined, along with Julian Huxley's involvement in the Eugenics Society. In the second, the policy outcomes of these views are considered, along with Huxley's views on both sterilization and birth control. Together, these sections provide important background on the scientific and political milieu surrounding the authorship of *Brave New World*, which can, in many ways, be read as a critique of the eugenics movement's goals and proposed methods.

The eugenics movement's origins lie in the late nineteenth-century work of Francis Galton, a relative of Charles Darwin and a dedicated Victorian polymath. Taking Darwin's theory of evolution by natural selection a step further, Galton proposed that human evolution could, and should, be regulated by rational processes to maximize social outcomes and improve society. His major exposition on the topic, a book entitled *Hereditary Genius*, traced historically high-achieving British families and concluded that genius was, in fact, transmitted through a biological process. Galton later helped establish a chair in eugenics at University College, London, and gave his blessing to the creation of the Eugenics Education Society (later renamed the Eugenics Society), a London-based propaganda society open to all who shared its goals.

Galton's original notion of eugenics revolved around the idea of encouraging the "best" members of society to reproduce in greater numbers than their inferior counterparts. This was the essential argument of *Hereditary Genius*, which presented a vast number of family lineages designed to demonstrate that "genius" and other desirable qualities were passed through hereditary mechanisms. In his memoirs, Galton divided married couples into three distinct categories: "a small class of 'desirables,' a large class of 'passables'… and a small class of 'undesirables.'" The state would benefit, he wrote, by redirecting its "social and moral support as well as timely material help" to the desirables from the other two groups (Galton, *Memories of my Life* 322).

For Galton, eugenics was more than a desirable social reform but was in fact akin to a religious awakening: "I take Eugenics very seriously, felling that its principles ought to become of the dominant motives in a civilized nation, much as if they were one of its religious tenets." (Galton, *Memories of my Life* 322) Further, he claimed, eugenics was a fundamentally humanitarian undertaking for both society and the individuals involved:

> Its first object is to check the birth rate of the Unfit, instead of allowing them to come into being, though doomed in large numbers to perish prematurely. The second object is the improvement of the race by furthering the productivity of the Fit by early marriages and healthful

rearing of their children. Natural Selection rests upon excessive production and wholesale destruction; Eugenics on bringing no more individuals into the world than can be properly cares for, and those only of the best stock (Galton, *Memories of my Life* 323).

The notion of the "unfit" was critical to Galton's understanding of eugenics and its later political incarnations. For many eugenicists, being "unfit" meant performing poorly on IQ tests or suffering from a specific mental illness that was deemed transmittable by hereditary means (Carlson). Having a large number of the "unfit" in society would lead to its downfall, Galton believed, and this danger was compounded by his fear that, in the modern world, the "fit" were actually breeding in smaller numbers than their inferiors. Eugenics, as a political process, intended to halt this trend by encouraging the "fit" to breed more and the "unfit" to breed less through whatever means this might be possible.

Galton, as a relative of Charles Darwin, was himself well acquainted with the Huxley family. Thomas Huxley, often nicknamed "Darwin's Bulldog" for his enthusiastic defense of evolutionary theory, was an associate and correspondent of Galton as well. In the twentieth century, this historical connection between the Huxley family and eugenics was largely continued by Julian Huxley, Aldous' brother. Born in 1887, Julian attended Eton and Balliol College, Oxford, before taking up a brief lectureship in biology at Rice University in Texas (J. Huxley, *Memories* 96–102). Julian was also an Oxford supervisor of Carlos Paton Blacker, an aspiring psychologist, who would later become the Eugenics Society's most significant interwar leader. Following World War I, Julian began publishing popular scientific works, many of which focused on using eugenics and evolutionary theory for racial betterment. By the late 1920s, he was a well-known popular commentator on scientific issues, with a reputation for advocating social reforms based in the lessons of science, much as his grandfather had done. Foremost among these reforms would become the advocacy of a voluntary eugenic sterilization law in Britain.

By background, Carlos Paton "C.P." Blacker had much in common with the younger generation of Huxleys. After attending Eton, Blacker joined the British Army and was wounded in World War I. After the war, he entered Balliol College, Oxford, and read zoology under Julian Huxley before entering Guy's Hospital Medical School and gaining a reputation as a leading birth control advocate ("Obituary"). In the early 1930s, Blacker became the *de facto* leader of the Eugenics Society, which he quickly placed on a more moderate political trajectory in a period of political strife.

Blacker's political moderation was largely born out of an effort to rehabilitate British eugenics from several decades of failure. By the early 1930s, the British eugenics movement had fallen far behind its foreign counterparts, despite Galton's personal involvement in its origins. Two decades earlier, a number of American states had passed laws allowing for the sterilization of citizens deemed "unfit" by the medical or judicial establishment. The state of California ultimately became the most aggressive sterilizer of its citizens in the world before Adolf Hitler's rise to power in 1933, and most eugenics advocacy groups outside the United States looked to California for a model of how they might proceed both medically and politically. One of the most influential accounts of California's sterilization movement came from Cora B. S. Hodson, a long-time member of the Eugenics Society, who traveled widely and provided background information for Society leaders considering their political options. In an influential book published in 1934, Hodson claimed that sterilization had been practiced so extensively in California that it had become routine and no longer required patient consent in some institutions:

> I asked the senior woman medical officer, who most kindly took me everywhere, whether I might hear her explaining the operation to some girl and trying to persuade her to accept it. I was startled at her reply. 'What do you mean? I never tell them about it.' She went on to say that the operation had been so long the general practice that it had become a tradition… it was regarded as a kind of first-class award and any who thought they were getting on particularly well would take a chance of asking the doctors 'how soon they might have their

operation.'... They were, without exception, very proud from their operation, and each one who had it was eager to inform me of the fact (Hodson 23).

Influenced by accounts such as this, eugenic sterilization quickly became the eugenics movement's principal goal. Julian Huxley and Blacker were largely the driving forces behind the beginnings of a vast political campaign to convince parliament to pass a sterilization bill that would allow the voluntary sterilization of the unfit on eugenic grounds. By late 1934 and early 1935, more than seventy-five percent of the public outreach events sponsored by the Eugenics Society focused on sterilization ("Addresses"). However, following several unsuccessful attempts to encourage the government to introduce a bill, by 1937, the campaign had essentially been defeated. The only direct vote on a bill had taken place prematurely, in 1931, when it had been rejected by the House of Commons with a final vote of 157 to 89.[2] Even following the defeat, however, the Eugenics Society was still encouraging the public to keep sterilization in mind. In 1938, the organization arranged for mass public showings of a propaganda film featuring Julian Huxley, entitled *From Generation to Generation*, which illustrated the basic principles of heredity and purported to show how both desirable and undesirable traits could be inherited. Showing footage of a crowded mental health facility and the grotesquely contorted faces of its patients, the film concluded simply that "it would have been better by far, for them and the rest of the community, if they had never been born" (*From Generation to Generation* pt. 2).

  With his brother Julian so closely associated with the Eugenics Society and the sterilization campaign, it is clear that Aldous Huxley kept a close eye on the events taking place both within parliament and the wider eugenics movement around the time he was writing and publishing *Brave New World*. In addition, Huxley had long shown an interest in his brother's work and the implications of hereditary theory, writing to Julian in 1925 to inquire "what's a good book on the effects of modern genetic discoveries on the Darwinian theory. How do organisms ever get out of that hereditary predestination exhibited by mendelism [*sic*]?" (Huxley, *Letters of Aldous Huxley* 250). The term Mendelism referred to a dominant theory of biological inheritance of the time, and, as will be shown, this interest in "hereditary predestination" and its implications would occupy Huxley's mind for decades after the publication of *Brave New World.*

In addition, it is clear from their correspondence that, while Aldous Huxley and Blacker were acquainted, probably through Julian's introduction, they were not particularly close; however, this did not preclude the existence of a significant relationship between the two. In late 1933, the year after *Brave New World*'s publication, Aldous Huxley wrote to Blacker inquiring about the status of the sterilization campaign, ostensibly for an article he had been commissioned to write for *Nash's Magazine.* Describing his interest in the matter, Huxley wrote:

> I am tolerably well up in the history of the sterilization movement in other countries and in the evidence in support of sterilization. What I should like to know, however, is this: whether the bill for the legalization of sterilization in England was actually introduced in the House of Commons. And if so, what was (and what is likely to be) its fate (Huxley, *Aldous Huxley: Selected Letters* 290).

As already noted, at this point, the first sterilization bill had already been defeated in the House of Commons two years prior. Noting this fact, Blacker took the opportunity to not only update Huxley on the status of the legislation, but also provide him with an analysis of the Society's future strategy. Blaming the left-wing Labour Party's opposition to the bill for its defeat, Blacker claimed that "since the last general election the matter has been taken up with a great deal more energy in the House of Commons." Predicting the introduction of a new bill within the foreseeable future, Blacker seemed confident of a more successful outcome in the near future.

However, Blacker's letter also alluded to an emerging problem the Eugenics Society was facing: the eugenics program being implemented by Adolf Hitler's government in Germany. Blacker enclosed a number of eugenic pamphlets in his letter to

Huxley, including a copy of the *Eugenics Review*, the Society's in-house publication. This, he noted, included the text of the German compulsory sterilization bill that Hitler's government had recently introduced a bill that would eventually deprive hundreds of thousands of Germans of their reproductive abilities. The clear and public embrace of eugenics by the Nazi State, Blacker, noted was already causing problems for the British eugenics movement. "The adoption of a drastic eugenic policy by the nazi [*sic*] had the not unnatural effect of still further antagonizing persons of Labour persuasion against eugenics," he told Huxley.[3]

Blacker was, of course, wrong in his optimism for the second sterilization bill's passage, as noted previously. What is intriguing, however, is what this correspondence reveals about Aldous Huxley's relationship with the eugenics movement. A year after *Brave New World*'s appearance, Blacker and the leadership of the Eugenics Society would almost certainly have been aware of the glaring similarities between their own advocacy of rationalized reproduction and the dystopian fantasy of the hatcheries presented in the novel. Indeed, in 1932, Henry Fairfield Osborn, a leading American eugenicist and birth control opponent, presented a paper entitled "Birth Selection versus Birth Control" at the Third International Congress of Eugenics in New York City. The paper directly referenced *Brave New World* to argue against the use of contraception on eugenic grounds (Osborn). Quoting an extended passage from the novel describing the human artificial incubation process, Osborn argued that "in young Huxley's satire extreme modernism enters the final phase of its logical consequences, from which he recoils while he satirizes" (Osborn 39). Osborn then proceeded to state that Thomas Huxley, Aldous' grandfather, would have been appalled by his grandson's vision of the future by comparing the use of birth control to the artificial fertilization and gestation processes described in the novel:

> I owe to Thomas Huxley the two outstanding principles of my own naturalistic philosophy; first, that nothing which is true can be harmful to the body, to the mind or to the soul; second, whatever is natural in the wondrous and beautiful order of nature can not [sic] be

fraught with danger. On the contrary, whatever is unnatural may not be essentially immoral but may be fraught with hidden dangers... birth-selection is natural; it is in the order of nature. Birth control is not natural and while undoubtedly beneficial and benevolent in its original purpose, it is fraught with danger to society at large and threatens rather than insures the upward ascent and evolution of the human race. Such ascent, it seems to me, is the greatest responsibility with which we biologist and eugenicists are charged today (Osborn 40).

Osborn's interpretation of *Brave New World* is so staggeringly superficial (essentially, eugenic selection is "natural" and, therefore, safe, while birth control is "unnatural" and dangerous, thus making it more similar to the dystopian technologies presented in the book) that one wonders whether he actually read the novel before formulating the lessons he wanted to take from its pages. Certainly, contraception plays an important role in the society presented in the novel, in the sense that it prevents the creation of traditional family units that might challenge the authority of the state and, secondarily, allows for the uninhibited sexual pleasure that keeps the populace occupied and sated. However, to interpret this aspect of *Brave New World* as its most "unnatural" aspect in comparison to the artificial breeding of human beings for specific social and economic functions is a stretch at best. Yet, for Osborn, this was precisely the lesson that *Brave New World* presented.

This rather unusual interpretation of Huxley's work demonstrates that, for eugenicists, *Brave New World* need not be seen as a direct attack on their scientific and political views but, instead, as simply an illustration of how society might change in the future, with both positive and negative aspects. Philip Ball, among other commentators, has observed that *Brave New World* was perhaps most directly a response to a short book, entitled *Daedalus, or Science and the Future*, by J.B.S. Haldane, a British biologist involved in the eugenics movement. In Haldane's account, a new technology called ectogenesis would allow for the creation of artificially gestated fetuses similar to Huxley's notions in *Brave New World*, with desirable eugenic outcomes (Haldane). While

Haldane's account was influential, however, ectogenesis was seen as science fiction by most mainstream eugenicists of the 1930s. Blacker, for instance, was far too focused on voluntary sterilization to concern himself with the possible implications of a technology that was far in the future. Thus, while *Brave New World* carried what appears to be a quite obvious satire on the very idea of eugenics, for eugenicists, this was less apparent, as Osborn's bizarre interpretation makes clear. In many senses, it seems that most eugenicists of the 1930s missed Huxley's point and instead focused on the individual aspects of Huxley's vision rather than the overall picture of the future he sought to paint.

Accordingly, Huxley's connections with the Eugenics Society, while never strong, did not sour with the publication of *Brave New World*. In 1936, Huxley accepted an invitation to attend the Society's flagship Galton Dinner and second a vote of thanks to his brother for a lecture he was to deliver on the progress of eugenics.[1] The following year, Blacker sent Huxley a copy of a book entitled *Sex and Culture* by J.D. Unwin, which Blacker had favorably reviewed for *The Lancet* in the hopes that Huxley might see fit to write a popular review of his own. Huxley later included his essay on the topic in his 1937 essay compilation, *Ends and Means: An Inquiry Into the Nature of Ideals and Into the Methods Employed for Their Realization* (Huxley, *Ends and Means* 311). Huxley's relationship with Blacker had clearly not been destroyed by *Brave New World*'s publication.

At the same time, Huxley's personal correspondence makes clear that his intent in *Brave New World* was to subject the entire notion of biologically managing the state, as eugenics itself sought, to satirical scrutiny. Writing to Julian in 1946, after the defeat of Nazi Germany and the discrediting of eugenics through its obvious connections with Nazism, Huxley's view was that his work was more relevant in the late 1940s than in the 1930s:

> The book has taken on a fearful topicality. For it looks as though, if we don't get blown up within the next few years, the Brave New World is only a couple of generations away, with really scientific dictatorships using all the resources of applied psychology and

biology to make their subjects like the slavery to which they have been reduced, instead of, as now, ineptly and unsuccessfully trying to bludgeon and liquidate them into acquiescence (Huxley, *Letters of Aldous Huxley* 539).

This sentiment effectively summarized Huxley's view of biology in *Brave New World*: in contrast to Haldane's optimistic vision that ectogenesis would help lead the world to a more eugenic future, in Huxley's view, the rational control of human reproduction would lead only to dictatorship and repression.

At the same time, however, there is evidence that Huxley himself was concerned by the same notions of degeneration and unfitness that had preoccupied the eugenicists of the 1930s. Writing to the author Alberto Bonnoli in 1948, Huxley essentially presented a Galtonian argument for concern over the direction of human development:

In the highly industrialized countries, there is a tendency for the less gifted members of society to have more children than the more gifted. As a result... there will be at the end of this century twice as many feeble-minded children in the schools as there are now and half as many children of outstanding ability. ... The question arises: can one have a democratic way of life in a population which is, biologically speaking, degenerating? (Huxley, *Letters of Aldous Huxley* 588).

Huxley's presentation of a classically eugenic/degeneration-oriented argument is intriguing and suggests a certain nuance in his views toward eugenics. On the one hand, the dystopian vision of *Brave New World* was deeply rooted in the state's control over reproduction and its rational management of the population. Yet in his letter to Bonnoli, Huxley seems to suggest that some form of rational management might indeed be necessary to ward off degeneration and social collapse.

The explanation for this apparent contradiction lies in Huxley's personal connections to the eugenics movement and background in the periphery of British science's leading circles. As demonstrated by his connections to Blacker, Aldous Huxley was well aware of the Eugenics Society's political aspirations and objectives. Through his brother Julian, he was personally acquainted with the most important eugenics advocates in the country, and his grandfather's connection to Darwin and Galton gave both brothers powerful voices within those circles. As demonstrated by his 1925 letter to Julian, Aldous Huxley had a long-standing interest in evolutionary theory and its implications for human society, specifically the implications of the "hereditary predestination" implied by the rigid biological determinism common in the eugenics movement. Thus, his interest in "degeneration" can be seen as a derivative of these high-level connections to British science and not necessarily a direct contradiction to his fears about increasing state control.

Indeed, while *Brave New World* could easily be read as a satire on the very notion of eugenics, it appears that many eugenicists read it instead as a cautionary tale about modern science taken too far, which they themselves did not associate with their own ideas in many cases. For eugenicists like Blacker, *Brave New World* was clearly not seen as significant enough an attack to justify Huxley's exclusion from Society events, and in 1933, it is clear that he still viewed the author as a possible ally in the political campaign for eugenic sterilization. For eugenicists such as Osborn, in fact, *Brave New World* could be read to demonstrate the correctness of eugenic birth selection in contrast to "unnatural" birth control. *Brave New World* was thus a sort of *tabula rasa* for eugenicists to interpret through their own views. For Huxley himself, *Brave New World* reflected both his deep-seated fears about the totalitarian potential of biology and his background in Britain's leading scientific circles and the outer periphery of the eugenics movement itself. As a result, he evidently saw little contradiction in expressing concern over both the dictatorial potential of biology and the alleged degeneration of the western world even after the end of World War II.

Notes

1. See correspondence concerning Galton Dinner, 9 Jan. 1936, Eugenics Society papers C. 184/Blacker papers A.2/1.

Critical Insights

2. See Letter from C.P. Blacker to Aldous Huxley, 4 Dec. 1933, Eugenics Society Archive, Wellcome Library, London, C. 184.
3. See Eugenics Society papers C. 184.

Works Cited

"Addresses Delivered by Lecturers of the Eugenics Society, December 1934–February 1935." *The Eugenics Review*, XXVII.1 (1935–36): 67–68.

"Obituary: Carlos Paton Blacker." *The Lancet* 305.7915 (1975): 1096–1097.

Ball, Philip. "In Retrospect: Brave New World." *Nature* 503 (2013): 338–339.

Carlson, Elof Axel. *The Unfit: A History of a Bad Idea.* New York: Cold Spring Harbor Press, 2001.

From Generation to Generation. Gaumont British Instructional for the Eugenics Society, 1935.

Galton, Francis. *Hereditary Genius: An Inquiry into Its Laws and Consequences.* London: Macmillan, 1925.

_____. *Memories of My Life.* London: Methuen & Co, 1909.

Haldane, John Burdon Sanderson. *Daedalus.* New York: E.P. Dutton & Co., 1924.

Hodson, Cora Brooking. *Human Sterilization Today: A Survey of the Present Position.* London: Watts & Co., 1934.

Huxley, Aldous. *Brave New World.* New York: Harper Perennial Classics, 2006.

_____. *Ends and Means: An Enquiry into the Nature of Ideals and into the Methods Employed for Their Realization.* New York: Harper & Brothers, 1937.

Huxley, Aldous and James Sexton. *Aldous Huxley: Selected Letters.* Chicago: Ivan R. Dee, 2007.

Huxley, Aldous and Grover Smith. *Letters of Aldous Huxley.* London: Chatto & Windus, 1969.

Huxley, Julian. *Memories.* New York: Harper & Row, 1970.

Osborn, Henry F. "Birth Selection versus Birth Control." *A Decade of Progress in Eugenics: Scientific Papers of the Third International Congress of Eugenics Held at American Museum of Natural History*

New York, August 21–23, 1932. Baltimore, MA: Williams & Wilkins, 1934. 29–41.

Soloway, Richard. "Blacker, Carlos Paton (1895–1975)." *Oxford Dictionary of National Biography.* Oxford, UK: Oxford UP, 2004.

Maternity as a Social Construct in *Brave New World*

Nicole Fares

Aldous Huxley's *Brave New World* begins with a telling scene, in which a government official, the Director of Hatcheries and Conditioning (D.H.C.), conducts a group of young schoolboys on a tour of the facility he directs. It quickly becomes clear that this is the facility, in which the new infants of this future society are scientifically manufactured to fulfill pre-defined roles in the world. Not only does the D.H.C. make clear that natural viviparous reproduction is a thing of the past, but that the very notion of motherhood, in the sense of both giving birth and childrearing, is now regarded as a form of "smut" (Huxley, *Brave New World* 17). Indeed, motherhood itself seems to be regarded as one of the most embarrassing and taboo ideas in this society, standing in stark contrast to the traditional glorification of motherhood that was typical of Huxley's own world. However, a close examination of these seemingly opposed attitudes toward motherhood reveals that both are based in fundamentally patriarchal notions about women.

An understanding of the complex hegemonic ideas of motherhood and normative ideals of family construction in modern Western society is essential in order to interpret the absence of traditional motherhood in *Brave New World*. This chapter applies Judith Butler's concept of maternity as a social construct to examine the figuration of motherhood in Huxley's novel, demonstrating that this construction is actually similar to that of motherhood in modern Western society, but representing the opposite extreme of the spectrum. I also draw upon Michel Foucault's idea of the gradual refinement and expansion of mechanisms of control and discipline in modern society, which reveals the micro-powers and technologies of control at work; I then argue that the vision of motherhood in any patriarchal society is going to be problematic for women. According to both Butler and Foucault, attempts at social reform in pursuit of greater personal freedoms are inevitably manipulated to become techniques of domination.

As opposed to the horror of motherhood in *Brave New World*, social pressure to have children has turned motherhood into an institution in modern Western society; the *need* for women to have children is a requirement for women and is regarded as a natural product of *maternal instinct*. In both cases, social and cultural perspectives demand that women adapt to certain cultural norms and principles that influence reproductive decision-making—whether or not to become a mother, and how to go about doing so. What I intend to show is that this social construction of motherhood manipulates language and symbology, in order to control women and to ensure a stability and emotional norm consistent with social ideologies.

The demography of motherhood in the United States has shifted strikingly within the past two decades. Eighty percent of American women are mothers, which is a decreased number from a study conducted in 1990 by Gretchen Livingston and D'Vera Cohn. For example, "today's mothers are older and better educated; they are also less likely to be Caucasian and less likely to be married" (Livingston and Cohn). However, the desire and instilled need to be a mother remain, and society still considers motherhood to be a woman's most important role—and her greatest accomplishment. In today's Western culture, the principal social role of women is and has been considered to be as the tenders and nurturers of children (Ehrenreich 494). Though more permissive than past decades, social norms demand that women raise children to the exclusion of roles and responsibilities outside the home; girls are brought up with the concept that motherhood is an inextricable part of a woman's identity, even to the point of being considered a second nature. In such culture, any woman who fails to adhere to this ideal is discriminated against socially.

The modern concept of motherhood is an all-encompassing identity rooted in self-sacrifice and infused with social and political meaning. It is a symbol of an "untainted humanity so powerful as to infatuate a century of European writers, philosophers, and thinkers"—an inspiration to men such as Freud, Darwin, Marx, and

Engels (Rubin 50). It is an idealized role, described as an expression of perfect love toward something or someone, for whom one actually has feelings of both love and hate. The hate is ignored and so kept from consciousness, while perfect love is unrealistic to achieve.

In patriarchal Western society, men are the primary policy makers, who govern most societal infrastructures. Under the modern patriarchal Western institution and its ideology of motherhood, the definition of *mother* is limited to heterosexual women who have biological children, while the idealized concept of *good* motherhood is further restricted to a select group of women who are white, heterosexual, middle-class, able-bodied, married, thirty-something, in a nuclear family with usually one to two children, and (ideally) full-time mothers. Clearly, while mothers are nominally celebrated, some are more celebrated than others. Mothers who do not fit normative requirements are looked down upon by society. Mothers who are single parents are socially stereotyped as inappropriate or incapable of properly raising children. In addition, adults and children in nuclear families are viewed more favorably than adults and children in other family structures (divorced, remarried, and single); voluntarily childless women are also stigmatized, and abortion is described as emotionally and psychologically injurious to women. On the other hand, women themselves continue to describe the "exhaustion, guilt, anxiety, and loneliness" that come with being a mother in contemporary Western society (O'Reilly, *Twenty-first-century Motherhood* 27).

The modern patriarchal social expectation is that a relationship and maternal bond will be created and shared between mother and son that will influence his future character, as well as his self-esteem and confidence—considered most important because men will inevitably exert the most control over the modern social structure. Feminist scholars over the last two decades have vigorously challenged this patriarchal construct and called for new and expansive definitions of maternal identity. For example, feminist mothering seeks to reclaim power for mothers; to implement a mode of mothering that mitigates the ways that patriarchal motherhood, both discursively and materially, regulates and restrains mothers and their mothering, drawing upon the distinction made between two meanings of motherhood, one superimposed on the other: "the potential relationship of any woman to her powers of reproduction and to children," and "the *institution*—which aims at ensuring that that potential and all women—shall remain under male control" (Rich 13).

In contrast to this utopian project, *Brave New World* is a dystopian account of scientific planning leading to dehumanization. Ten controllers of the World State determine all aspects of society; children are born in state hatcheries, where they are given or denied certain elements that are critical to proper development, according to the social class pre-determined for them. These decanted babies are medically and psychologically manipulated, so that they have only the appropriate intelligence, strength, and attractiveness to fill the social and economic positions for which they are intended. They are raised and indoctrinated in conditioning centers so that, by the time they are old enough to work, their only ambitions are to perform the tasks for the positions they were raised to fill. Their loyalty is to the state and to the preservation of the community and stability.

The citizens of *Brave New World* are happy and content with their simple lives: "We don't want to change. Every change is a menace to stability" (172). In order to maintain that stability, the World State has severed all personal ties among its citizens and manipulated the language itself so that "family" and associated terms have become obsolete concepts. The result, however, is more sinister than simple obsolescence; the World State maintains stability by obliterating individual personality. Persons of the same caste are largely interchangeable by design, literally manufactured in identical batches via the "Bokanovsky process." Few personality traits are left to chance, and people are encouraged (through promiscuity, which spreads their emotional energies among multiple partners) not to form strong bonds with other individuals.

As familial bonds are perceived to be strong, as well as major factors in self-identification, familial terms such as "father" and (especially) "mother" are transformed into profanities in order to eliminate them. David Sisk asks, "By controlling language, can a speaker also control the thoughts of others who speak that language?" (Sisk 1). Dystopian societies, of course, often seek to manipulate language. This language can thus control the thoughts of the people in these societies; and if a society is conditioned into thinking through the filter of the official ideology, then the state has the ultimate power to manipulate the people. Most famously, in George Orwell's *Nineteen Eighty-Four*, for instance, the totalitarian government attempts to do away with the common language and replace it with the artificial and highly restrictive Newspeak to achieve control over the people. *Brave New World* also depicts language as a means of control, though a somewhat more complex one that arguably started out with at least *some* good intentions. One might compare here the presumably utopian society of Anarres in Ursula K. Le Guin's *The Dispossessed*, in which the very language ("Pravic") has been structured to reflect complete gender equality. Thus, there are no words in Pravic for sexual intercourse that indicate possession of one person by another or something being done by one person to another, except for one indicating rape. Instead, sexual verbs in the language are all plural, indicating mutual activity. Still, as Walter Meyers has pointed out, even this well-intentioned strategy has a downside: since languages tend to evolve over time, the society of Anarres is forced to adopt extreme measures to prevent its ideal language from changing (Meyers 208).

The situation in Huxley's novel is similarly problematic. The paternal law in *Brave New World* structures all linguistic significations and so becomes a universal organizing principle of culture itself. It influences meaningful language, and hence meaningful experience, through the repression of primary libidinal drives, including the dependency of the child on the maternal body. As Judith Butler points out, this could theoretically be a good thing: once the latter ceases to be socially influenced, "the culturally constructed body will then be liberated, neither to its 'natural' past, nor to its original pleasures, but to an open future of cultural possibilities" (*Gender Trouble* 119). Unfortunately, while the elimination of motherhood could be seen as part of an attempt to achieve gender equality, the society of *Brave New World* is still, in fact, highly patriarchal, as critics, such as June Deery, have shown.

The concept of maternity in *Brave New World* can be thus explained by applying Butler's argument that the notion of "maternity" is a social construction, and that maternity preceding or defining women is itself a product of discourse (Butler, "Body Politics" 115). Today's traditional Western social representation of motherhood is compulsory in ways that limit women and ascribe to them a pre-defined set of expectations upon which their subjectivity depends. It is a "compulsory cultural construction," one that assumes "the female body as a maternal body" (Butler, "Body Politics" 115). This body is a cultural construct, both prone to cultural variations in how it is understood and amenable to alternative cultural possibilities. The presumption of the female body as dominated by drives is the effect of "a historically specific organization of sexuality" (Butler, "Body Politics" 118), one that establishes motherhood as mandatory for all women and therefore creating a "compulsory obligation on women's bodies to reproduce" (Butler, "Body Politics" 115).

The concept of motherhood is defined by specific social rules; the role of 'mother' is thereby institutionalized. Motherhood is one of the most enduring roles in human societies; its definition and resulting expectations have been constructed and reconstructed with each passing political, social, and cultural wave, partly because it has traditionally been necessary for the survival of the species, regardless of the social context. In *Brave New World*, this necessity is removed, presumably changing everything in this regard. Motherhood has been redefined to the point of removal from society and from the identity of women entirely, dramatizing Butler's argument that the concept of motherhood is a social construct that can be instilled or removed from society through means of social manipulation.

In both modern Western society and the society of *Brave New World*, the social construction of maternity is dominated by patriarchal ideologies and is thus limiting and damaging to women. Normative social influence is a type of conformity that leads people to exhibit public compliance—but not necessarily private acceptance—of the group's social norms. The implication seems to be that the imposition of any normative vision of motherhood is problematic, no matter what that vision might be because it positions any woman who does not meet that normative vision in a difficult situation. "Normal" is also used to describe behavior that conforms to the most common behaviors in society—known as conforming to the social norm. In the case of contemporary Western society, the concept of a normal woman is one who desires to become a mother and naturally possesses motherly instincts. The "normal" mother is married, naturally loving, and devoted to nurturing her children (and, by extension, her spouse). Any woman who does not fit into these normative visions is regarded as abnormal, and is, therefore, denied the approval of society. As long as there is a fixed vision of what is "normal," there will be a counterpoint notion that everything else is "abnormal," possibly even morally deviant, as in the suspicion directed toward single mothers and the downright demonization of "welfare" mothers by the American political right in recent years. Norms imply that violators will be punished or sanctioned. Most norms attempt to encourage behavior that neither directly harms anyone, nor threatens the society with chaos and disintegration. They are intended to make a statement about what is considered by some, many, or most members of a society to be the normal and correct behavior. They embody certain principles of moral correctness that is separate from and independent of what they do for the society's physical survival (Butler , *Gender Trouble* 93).

Foucault repeatedly frames his work as an examination of the relations among knowledge, power, and human subjects. One of Foucault's crucial concerns in *Discipline and Punish* and elsewhere is with the role played by the "normal" in modern Western societies— defining "deviants" and "delinquents" as "abnormal." The power is that of disciplinary technology and its aim is normalization. The concept of norm violation appears to be a simple, objective criterion for determining what is deviant and what is not. This term refers to rules or expectations for behavior that are shared by members of a group or society. The concept of social norm has been honored by a long tradition of sociological theory and research that views *consensus* as a basic fact of organized social life. According to this sociological tradition, consensus, or shared agreement, exists in all organized groups and societies about what behaviors are appropriate and expected of members. This consensus is expressed through social norms; shared rules that channel behavior in various areas of social life into orderly and predictable patterns. Behavior that deviates from these normative patterns, according to the normative definition, is deviant behavior; deviants are those people who violate the normative consensus of organized society. In *From Motherhood to Mothering*, Adrienne Rich distinguishes between "motherhood" as experience, "motherhood" as enforced identity, and "motherhood" as political institution by using the example of an unwed teenager who may experience motherhood as a rare source of self-affirmation, while society deems her motherhood to be illegitimate and deviant. Society's construction of motherhood and its image of what constitutes a good mother versus a bad mother facilitates male control over all women. Women who fail to meet the ideal of motherhood (unwed mothers, "unfit" mothers, and women who do not become mothers) are stigmatized for violating the dominant norm and considered deviant or criminals (Roberts 5). Martha Fineman calls motherhood "a colonized concept—an event physically practiced and experience by women, but occupied and defined, given content and value, by the core concepts of patriarchal ideology" (Fineman 289–90).

This concept of social normalization is well described by Foucault's account of disciplinary power, which is related to punishment and, more specifically, part of the prison model. However, disciplinary power is also tied to normalization. This involves the construction of an idealized norm of conduct and then rewarding or punishing individuals for conforming to or deviating from this ideal. This normalization, exercised in both contemporary Western society and in *Brave New World*, is one of an ensemble of tactics for exerting the maximum social control with the minimum expenditure of force, which Foucault calls "disciplinary power" (Foucault 27). This is a crucial aspect of social structure in modern societies; normalization is what distinguishes the abnormal, the delinquents, and the deviants, from the rest of society—the "normal." In a similar

---

manner, a specific action is deemed a crime when society decides that the action is not "normal" behavior. Those who do not act in the "normal" manner of society are locked up, shipped off, or placed into mental institutions. Without normalization, the manipulation of the individual by the power structure would be minimal. Control of the society's power emerges from the ability to manipulate the individual into the larger social norm, but this normalization can only be established by the dominant aspects of society (Foucault 30). What is crucial, of course, is the internalization of the "normal," causing individuals to desire to be normal, even without coercion. This can be seen very clearly in *Brave New World* in the way individuals have accepted the notion that motherhood is obscene and disgusting.

Foucault argues that the eighteenth century introduced a new form of power: discipline, a power relation, in which the subject is complicit (Foucault 55). Literally manufactured to be happy with the roles intended for them in society, the citizens of Huxley's World State are the ultimate complicit subjects, so Foucault's vision of the working of disciplinary power in modern bourgeois societies describes them well. Of course, given M. Keith Booker's description of the World State as a "bourgeois dystopia," one would expect this to be the case (Booker 47–67). Indeed, in the case of *Brave New World*, the exercise of power is a paradigmatic case of what Foucault refers to as "productive": citizens are conditioned to obey happily, not coerced against their wills. If they do not conform, they are simply excluded from society, exiled to a place of misfits.

This system is very good for enforcing conformity; it does, however, make it difficult to fit in for those who deviate from the norm for any reason. Bernard, for example, is extremely troubled by his obvious difference from other "Alphas." Similarly, Linda, having been abandoned, pregnant, on the Savage Reservation, cannot function well on the Reservation due to her prior conditioning; on the other hand, she cannot successfully return to her old society after years of absence and retreats into a drug-induced haze. Much of her difficulty surrounds her role as the mother to John, the son born to her on the Reservation. Shamed by the fact that she has given natural birth to her son, she chooses to withdraw and deal with the repercussions of her abnormal and perverted act of mothering. We see the character struggle to figure out her role as a mother, which brings with it guilt, anger, and helplessness; she has never had a mother herself and was programmed to consider that same act or role as a deviance and abnormality. In her son's reminiscence, she becomes upset with him because his very existence reminds her that she's broken a fundamental rule of society. In one instance, however, as she reaches to hit him, she finds herself suddenly overcome with maternal joy and instead hugs and kisses him all over.

Once Linda had violated the social rule against motherhood, there was little chance she could be reintegrated into the society of the World State. But, as she had been conditioned in the state, there was little chance that the "Savages" would accept her into their world, unaccustomed as they were to her strange behavior, promiscuity, and lack of emotion. Instead, she was mistreated and ridiculed for not fitting into their society's own concept of "normal." Her passionate, intense, and sometimes incoherent narration to Bernard and Lenina captures effectively her plight among the Savages. Like her son, she dreamt of escaping the reservation and returning to the new world. When Linda returns to London, however, the society of the World State rejects her as well and ridicules her for the flabbiness and slovenliness acquired from living long years at the reservation. Unable to show emotion, she cannot even turn to her son John for comfort, even though he longs for closeness with his mother. As a result, she lives in a soma stupor in order to be able to tolerate her existence. Her perpetual overdosing leads to ill health and eventually death, arousing the reader's sympathy and understanding her as the victim of both worlds/societies.

The World State in *Brave New World* has consciously and intentionally constructed a new vision of maternity as disgusting and horrifying in order to prevent strong individual emotional attachments, which enhances the concept of motherhood as a product of discourse. The novel implies that the key to stability is the absence of individuality. The government has internalized this concept; one of the ten controllers of the World State declares that there is "no civilization without social stability. No social stability without individual stability" (Huxley, *Brave New World* 31). The need for stability creates a government that believes stability to be achievable if people think and look the same. Stability, in effect, prevents chaos—and in particular prevents the repetition of the conditions of the apocalyptic Nine Years' War that haunts the deep memory of this society, nearly 600 years after it occurred. The main source of personal chaos is emotion. Watts echoes this as he defines man as "a creature marked by confusion, fear, and deathlessly individual awareness" (Watts 79). Emotions drive a person to act, to assess their life, to grow, to learn, and to love. Emotions are so personal and intimate that the government in *Brave New World* (like the governments of many dystopian societies) discourages these intense human characteristics and regards them as a threat to the stability of their world. Emotions are thus controlled in *Brave New World*.

> To compensate for the restraints placed upon him by the extant social ideals and to fill the leisure time produced by specialized functioning, man has surrounded themselves with substitutes for real emotions. This compensation is necessary because of the worship of success and efficiency, which brought in its wake the exaltation of the machine with its concomitant, standardization (Rogers 270).

Control and stability can best be achieved when everyone is contented. The government attempts to eliminate any painful emotion, which means every deep feeling, every passion, is removed. Huxley shows that the government recognizes the dangers of negative emotions when the controller states, "actual happiness always looks pretty squalid in comparison with the over-compensations for misery" (Huxley, *Brave New World* 170).

In this society, the suppression of emotion begins even before birth, by ensuring that embryos grow in a sterile, artificial environment, rather than inside the wombs of mothers who will already have developed an emotional attachment to them by the time of birth. As Schmerl puts it, "Humanity is dead; the creatures of *Brave New World*, spawned in bottles, fed on slogans and drugs, leading an utterly meaningless life whose only purpose is to perpetuate the meaninglessness" (Schmerl 37). The implications of the engineered cloning process of babies are tremendous; with the destruction of the family, the government has single-handedly prevented family emotions and ensured that the only loyalties felt by individuals are to the state. There are no mothers, fathers, brothers, sisters, uncles, aunts, cousins, or grandparents. There are no husbands or wives, or even committed lovers. Individuals are raised to consider the language of sexual promiscuity as normal, expected, and accepted, while the language of the family is obscene. The rulers of the World State clearly believe that, in order for a society to achieve complete social stability, a loss of individuality and the outlawing of natural biological function must occur. Successfully engineering these conditions produces a world where people live contentedly, free of disease and crime, but at the cost of close familial or other personal bonds.

On the surface, the figuration of motherhood in the society of *Brave New World* is precisely the opposite of that in modern Western society, though both are ultimately patriarchal and limiting to women. However, the cognitive estrangement produced by *Brave New World* can potentially give us a different perspective from which to view the apparent glorification of motherhood in our world, enabling us to see that there might be an element of revulsion just beneath the surface there as well. The virtual demonization of welfare mothers as expressed by the political right in the U.S. demonstrates this quite clearly, showing that mothers who have escaped patriarchal control by having children within a family structure that is not dominated by fathers are particularly disturbing to our own social order. Thus, the divide between the disgust shown toward motherhood in *Brave New World* and the apparent elevation of motherhood in our society is not as clear as it seems.

The patriarchal construct of "mother" as a biological and essential category is problematic to women by its very nature, regardless of its specific contents. In *Of Woman Born*, Rich writes: "We do not think of the power stolen from us and the power withheld from us in the name of the institution of motherhood" (275). There are many ways that patriarchal motherhood, both discursively and materially, regulates and restrains mothers and their mothering. Motherhood as it is currently perceived and practiced in patriarchal societies is disempowering if not downright oppressive for a multitude of reasons, ranging from the societal devaluation of a mother's domestic work to the endless tasks of privatized mothering and the impossible standards of idealized motherhood. O'Reilly argues that modern motherhood functions as a patriarchal institution, "one that has largely been impervious to change despite forty years of feminism, because of the gender ideology that grounds it: namely, gender essentialism and the resulting naturalized opposition of the public and private spheres" (O'Reilly, *Twenty-first-Century Motherhood* 19). Only by unearthing and severing the ideological underpinning of patriarchal motherhood can we develop a politics of maternal empowerment and a practice of outlaw motherhood.

Scholarship on motherhood, whether concerning mothering as institution, experience, or identity, has focused on how motherhood is detrimental to women because of its construction as a patriarchal entity. Scholars, such as Julia Kristeva—who have seen motherhood as a very positive experience for women and are interested in the experience of motherhood—argue that the gender inequities of patriarchal motherhood cause the work of mothering to be both isolating and exhausting for women, while those concerned with ideology call attention to the guilt and depression that is experienced by mothers who fail to live up to the impossible standards of patriarchal motherhood (O'Reilly, *Twenty-first-Century Motherhood* 2). Any form of patriarchal society denies women their potential as full human beings. As Adrienne Rich argues, institutionalized motherhood demands of women maternal "instinct" rather than intelligence, selflessness rather than self-realization, and relation to others rather than the creation of self. Motherhood is 'sacred' so long as offspring are "legitimate"—that is, as long as the child bears the name of a father who legally controls the mother (42). As long as society is patriarchal, any vision of motherhood (or any other role for women that is defined by men) is going to be problematic. This simple fact is one of which Huxley, in *Brave New World*, seems blissfully unaware.

Works Cited

Booker, M. Keith. *The Dystopian Impulse in Modern Literature: Fiction as Social Criticism.* Westport, CT: Greenwood Press, 1994.

Butler, Judith. "The Body Politics of Julia Kristeva." *Hypatia.* 3.3 (1989): 104–118. *JSTOR.* Web. 19 Nov. 2013.

———. *Gender Trouble: Feminism and the Subversion of Identity.* New York: Routledge, 1990.

Deery, June. "Technology and Gender in Aldous Huxley's Alternative Worlds." *Extrapolation: A Journal of Science Fiction and Fantasy* 33.3 (1992): 258–273.

Ehrenreich, Nancy. "The Colonization of the Womb." *Duke Law Journal* 43.3 (1993): 492–587. *JSTOR.* Web. 19 Nov. 2013.

Fineman, Martha L. "Images of Mothers in Poverty Discourses." *Duke Law Journal* 40.2 (1991): 274–90.

Foucault, Michel. *Discipline and Punish: The Birth of the Prison.* 1975. New York: Vintage Books, 1995.

Fraser, Nancy. *Unruly Practices: Power, Discourse, and Gender in Contemporary Social Theory.* Minneapolis: U of Minnesota P, 1989.

Huxley, Aldous. *Brave New World & Brave New World Revisited* New York: Harper Colophon, 1965.

Le Guin, Ursula K. *The Dispossessed: An Ambiguous Utopia.* New York: Harper & Row, 1974.

Livingston, Gretchen and D'Vera Cohn. "The New Demography of American Motherhood." *Pew Research Social & Demographic Trends.* Pew Research Center, 6 May 2010. Web. 17 Nov. 2013. <http://www.pewsocialtrends.org/2010/05/06/the-new-demography-of-american-motherhood/>.

Meyers, Walter E. *Aliens and Linguists: Language Study and Science Fiction.* Athens: U of Georgia P, 1980.

O'Reilly, Andrea. *Twenty-first-century Motherhood: Experience, Identity, Policy, Agency.* New York: Columbia UP, 2010.

———, ed. *From Motherhood to Mothering: The Legacy of Adrienne Rich's of Women Born.* Albany: State U of New York P, 2004.

Rich, Adrienne. *Of Woman Born: Motherhood as Experience and Institution.* New York: Norton, 1986.

Roberts, Dorothy E. "Racism and Patriarchy in the Meaning of Motherhood." *The American University Journal of Gender, Social Policy & the Law* 1.1 (1992): 1–38.

Rogers, H. Winfield. "Aldous Huxley's Humanism." *The Sewanee Review* 43.3 (1935): 262–272. *JSTOR.* Web. 20 Nov. 2013.

Rubin, Stuart Nancy. *The Mother Mirror: How a Generation of Women Is Changing Motherhood in America.* New York: Putnam, 1984.

Schmerl, B. Rudolf. "Aldous Huxley's Social Criticism." *Chicago Review* 13.1 (1959): 37–58. *JSTOR.* Web. 19 Nov. 2013.

Sisk, W. David. *Transformations of Language in Modern Dystopias.* Westport, CT: Greenwood Press, 1997.

Watts, Harold H. *Aldous Huxley.* New York: Twayne, 1969.

The Burden of Science and Biology in *Brave New World*

Josephine A. McQuail

To be the child—or even grandchild—of greatness is a burden. The grandson of Thomas Henry Huxley, autodidact anatomist, and colleague and supporter of Darwin—known, in fact, as "Darwin's bulldog" in his time, meaning, not just an advocate of evolution, but of scientific inquiry in general—Aldous Huxley had a lot to live up to. And the legacy was not only on his father's side; his great grandfather on the maternal side was Thomas Arnold (headmaster of Rugby and revered by Thomas Hughes in Tom Brown's School Days), not to mention that Aldous was grandnephew to Matthew Arnold. T. H. Huxley was a brilliant anatomist, who theorized, among other things, that birds evolved from small, carnivorous dinosaurs, an idea that is generally accepted today. T.H. Huxley was also instrumental in establishing the widespread, free public education that came to the fore in England in the late nineteenth century— thus Aldous Huxley had a legacy involving not just science, but education, and the latter from both sides of his family. As Aldous Huxley was aware, Thomas Arnold, senior, and T.H. Huxley also were involved in a debate between the merits of a classical versus a scientific education. The Victorian patriarch Huxley dismissed critics' fears that "'man's moral nature [would] be debased by the increase of his wisdom'" (Woodcock 15). This dilemma would concern Aldous Huxley throughout his career as writer and thinker.

Despite his brilliance, T. H. Huxley experienced bouts of debilitating depression, a tendency that was to haunt Aldous's brother Julian, who took up his grandfather's vocation of biologist, and suffered numerous nervous breakdowns. Their brother, Trevenen, also committed suicide as a young man while confined for nervous depression. Sensitivity toward those suffering from mental anguish, fear of death, and forbidden love is evident even behind the bizarre convolutions of *Brave New World*. Aldous suffered not only the loss of his brother Trev, who (in love with a servant girl who was bearing his child and prevented by his family from committing himself to her at the time of his suicide) hanged himself, Aldous also endured the loss of his mother from cancer. And, before graduating college, he also experienced partial loss of his sight from (apparently) a strep infection of both eyes. *Brave New World* is a strange compendium of these family traumas; it is also a bizarre twist on his grandfather's cheerleading of Darwin's *Origin of Species*, showing the strategy of the society of *Brave New World* to be a deliberate devolution. Aldous Huxley's grandfather, like Darwin, also undertook a voyage to exotic locales; in Huxley's case, not on the Beagle, but on the HMS Rattlesnake, and not to the Galápagos and South America, but to Australia and New Guinea. Though the direct object of his scientific study at the time was the jellyfish, T. H. Huxley sketched the aborigines of Australia and New Guinea, and was later to construct an ethnography of human races. Suicide by hanging, depression, nihilism, death of a mother, depictions of "savages" in a foreign land—all of these things are featured in *Brave New World*, and all of these things were crucial to the psychological makeup of Aldous Huxley. Of all of Huxley's novels, *Brave New World*, which seems furthest from a realistic depiction of his milieu, is probably psychologically closest to Huxley's core.

The opening scene of *Brave New World* occurs in the "LONDON HATCHERY AND CONDITIONING CENTER" (Huxley, *Brave New World* 3). Given Huxley's family background in education (his mother, Julia, also ran a girls' school of some repute), can it be entirely coincidental that the opening of *Brave New World* is also a scene of instruction, with the Directory of Hatcheries and Conditioning (D.H.C.) giving students new to the Hatchery a tour? Of course, by and large, the "education" provided by the 'Brave New World' (or World State as it's officially known) society to children is "hypnopaedia," or sleep-teaching, as well as behavioral conditioning. The Hatchery has replaced the need for human reproductive biology primarily by replacing the biological necessity for mothers to host the developing human embryo and then give birth. In this, *Brave New World* resembles Mary Shelley's

Frankenstein, where the innovations of the scientist Frankenstein subvert female gestation and birth in procreation by assembling parts of cadavers and by somehow imbuing the resultant creature with life. Huxley's horrifying vision of a society, which has bioengineered an alternative to fetal development in the womb had itself gestated for a while in his mind, apparently, but a look at the germ of the idea tells us that it comes from a projection of horror at mechanistic evolution and sexual reproduction. In Huxley's very first novel *Crome Yellow* (1921), his irascible character, the elderly Scogan, is the oracular prophet of the future, whose vision comes true in the future projected in Huxley's *Brave New World* a decade later:

> An impersonal generation will take the place of Nature's hideous system. In vast state incubators, rows upon rows of gravid bottles will supply the world with the population it requires. The family system will disappear: society, sapped at its very base, will have to find new foundations; and eros, beautifully and irresponsibly free, will flit like a gay butterfly from flower to flower through a sunlit world (Huxley, *Crome Yellow* 22).

"Nature's hideous system" is, of course, that predicted by evolutionary biology. Although Darwin's *Origins of Species* was not published in 1859, fossil discoveries had obviated much earlier the fact that Nature's plan was distinct from God's, at least God's plan as described in the Bible. The philosophical effect of such discoveries goes back much further than the nineteenth century; Darwin's own grandfather, Erasmus Darwin, devised a coat of arms, which said "Everything from shells" and proudly sported it on his carriage (King-Hele; Grigg). Just as his grandson would withhold publication of *Origin of Species* for fear of its implications for human belief systems (particularly religion), Erasmus Darwin felt pressure to paint over his coat of arms on his carriage after hostile remarks and ridicule by colleagues and neighbors (King-Hele; Grigg).

Aldous Huxley never quit thinking about the ideas that, post-Darwin, have continued to concern humanity, just as they concerned his grandfather. In *Ape and Essence* (1948), Huxley would refer to many of the themes he explored in *Brave New World*. The year is

2108, and after the Third World War, New Zealanders on a ship called Canterbury arrive to a post-apocalyptic, irradiated California, and the botanist Dr. Alfred Poole falls behind his scientific companions as they explore what remains of civilization. Dr. Poole is captured and has a visitation with the Arch-Vicar of the Church of Belial. World War III and its aftermath have made it clear that Satan is the God of this world. The Arch-Vicar traces the rise of Moloch back to "'Man pitting himself against Nature'" (Huxley, *Ape & Essence* 120), asserting "'It began with machines and the first grain ships from the New World. Food for the hungry and a burden lifted from men's shoulders'" (Huxley, *Ape & Essence* 121). The Arch-Vicar tells Dr. Poole that "'. . . Belial knew that feeding means breeding'" (Huxley, *Ape & Essence* 121-122). Since this is a screenplay we have instructions for a

> ...dissolve to a shot through a powerful microscope of spermatozoa frantically struggling to reach their Final End, the vast moonlike ovum in the top left-hand corner of the slide. On the sound track we hear the tenor voice in the last movement of Liszt's Faust Symphony: *La femme éternelle toujours nous élevé. La femme éternelle toujours . . .* Cut to an aerial view of London in 1800. Then back to the Darwinian race for survival and self-perpetuation. Then to a view of London in 1900—and again to London, as the German airmen saw it in 1940. Dissolve to a close shot of the Arch-Vicar (Huxley, *Ape & Essence* 122).

If the "Darwinian race for survival and self-perpetuation" is all that exists, life is very bleak, indeed. In fact, that Huxley is just as stuck on these ideas at this point in his philosophy as the generations who were first shocked by the theory of evolution is underscored by the fact that the "outsider" figure here, the fictional Alfred, reveals that he was named for Alfred, Lord Tennyson, by his mother, who was "'a great admirer of *In Memoriam*'" (Huxley, *Ape & Essence* 79). Tennyson's poem *In Memoriam: A.H.H.* (1850), of course, presents an early reaction to the theory of evolution (before *Origin of Species* was published, even) with its most famous line indicting "Nature red in tooth and claw" (Canto 56, l. 15). Tennyson's poem was known as the great agnostic poem, and it pits religious faith against scientific knowledge; in the poem's poetic preface, Tennyson opts for faith, while admitting that faith cannot withstand the scrutiny of science.

For Huxley, the product of a later generation, the choice of faith is virtually impossible at this point in his thinking (though he would come to embrace a mystical belief expressed in his *The Perrennial Philosophy*). For Huxley as an intellectual, mind and body are divided. Not only is human biology more than a little disgusting, it is also—specially sexual intercourse for Huxley—ridiculous. We are all slaves to the body. A member of the same generation that spawned the Bloomsbury Group—the Stephens sisters (later known by their married names as Virginia Woolf and Vanessa Bell); Lytton Strachey; Clive Bell; and others; and, in fact, loosely affiliated with them, Huxley himself joined his generation in rejecting Victorian values of propriety and conformity and, certainly, chastity. The promiscuous sex of *Crome Yellow, Eyeless in Gaza, Brave New World*, and, in a more exaggerated form, the horrifying vision of brutal orgies occurring yearly as the post-Armageddon human females come into heat in *Ape and Essence*, are a manifestation of this new attitude toward sexuality. Yet, the way that Huxley uses enforced promiscuity in both *Ape and Essence* and *Brave New World* indicates that he is ambivalent about it. Albert's true love for Loola in *Ape and Essence* and, in *Brave New World*, that of Bernard Marx and, later, of John the Savage for Lenina Crowne show the idealization of romantic love. Even when the possibility of romantic love exists, however, the grossness of the body intervenes.

One of the most horrifying examples of disgust for the body and the ridicule of sexuality coinciding comes in the novel *Eyeless in Gaza*, where the post-coital bliss of the characters Helen Amberly and Anthony Beavis, who have just made love on a rooftop, is accentuated by an airplane droning above when suddenly:

A strange yelping sound punctuated the din of the machine. Anthony opened his eyes again, and was in time to see a dark shape rushing down towards him. He uttered a cry, made a quick and automatic movement to shield his face. With a violent but dull and muddy impact, the thing struck the flat roof a yard or two from where they were lying. The drops of a sharply spurted liquid were warm for an instant on their skin, and then, as the breeze swelled up out of the west, startlingly cold. "Christ!" Anthony whispered at last. From head to foot both of them were splashed with blood. In a red pool at their feel lay the almost shapeless carcass of a fox terrier (Huxley, *Eyeless in Gaza* 113).

Ironically, it is at this moment that Anthony realizes that he truly loves Helen, yet she takes the grotesque incident as a sign that their relationship is doomed and flees. It is hard to think of a more bizarre disruption of a love scene in a novel, or of a better example of the discordant interventions made possible by the technology of the modern world.

But if men are preoccupied with and enslaved by biology, if anything, women are more so. Women in particular are enslaved to biological reproduction in a way that men are not. *Brave New World* liberates women from both childbearing and childbirth. Famously, the World State society has accomplished "the principle of mass production applied to biology" (7). Women are either "free martins" or sterile, or equipped with a "Malthusian belt," or birth control. As Scogan had predicted in Huxley's earlier novel, *Crome Yellow*, eros, or sex, is liberated from consequences of childbearing and can "flit like a gay butterfly from flower to flower through a sunlit world" (Huxley, *Brave New World* 22). Now, the production of human babies is the work, literally, of both genders on a factory floor. Besides the universal "soma" given to everyone to induce the feeling of euphoria and well-being, women may receive special "pregnancy surrogacy" treatments if they are feeling down or alienated (the word "hysteria" after all, derives from the Latin word for "uterus"). If women's bodies are "designed" to make babies, every consideration is given to satisfying that biological need in the *Brave New World*, just as no one, male or female, is to repress the urge to have sex. Because babies are conceived and born in vitro ("bottled" and "decanted") and not in utero, the Freudian Oedipal and Electra complexes are ostensibly avoided (though both John the Savage, even though he is born from Linda on the Savage Reservation by mistake, has an Oedipal relationship with Popé, his mother's lover; and Bernard

Marx has a bit of a conflict with John's biological father, the Director of the Hatcheries and Conditioning Centre itself, suggesting that such rivalries are inevitable with humans).

It may be a little difficult to conceptualize the floor of the Hatchery, but it is laid out like a car assembly plant. "Ford" is the god of the 'Brave New World' (all crosses have had the top cut off to become "T"s, as in the "Model T Ford") because of his innovation of the assembly line.

Due to human engineering, the survival of the fittest is no longer guaranteed in the 'Brave New World' society. However, Huxley, himself the product of an elite education and destined (had it not been for the unlucky accident of his near blindness) to the managerial class of the British elite, recognized that, already in his society, not everyone is explicitly given the support they need to succeed. That he was prophetic sometimes is hard to deny, but the vision of social engineering he provides would truly be a nightmare if realized. There were seeds of such a utilitarian vision of society in the eugenics movement and, of course, in Nazi experiments involving sterilization and other conditions that would be performed in the 1940s—chillingly, some specifically using twins ("Nazi Human Experimentation"). Incredibly, some of his contemporaries believed that Huxley was actually advocating the *Brave New World* society as utopic (Watt 16). This is proof that some people just don't get irony because there is nothing ideal about the new World State. It is a world where human beings are regulated, measured, and conditioned from conception. Fetuses are graded and sometimes deliberately stunted, as when we observe a mechanic adjusting the "blood-surrogate pumps" of some embryos:

> "Reducing the number of revolutions per minute," Mr. Foster explained. "The surrogate goes round slower, therefore passes through the lung at longer intervals; therefore gives the embryo less oxygen. Nothing like oxygen-shortage for keeping an embryo below par." Again he rubbed his hands (14).

These are some of the most horrifying scenes in *Brave New World*. Also horrifying, but, at the same time, one of the most intriguing of the Machiavellian interventions in the 'Brave New World,' is the stunting of embryos via "alcohol in the blood surrogate." This instance in the novel, where alcohol is introduced into the fetal environment to induce the retardation of the embryos, shows Huxley at his most prophetic. Of course, today we know about Fetal Alcohol Syndrome, but it was actually unknown in Huxley's day. The very term "Fetal Alcohol Syndrome" was first used, in fact, in an article in *Lancet* published in 1973 (O'Neil). *Brave New World* was published, of course, in 1932, more than forty years before Fetal Alcohol Syndrome was recognized. Huxley, no doubt, became aware of speculation about the effects of alcohol on a fetus from the eugenics movement. Alcohol abuse was thought by eugenicists to result in damage that was hereditary—including "heritable imbecility" (O'Neil)—but Huxley seems to get closer to the truth as we know it today regarding Fetal Alcohol Syndrome, since it is "alcohol in the blood surrogate," which causes the damage desirable in the Delta, Epsilon, and Gamma fetuses. Indeed, our "antihero" in *Brave New World*, Bernard Marx, though an "Alpha," is unusually small in stature and therefore disaffected, and the rumor is that somehow, by mistake, alcohol was put in his blood surrogate.

The conditioning of children by unpleasant noise and by electric shock to cause them to detest both flowers and books is also horrifying. The D.H.C. once again presides over the scene; the infants are turned so that they can see some books set among roses, to which they at first react quite happily, then, on the signal of the Director, the Head Nurse presses a level that sets off a violent explosion and some shrill alarms:

The children startled, screamed; their faces were distorted with terror.

"And now," the Director shouted (for the noise was deafening), "now we proceed to rub in the lesson with a mild electric shock."

He waved his hand again, and the Head Nurse pressed a second lever. The screaming of the babies suddenly changed its tone. There was something desperate, almost insane, about the sharp spasmodic yelps to which they now gave utterance. Their little bodies twitched and stiffened; their limbs moved jerkily as if to the tug of unseen wires (Huxley, *Brave New World* 21).

The introduction of Bokanovsky's process (a fictional innovation of cloning) combined with "Podsnap's technique" allows for the creation of sometimes hundreds of identical "twins," which results in more efficient reproduction and labor—the kind, of course, that involves a job. After all, having identical human workers working the same task makes for a smoother running machine, as when we are treated to a description of a "small factory of lighting-sets for helicopters," in which various tasks are performed by work groups made up entirely of clones, like the "eighty-three almost noseless, black brachycephalic Deltas were cold-pressing. The fifty-six four-spindle chucking and turning machines were being manipulated by fifty-six aquiline and ginger Gammas. One hundred and seven heat-conditioned Epsilon Senegalese were working in the foundry" and so on (Huxley, *Brave New World* 159–60).

Huxley's solution to the problem of finding contented and efficient workers seems improbable, but, via such procedures as mandatory personality tests to gauge job suitability, invasive drug testing to gauge supposed competency, and even surveillance to test honesty, workers today are scrutinized in unprecedented ways. What employer wouldn't like to mold workers to suit its needs? In the early twentieth century, this desire was evinced by a Frenchman; like many of Huxley's characters, Maurice Bokanovsky was a real figure; this time, not a scientist, but a French bureaucrat, who believed in government efficiency (Sexton 85). "Podsnap," it can be conjectured, is a reference to the beans used by pioneering geneticist Gregor Mendel to study genetics. But "Podsnap's technique" is the process used to ripen ova (eggs) from the human ovaries. What Huxley calls "Podsnap's technique" was done outside of the body in *Brave New World*; today, the technique for ripening eggs for fertilization must be done within the body, when women wishing to either conceive or to donate eggs must undergo a series of difficult injections which often lead to weight gain and depression, among other symptoms.

The ethical questions brought up by Huxley's exploration of what was essentially the Fordist manufacture of human beings arise today in a very different context with fertility treatments and in vitro fertilization. These processes oftentimes result in the potential for multiple births, though, usually, not identical multiple births. The "Octamom" (Nadya Suleman), who gave birth to eight infants at one time, was vilified, but she faced the same dilemma that other women who receive fertility treatments often do: the choice between the potential for multiple births (which also involves problems like cerebral palsy, premature birth, and so on) and selectively "culling" or aborting fetuses to avoid the risks inherent in a pregnancy with multiple fetuses.

In *Brave New World*, with the application of both Bokanovsky's process and Podsnap's technique, many hundreds of fetuses can be created from one egg; statistics are even kept for how many identical babies result from one ovary. It's hard sometimes to tell if Huxley is joking, being ironic, or is actually racist. In the opening chapter, as the D.H.C. recounts for the students the astounding numbers of exact replicas, which have sprung from either one ovum or from one ovary, we learn that the largest numbers of replicas have been achieved:

in some of the tropical Centres. Singapore has often produced over sixteen thousand five hundred; and Mombasa has actually touched the seventeen thousand mark. But then they have unfair advantages. You should see the way a negro ovary responds to pituitary! It's quite astonishing, when you're used to working with European material (Huxley, *Brave new World* 8–9).

Although Aldous Huxley's grandfather T.H. Huxley was as much an ethnologist as an anatomist or biologist, it is important to note that he was not a proponent of this view of Geographical Determinism; in fact, T. H. Huxley insisted on the link between different races as part of the human family, and refused to justify slavery or racism by calling negroes an inferior race. It is not as easy for today's readers to see such a perspicacious view in Aldous Huxley's portrayal of the inhabitants of the Native reservation. Then again, *Brave New World* is a satire, and, as such, we cannot take Huxley literally. From Linda's perspective, compared to her former home in the new World State, the Native Americans are incomprehensible because of their values of monogamy, and compared to the *Brave New World* society, their religion is authentic; their work (the women work with looms to make cloth) is meaningful. Yet, the Native Americans exclude both Linda and her son John, since they are "outsiders" and non-native. Huxley recognizes that all human societies can be cruel, as indeed, someone who grew up in an English boarding school environment *would* know (particularly awful examples of humiliation in such a setting occur in *Eyeless in Gaza*).

Among the multiplicity of images in *Ape and Essence* was one that apparently caused offence to one of the twentieth century's most prominent scientists, Albert Einstein. To dramatize the final nuclear war, Huxley shows "Dr Albert Einstein, on a leash, behind a group of baboons in uniform" (40). There is "a second group of animals, wearing different decoration and under another flag, but with the same Dr. Albert Einstein, on an exactly similar string, squatting at the heels of their jack boots" (40). To Amiya Chakravarty, Huxley wrote in May 1950 (quoting from his own novel at one point in the letter):

> What you say about Einstein having been offended by my use of his name in *Ape and Essence* distresses me very much. I thought that I had made it perfectly clear that I was using him—just as I had used Faraday and Pasteur—as an embodiment of science. ... The purely allegorical nature of my Einstein figures is clearly indicated, first, by the fact that there are two of them, one in servitude to each army, and, second, by the narrator's remark, after quoting Pascal on the idolatrous nature of the worship of truth without charity, that the death of the two Einsteins is in fact the suicide of modern science. Einstein as a person never enters into the book; his name is employed exclusively as a symbol and personification of Modern Physics (*Selected Letters* 412–413).

Huxley in *Brave New World* gave voice to his generation's fear about modern science. He also foresaw that not only was "science committing suicide," but humanity itself was rapidly driving itself to extinction. Prophetically, in his 1956 *Tomorrow and Tomorrow and Tomorrow* (published in the U.S. as *Adonis and the Alphabet*), Huxley takes humanity to task for wasting resources, living like "drunken sailors," … "the irresponsible heirs of a millionaire uncle" (Rolo xiii). In "What Can the Scientist Do?," Huxley echoes Dr. Gene Weltfish, who, in 1945, came up with a simple and ingenious formula, to which "[t]echnicians and scientists" should swear, just as medical doctors have the Hippocratic oath:

> I pledge myself that I will use my knowledge for the good of humanity and against the destructive forces of the world and the ruthless intent of men; and that I will work together with my follow scientists of whatever nation, creed or color for these our common ends (Rolo 543–4).

As they say in acting, "Timing is everything" and this oath was published by Dr. Weltfish in *Scientific Monthly* in September 1945, in other words, just after the United States had dropped hydrogen bombs on Hiroshima and Nagasaki.

In this year of 2013, the fiftieth anniversary of Huxley's death, how many remember that he died the very same day John F. Kennedy was assassinated: November 22, 1963? C.S. Lewis also died the very same day. That was a day that the world lost three exceptional men, who promised hope for the future. In *Science, Liberty and Peace*, published in 1946, Huxley pointed out simply that:

> up to the present time applied science has not been used mainly or primarily for the benefit of humanity at large, or (to put the matter less abstractly) for the benefit of individual men and women, considered as personalities each one of which is capable, given suitable material and social conditions, of a moral and spiritual development amounting, in some cases, to a total transfiguration . . . . (Rolo 538).

In other words, if science and biology ceased being burdens on humanity and became liberators, it is possible to imagine a true utopia, which supports human potential rather than the false one offered by *Brave New World* and, too often, by our own world.

Works Cited

Atkins, John. *Aldous Huxley: A Literary Study*. New York: Orion Press, 1967.

Baker, Robert S. *Brave New World: History, Science, and Dystopia*. Boston: Twayne Publishers, 1990.

Bedford, Sybille. *Aldous Huxley: A Biography*. New York: Carroll & Graff, 1973.

Dunaway, David King. *Huxley in Hollywood*. New York: Harper & Row Publishers, 1989.

Firchow, Peter. Science and Conscience in Huxley's *Brave New World*. *Contemporary Literature*. 16.3 (Summer 1975): 301–16. *JSTOR*. Web. 9 Dec 2013.

Greenblatt, Stephen Jay. *Three Modern Satirists: Waugh, Orwell, and Huxley.* New Haven & London: Yale UP, 1965.

Grigg, Russell. "It Was All in the Family: Erasmus Darwin's Grandson Learned Early About Evolution." *Creation Ministries International*. Web. 6 Dec. 2013.

Henderson, Alexander. *Aldous Huxley*. 1936. New York: Russell & Russell, 1964.

Huxley, Aldous. *After Many a Summer Dies the Swan*. 1939. New York: Harper & Row, 1965.

———. *Ape and Essence*. New York: Harper & Brothers, 1948.

———. *Brave New World*. 1932. New York: Harper Perennial, 2006.

———. *Crome Yellow*. 1921. *Project Gutenberg*. September 3, 2012. Web. 10 Dec. 2013.

———. *Eyeless in Gaza*. 1936. New York: Carroll & Graf, 1995.

———. *Selected Letters*. Ed. James Sexton. Chicago: Ivan R. Dee, 2007.

Huxley, Julian, ed. *Aldous Huxley 1894-1963: A Memorial Volume*. New York: Harper & Row, 1965.

King-Hele, Desmond. *Erasmus Darwin*. New York: Charles Scribner's Sons, 1963.

Meckier, Jerome. "Aldous Huxley's Americanization of the 'Brave New World' Typescript." *Twentieth-Century Literature*. 48. 4 (Winter 2002): 427–460. Web. 10 Dec. 2013.

"Nazi Human Experimentation." *Wikipedia*. Last updated Nov. 18, 2013. Web. 11 Dec. 2013.

O'Neil, Erica. "The Discovery of Fetal Alcohol Syndrome." 25 Sept. 2013. Web. 21 Nov 2013. <http://embryo.asu.edu/pages/discovery-fetal-alcohol-syndrome>.

Rolo, Charles J. *The World of Aldous Huxley: An Omnibus of His Fiction and Non-Fiction Over Three Decades*. New York & London: Harper & Brothers, 1947.

Sexton, James. "Aldous Huxley's Bokanovsky." *Science Fiction Studies* 16. 1 (Mar. 1989): 85–89. *JSTOR*. Web10 Dec. 2013.

Thody, Phillip. *Huxley: A Biographical Introduction*. New York: Charles Scribner's, 1973.

Wagner, Erica. *Ariel's Gift: Ted Hughes, Sylvia Plath and the Story of Birthday Letters*. London: Faber & Faber, 2000.

Watt, Donald, ed. *Aldous Huxley: The Critical Heritage*. London & Boston: Routledge & Kegan Paul, 1975.

Woodcock, George. *Dawn and the Darkest Hour: A Study of Aldous Huxley*. Montreal, New York, London: Black Rose Books, 2007.

Penitentes at the Snake Dance: Native Americans in *Brave New World*_____

Katherine Toy Miller

One of the major plot points in *Brave New World* occurs when Bernard Marx and Lenina Crowne vacation at the New Mexico "Savage Reservation." Here Huxley's young, failed hero, John, modeled on Huxley's close friend, British author D. H. Lawrence, enters the novel. John then travels with Bernard and Lenina from his native world to the brave new world, from where his mother and father come. Lawrence had lived in New Mexico and frequently wrote and spoke about the southwestern reservations, particularly in the letters Huxley collected and edited after Lawrence's death in 1930. All together, this inspired many aspects of *Brave New World*, begun in 1931.

Through Lawrence, Huxley was also likely aware of other accounts written by early Anglo visitors to the area and drew heavily on all of these sources, as he said:

> I had no trouble finding my way around the English part of Brave New World, but I had to do an enormous amount of reading up on New Mexico, because I'd never been there. I read all sorts of Smithsonian reports on the place and then did the best I could to imagine it. I didn't actually go there until six years later, in 1937, when we visited Frieda Lawrence [D. H. Lawrence's wife] (Huxley 2011).

. Huxley conflated this information about the remote, impoverished reservations in ways that are culturally derogatory and inaccurate to create a Savage Reservation that, though rich in traditions, human relationships, and contact with nature, is dirty and violent in contrast to the prosperous brave new world that is clean, efficient, and sterile, creating conflict for John and the reader, so both reject these dystopian situations.

Huxley never acknowledged or apologized for his maligning and misrepresenting the Pueblo people of the Southwest—particularly their spiritual practices—not in his 1946 *Brave New World* foreword, his 1958 *Brave New World Revisited*, or anywhere else. What Huxley called "the most serious defect" in *Brave New World* was that John:

> is offered only two alternatives, an insane life in Utopia, or the life of a primitive in an Indian village. . . . [The idea] that human beings are given free will in order to choose between insanity on the one hand and lunacy on the other, was one that I found amusing and regarded as quite possibly true (Huxley, *Brave New World* viii).

Retrospectively, he would have offered John a third alternative, in which "[r]eligion would be the conscious and intelligent pursuit of man's Final End, the unitive knowledge of the immanent Tao or Logos, the transcendent Godhead or Brahman," similar to the beliefs of the people he denigrated (Huxley, *Brave New World* ix).

Huxley's reservation pilot tells Bernard and Lenina that Indians are "perfectly tame; savages won't do you any harm" (Huxley, *Brave New World* 106), just as Lawrence concludes in a August 1924 letter Huxley collected that the Indian is "a wonderful live toy to play with. More fun than keeping rabbits, and just as harmless" and describes seeing the snake dance in a Hopi village as "Like being right inside the circus-ring: lots of sand, and painted savages jabbering, and snakes and all that" (D. H. Lawrence, *Letters* 609). But Lawrence soon wrote a more reflective piece, "The Hopi Snake Dance":

> [The Hopi] has the hardest task, the stubbornest destiny. Some inward fate drove him to the top of these parched mesas, all rocks and eagles, sand and snakes, and wind and sun and alkali. These he had to conquer. Not merely, as we would put it, the natural conditions of the place. But the mysterious life-spirit that reigned there. The eagle and the snake (D H. Lawrence, "Hopi Snake Dance" 152).

He then explains his understanding of the Hopi religion:

The animistic religion, as we call it, is not the religion of the Spirit. A religion of spirits, yes. But not of Spirit. There is no One Spirit. There is no One God. There is no Creator. There is strictly no God at all: because all is alive. In our conception of religion there exists God and His Creation: two things. We are creatures of God, therefore we pray to God as the Father, the Savior, the Maker. . . . The American-Indian sees no division into Spirit and Matter, God and not-God. Everything is alive, though not personally so. Thunder is neither Thor nor Zeus. Thunder is the vast living thunder asserting itself like some incomprehensible monster, or some huge reptile-bird of the pristine cosmos (Lawrence, "Hopi Snake Dance" 147, 149).

Because Western civilization attempts to control natural forces not with prayer but with science and machines "we die of ennui," Lawrence points out, while "This was a capital in the original: An Indian with his own religion inside him cannot be bored. The flow of the mystery is too intense all the time" (Lawrence, "Hopi Snake Dance" 153, 178). This is the dilemma Huxley struggles with in *Brave New World*—how to make life worth living. And as he admits, he fails to create a viable option.

Bernard and Lenina visit the pueblo of Malpais, modeled on Acoma Pueblo—the adobe "Sky City" in west-central New Mexico. Continuously inhabited since before the twelfth century, with a large Franciscan mission church, San Estevan, established in 1629, it is a National Historic Landmark and a major tourist attraction. Acoma has always left a favorable impression on visitors from Coronado's army in 1540 (who arrived there after crossing the nearby volcanic field they named "Malpais" or "badlands,'" now a National Monument) to writer Willa Cather, who depicted it in her novel *Death Comes for the Archbishop* (1927), and photographer Ansel Adams (1941). When Lawrence was first invited to New Mexico, he was sent a photo of Acoma Pueblo as an enticement (Frieda Lawrence 306–7).

Huxley had Bernard and Lenina fly over Acoma and surrounding locations (*Brave New World* 105) and writes of "Our Lady of Acoma," (*Brave New World* 128) presumably conflating Acoma and Our Lady of Guadalupe, a manifestation of the Virgin

Mary important to Catholics throughout Mexico and the Southwest. He may have read L. Bradford Prince's 1915 description of Acoma:

The giant rock on whose summit it has its seat, rises perpendicularly nearly four hundred feet from the great plain below, which is itself over seven thousand feet above the sea. The cliff, or mesa, as every elevation with a level top is called in New Mexico, has been well compared to a lofty rocky island of the sea; the only difference being that one is surrounded by water and the other by air. The area of its summit is not far from a hundred acres, but it has a remarkably rough and irregular contour, indented by deep bays which almost bisect it, and by a multitude of lesser chasms; so that its circumference resembles that of the rocky islets on the coast of Maine or of Norway (Prince 214–215).

Huxley, using similar oceanic metaphors, writes less enthusiastically that "the mesa was like a ship becalmed in a strait of lion-colored dust. . . . On the prow of that stone ship in the centre of the strait, and seemingly a part of it, a shaped and geometric outcrop of the naked rock, stood the pueblo of Malpais." As Bernard and Lenina walk towards the outcropping "The sides of the great mesa ship towered over them, three hundred feet to the gunwale." They reach the top by climbing "a very steep path that zigzagged from side to side of the gully." When they emerge from the ravine the "top of the mesa was a flat deck of stone" (*Brave New World* 107–8).

For John to have sufficient motivation to leave, Huxley must depict his life in Malpais as unpleasant: "The squalor of that little house on the outskirts of the pueblo! A space of dust and rubbish separated it from the village. Two famine-stricken dogs were nosing obscenely in the garbage at its door. Inside, when they entered, the twilight stank and was loud with flies" (118).

Charles F. Lummis wrote of Acoma very differently in The Land of Poco Tiempo (land of "pretty soon"), a popular book published in 1893 which Lawrence also received as an enticement (Merrild 28).

The dark store-rooms in their curious houses are never empty; and in the living-rooms hang queer tasajos (twists) of dried muskmelon for dwarf pies, bags of dried peaches for the same end, jerked mutton from their own flocks, jerked venison from the communal hunt, parched chile, and other staples. . . . The cleanly and comfortable wool mattresses are rolled and laid on benches with handsome and often costly Navajo blankets, for a daytime sofa. By night they are unrolled upon rugs or canvases on the floor. . . .(Lummis 69–70).

When Bernard and Lenina arrive at the valley of Malpais they are told "there's a dance this afternoon at the pueblo" (Huxley, *Brave New World* 105). What they encounter is Huxley's distortion of the Hopi Antelope-Snake ceremony, the last major ceremony in the Hopi annual cycle. According to critic Leah Dilworth "From 1880 to 1920, the Hopi Snake and Antelope ceremony, popularly known as the Snake dance, was far and away the most widely depicted Southwest Native American ritual" (Dilworth 21). Captain John Gregory Bourke published his popular book, *The Snake-Dance of the Moquis [Hopis] of Arizona* in 1884, which sparked increased interest. Jesse Walter Fewkes, a Smithsonian Bureau of American Ethnology anthropologist/ethnologist, studied the Antelope-Snake ceremony from 1891–1897 and published reports in 1894–95 and 1897–98 which Huxley likely saw.

A likely similar ceremony was first recorded by the Spaniard Antonio Espejo in 1582; Espejo "wrote admiringly of an Acoma ceremony in which people danced and juggled with live snakes" ("Acoma"). According to Fewkes, other pueblo villages had a snake dance; the Hopi custom of carrying the snakes in their mouths is a local variant (Fewkes 305): "The Hopi or so-called Moqui Indians of Arizona are among the few surviving tribes of American aborigines which still retain an ancient ritual that is apparently unmodified by the Christian religion" (Fewkes 963). The Hopi, believing that being forced by the Spanish soldiers and priests to accept Christianity and stop their ceremonies had caused the rains to stop, the crops to fail, and famine to spread, secretly returned to their practices. The rains returned, "proving to the Hopis that their own ceremonies brought rain and that the Christian religion of the Castillas [Castilian Spanish] was not good for them" (Waters 253–254). After the Pueblo Revolt of 1680, in which the southwestern pueblos united to drive the Spanish out of their territory, the normally peaceful and tolerant Hopi killed the four priests and completely dismantled the Catholic Church at their village of Oraibi. They then had little contact with whites for another two hundred years.

The ceremony takes place over as many as twenty days and involves the creation of altars in the kivas (underground chambers) of the men of the Antelope and Snake clans, who then gather and wash the snakes, perform a symbolic marriage between a young tribal male and female, and conduct the Antelope race and dance followed by the Snake race and dance. The ceremony's immediate purpose it to bring rain and ensure the fertility of the crops, particularly the staple crop of maize. As Lawrence wrote in a letter Huxley edited, "the snakes are emissaries to his rain god to tell him to send rain to the corn on the Hopi Reservation" (D. H. Lawrence, *Letters* 610).

Hopi expert Frank Waters explains that the snake symbolizes life-giving mother earth while the antelope, which usually bears twins, symbolizes fruitful reproduction. Like the Hindu goddess Kundalini, the snake represents the generative organs and the life force curled at the base of the spine (the root chakra) while the antelope with its horns at the crown chakra represents the highest psychic powers of the brain, the doorway between the physical and spiritual realms. "Throughout the whole ceremony it is always the Antelope which takes precedence over the Snake, and day after day the Snake chief dutifully presents himself at the kiva of the Antelope chief—the lower self before the higher" (Waters 226).

When Bernard and Lenina reach the mesa top at Malpais pueblo, two pueblo men in ceremonial dress carrying writhing ropes of snakes "came nearer and nearer" Lenina: "their dark eyes looked at her, but without any sign of recognition, any smallest sign that they had seen her or were aware of her existence" (Huxley, *Brave New World* 109). Similarly, Lawrence writes in "The Hopi Snake Dance": "We say they look wild. But they have the remoteness of their religion, their animistic vision, in their eyes, they can't see as we see. And they cannot accept us. They stare at us as the coyotes stare at us: the gulf of mutual negation between us" (D. H. Lawrence, "Hopi Snake Dance" 178–179).

"'I don't like it,'" Lenina says after the men with snakes pass. "'I don't like it at all'" (Huxley, *Brave New World* 109), a reaction somewhat like Lawrence's initial response to the Hopi snake dance: "And what had they all come to see?—come so far, over so weary a way, to camp so uncomfortably?" (D. H. Lawrence, *Letters* 608).

Soon Bernard and Lenina arrive on a pueblo roof: "Below them, shut in by the tall houses, was the village square, crowded with Indians" (Huxley, *Brave New World* 112). Lawrence wrote "Hotevilla is a scrap of a place with a plaza no bigger than a fair-sized back-yard: and the chief house on the square a ruin. But into this plaza finally three thousand onlookers piled" (D. H. Lawrence, *Letters* 607).

Fewkes observed the same overcrowding nearly three decades earlier:

> The number of white spectators of the Walpi Snake dance in 1897 was more than double that during any previous dance, and probably two hundred would not be far from the actual enumeration. An audience of this size, with the addition of various Navaho and the residents of Walpi and neighboring pueblos, is too large for the size of the plaza, and it became a matter of grave concern to those who are familiar with the mode of construction of the walls and roofs of the pueblo whether they would support the great weight which they were called upon to bear (978).

Nearly a century later, in the mid-1980s, Hopis began restricting and even barring attendance by non-natives at the dance.

Though Lawrence emphasizes that "It is a capital in the original: There there are no drums, no announcements" which is partly why he dislikes this ceremony, arguing "From the cultured point of view, the Hopi snake dance is almost nothing" and calling it "uncouth rather than beautiful, and rather uncouth in its touch of horror. Hence the thrill, and the crowd" (D. H. Lawrence, "Hopi Snake Dance" 155, 146), Huxley includes drums and a "subterranean flute" (*Brave New World* 113) to heighten the drama and quickens the pace of the singing, stepping, and drumming until "first one woman had shrieked and then another and another, as though they were being killed; and then suddenly the leader of the dancers broke out of the line, ran to a big wooden chest which was standing at one end of the square, raised the lid and pulled out a pair of black snakes" (Huxley, *Brave New World* 114).

In "The Hopi Snake Dance" Lawrence writes that the snakes are brought out of the kisi or snake bower: "And before the crowd could realize anything else a young priest emerged, bowing reverently, with the neck of a pale, delicate rattle-snake held between his teeth" (164). The young priests circle around with the snakes in their mouths while an older priest accompanies each young one from behind, dusting his shoulders with "the feather-prayer-sticks, in an intense, earnest anxiety of concentration" (D. H. Lawrence, "Hopi Snake Dance" 165). The young men release their snakes which are caught up again by snake-catching priests: "And all the time, the snakes seemed strangely gentle, naïve, wondering and almost willing, almost in harmony with the men. Which of course was the sacred aim" (D. H. Lawrence, "Hopi Snake Dance" 167).

Lawrence records that the plaza is cleared, two Hopi women scatter white corn meal on the ground, the two snake-catchers, their arms full of snakes, turn them loose: "And before we who stood had realized it, the snakes were all writhing and squirming on the ground, in the white dust of the meal, a couple of yards from our feet." The snake-catchers take the snakes up again and run out of the plaza to the mesa where the snakes are released (D. H. Lawrence, "Hopi Snake Dance" 170–171). But in Huxley's invented ritual, which might seem accurate to the uninformed, "the snakes were flung down in the middle of the square; an old man came up from underground and sprinkled them with corn meal, and from the other hatchway [modeled on the underground kiva where the males hold their spiritual rituals] came a woman [a woman would almost never be in a kiva] and sprinkled them with water." Then the old man raises his hand for silence: "The drums stopped beating, life seemed to have come to an end" (Huxley, *Brave New World* 114).

In the most offensive scene of the book, Huxley combines native imagery and ritual with Christian symbolism and Penitente practices, which makes no sense to anyone familiar with both the

Hopis, who rejected the Spanish and Catholicism, and the Penitentes, southwestern lay male Spanish-American Roman Catholics known for self-flagellation and other self-chosen forms of torture: Up from the kivas, "the lower world," emerge "a painted image of an eagle" and "a man, naked, and nailed to a cross" (Huxley, *Brave New World* 114). A native boy of about eighteen, later identified as Palowhtiwa (the name of a Zuni chief, Pa-lo-wah-tiwa, Huxley must have read about in a Smithsonian Institution report), steps before the old man leading the ceremony who makes the sign of the cross over him. Walking around a "writhing heap of snakes," Palowhtiwa is lashed by a man wearing a coyote mask until he "pitched forward on his face. Bending over him, the old man touched his back with a long white feather, held it up for a moment, crimson, for the people to see, then shook it thrice over the snakes. A few drops fell. . ." (Huxley, *Brave New World* 115).

After this sacrifice, the drums break out; there is a great shout; the dancers rush forward, pick up the snakes, and run out of the square; the crowd runs after them and "only the boy remained, prone where he had fallen, quite still." Three old women "with great difficulty" carry him into a house. "The eagle and the man cross kept guard for a little while over the empty pueblo; then, as though they had seen enough, sank slowly down through their hatchways, out of sight, into the nether world" (Huxley, *Brave New World* 116).

Lawrence's record of the snake dance, rather than ending with near-death or possibly death, ends with the snakes free:

> Free to carry the message and thanks to the dragon-gods who can give and withhold. To carry the human spirit, the human breath, the human prayer, the human gratitude, the human command which had breathed upon them in the mouths of the priests, transferred into them from those feather-prayer-sticks which the old wise men swept upon the shoulders of the young, snake-bearing men, to carry this back, into the vaster, dimmer, inchoate regions where the monsters of rain and wind alternated in beneficence and wrath" (D H. Lawrence, "Hopi Snake Dance" 171–172).

The practices of the Los hermanos penitentes de la tercer orden de San Francisco were brought to the natives of Mexico and New Mexico by the Franciscan friars near the beginning of the Spanish Conquest (1519–1521). When the Spanish departed after Mexico's independence from Spain in 1821, many priests left, leading to the rise of the Penitente brothers as lay priests in New Mexico, where their practices, rather than dying out, became more extreme in the isolated Hispanic (not Native American) villages.

Huxley likely learned about the Penitentes from Lawrence who could view a Penitente morada (chapel) from the window of the Taos home where he was a frequent guest. His host, a Native American of Taos Pueblo, said, "'Indians got different ways. ... We have springtime too, but not like that'" (Luhan 145). In Lawrence's story about his hostess, "The Wilful Woman," the woman passes a "sort of church place where the Penitentes scourge and torture themselves, windowless so that no-one shall hear their shrieks and groans" (Finney 201). In his story "The Princess," Lawrence describes some of the Mexican-Americans as having in their black eyes "a queer, haunting mystic quality, somber and a bit gruesome, the skull-and-crossbones look of the Penitentes. They found their raison d'être in self-torture and death-worship" (Finney 168). His poem, "Men in New Mexico," says "The Penitentes lash themselves till they run with blood in their efforts to come awake for one moment" (D. H. Lawrence 359). There was also a Smithsonian Institution report about them (Robertson), which Huxley may have read. In *Brave New World*, when John visits Eton, Huxley's former school, he sees a film of the Penitentes of Acoma whipping themselves (Huxley, *Brave New World* 162), but there are no Penitentes at Acoma, since it is a Native American, not a Hispanic, community.

In his 1946 Foreword, Huxley acknowledges conflating the Penitentes with the spiritual practices of the Pueblo Indians, but he doesn't acknowledge that these two traditions are now practiced by different cultures in different languages:

> For the sake, however, of dramatic effect, the Savage [John] is often permitted to speak more rationally than his upbringing among the practitioners of a religion that is half fertility cult and half

Penitente ferocity would actually warrant. Even his acquaintance with Shakespeare would not in reality justify such utterances. And at the close, of course, he is made to retreat from sanity; his native Penitente-ism reasserts its authority and he ends in maniacal self-torture and despairing suicide (viii).

Huxley may have drawn connections between Aztec sacrifices, which Lawrence read and wrote about, and those of the Penitentes, called "the Christianized descendants of the Aztecs" (Robertson). The Penitente's extreme forms of torture, including being lashed with or to cactus, may have had roots in the Aztec sense of sin and atonement which had an emphasis on extreme violence. The early Franciscans may have allowed this "in the hope of gaining Indian converts": "The penances of the Penitentes reflect more of Indian than of Franciscan practice" scholar Mary Watters argues (254).

Aztec human sacrifice rose to prominence from the early fourteenth century, about two hundred years before the Conquest. To be sacrificed was an honor: "it was sometimes voluntarily embraced by them, as the most glorious death, and one that opened a sure passage into paradise" (Prescott 51) as it was at the Savage Reservation (*Brave New World* 116–117). The handsome, young impersonator of the Aztec god Tezcatlipoca, selected for his flawless physical beauty, was regaled during the year prior to his sacrifice (Prescott 46–47).

Self-sacrifice, more prominent than ritual human sacrifice, was practiced as penitence or debt payment toward the Aztec gods: "in many places in Mesoamerica, the act of bloodletting, performed by piercing various parts of one's own body with a sharp object, had been expected to promote agricultural and reproductive fertility, good health, and longevity. . . . [T]he blood shed in self-sacrifice was 'exchanged' for supernatural aid" (Klein 293–294). But in *Brave New World* Palowhtiwa's and John's sacrifices, devoid of cultural context and meaning, seem "maniacal."

In contrast, Watters, publishing at Oxford University Press five years before *Brave New World*, commends the Penitentes: "They are among the few who have not succumbed to our modern mechanical madness and mental and spiritual standardization. They have preserved their individuality as a group better than most of us." She concludes with questions that *Brave New World* also raises: "Who shall say which belief or which practice is civilization? Henry Ford's or Mahatma Gandhi's? The materialistic scientist's or the Penitentes'?" (Watters 256).

The Hopis did engage in a rite of passage involving flogging as part of the spring planting ritual, the Powámû ceremony, but it was never a public spectacle. Both boys and girls between the ages of eight and ten were lashed four times with a yucca wand by a tribal elder dressed in a Katcina costume. Boys were naked; girls remained clothed. Various reports describe differently the intensity of this flogging, which took place within the kiva. An account is given by Henry R. Voth, a Mennonite missionary among the Hopi people from 1893–1903, who witnessed the events in 1894 and 1899.

> The dreaded moment which the candidates have so often been told about and of which they stand in such great fear has arrived. They are about to go through the ordeal of being flogged. Presently a loud grunting noise, a rattling of turtle shell rattles and a jingling of bells is heard outside [the kiva] (Voth).

Three tribal elders in Katcina costumes run, dance, howl, and whip the roof of the kiva then enter with a supply of whips. The children tremble, some crying and screaming, as two Katcinas "keep up their grunting, howling, rattling, trampling and brandishing of their yucca whips" (Voth 103). Each child is brought forth, and, hands turned upward, severely whipped, while their guardians shout encouragement and criticism at the Katcinas: "in short, pandemonium reigns in the kiva during this exciting half hour." The Katcinas flog each other "to the great satisfaction of the little novitiates who have just been so cruelly treated" then depart, making a great deal of noise outside the kiva again (Voth 103–4). After this the children "learn for the first time that Kachinas, whom they were taught to regard as supernatural beings, are only mortal Hopis" (Voth 120).

This Hopi ritual is similar to the Aztec mimetic sacrifice of children, which came at the same time of year and for the same purpose: to ensure the fertility of the crops and bring the spring rains. The young Hopis, and those of other peaceful Pueblo tribes, such as the Zuni, were made to cry to sympathetically invoke the rain; this did not include human sacrifice, which the Aztecs initiated after the Pueblo tribes were well-established in America. A modern Zuni man recalled being lashed with a yucca whip when he was a boy of twelve and joining the men's kiva society. He understood it as a ritual cleansing never used for punishment. Old men would ask the boys—too young to have done anything wrong and pure from the kiva initiation ritual—to whip them in blessing (Wyaco 16). In Huxley's decontextualized, sadomasochistic version, after the snake dance, John performs flagellation and other forms of bodily mortification to punish and purify himself (and Lenina) throughout the rest of the novel. The attention it attracts helps bring about his suicide.

Works Cited

"Acoma." *Southwest Crossroads*. School for Advanced Research on the Human Experience, 2007. Web. 12 Nov. 2013.

Dilworth, Leah. *Imagining Indians of the Southwest: Persistent Visions of a Primitive Past*. Washington, DC: Smithsonian Institution Scholarly Press, 1997.

Fewkes, Jesse Walter. *Hopi Snake Ceremonies*. Rev. ed. Albuquerque: Avanyu Publishing, Inc., 2000.

Fraser, Raymond and George Wickes. "Aldous Huxley, The Art of Fiction No. 24." *The Paris Review.* Spring 1960. The Paris Review Online. Web. 13 March 2011.

Finney, Brian, ed. *The Cambridge Edition of the Letters and Works of D. H. Lawrence: St. Mawr and Other Stories*. Cambridge, UK: Cambridge UP, 1983.

Huxley, Aldous. *Brave New World*. 1932. New York: HarperCollins, 1998.

Klein, Cecelia. "The Ideology of Autosacrifice at the Templo Mayor." *The Aztec Templo Mayor.* Ed. E. H. Boone. Washington, D.C.: Dumbarton Oaks. 1987. 293–370.

Lawrence, D. H. "The Hopi Snake Dance." *Mornings in Mexico*. New York: Alfred A. Knopf, 1927. 141–179.

———. *The Letters of D. H. Lawrence*. Ed. Aldous Huxley. London: William Heinemann Ltd., 1932.

———. "Men in New Mexico." *The Cambridge Edition of the Works of D. H. Lawrence: The Poems*. Ed. Christopher Pollnitz. 2 vols. New York: Cambridge UP, 2013. 359–360.

Lawrence, Frieda. *Frieda Lawrence: The Memoirs and Correspondence*. Ed. E. W. Tedlock, Jr. New York: Alfred A. Knopf, 1964.

Luhan, Mabel Dodge. *Edge of Taos Desert*. Albuquerque: U of New Mexico P, 1987.

Lummis, Charles F. *The Land of Poco Tiempo*. 1928. Albuquerque: U of New Mexico P, 1966.

Merrild, Knud. *A Poet and Two Painters: A Memoir of D. H. Lawrence*. New York: The Viking Press, 1939.

Prescott, William H. *History of the Conquest of Mexico and History of the Conquest of Peru*. New York: Random House, 1948.

Prince, L. Bradford. *Spanish Mission Churches of New Mexico*. Cedar Rapids, Iowa: The Torch Press, 1915. Southwest Electronic Text Center. University of Arizona Library, 23 June 1998. Web. 27 Nov. 2013.

Robertson, John M. *Pagan Christs: Studies in Comparative Hierology*. 2nd ed. London: Watts & Co., 1911. Internet Sacred Text Archive. Web. 20 Nov. 2013.

Voth, Henry R. *The Oraibi Powamu Ceremony*. Field Museum of Natural History Publication 61, 3.2 (1901): 67–158. Internet Archive. Web. 28 Nov. 2013.

Waters, Frank. *The Book of the Hopi*. New York: Penguin Books, 1963.

Watters, Mary. "The Penitentes: A Folk-Observance." *Social Forces* 6:2 (Dec. 1927): 253–256. JSTOR. Web. 25 Nov. 2013.

White, Leslie A. "The Acoma Indians." *The Forty-Seventh Annual Report of the Bureau of American Ethnology, 1929-1930*. Washington, D. C.: Smithsonian Institution, 1932. 17–193. Internet Archive. Web. 25 Nov. 2013.

Wyaco, Virgil. *A Zuni Life: A Pueblo Indian in Two Worlds*. Albuquerque: U of New Mexico P, 1998.

Film Adaptations of *Brave New World*_____
Alexander Charles Oliver Hall

Although it was published in 1932, *Brave New World* has yet to inspire any major Hollywood adaptations. Nevertheless, two made-for-television adaptations have been produced—one in 1980 and the other in 1998. The 1980 adaptation, directed by Burt Brinckerhoff, stays very close to its source, seeming merely to disseminate its content, while the 1998 adaptation, directed by Leslie Libman and Larry Williams, takes several liberties with Huxley's novel, presenting new content within the source's frame. With contemporary adaptation studies having shaken loose the constraints of fidelity criticism—which concentrates on the adaptation's fidelity to the source text—scholarly interest in film adaptations of *Brave New World* should not be based solely on their fidelity to the novel. Instead, both adaptations of the novel can be judged by the utopian maneuvers—or attempts to proffer utopian content—mounted by each adaptation. Brinckerhoff, for instance, would seem to have maintained fidelity to the novel in his adaptation, thereby disseminating the utopian maneuver contained in the source, which is its warning against a dystopian reality, a utopian maneuver in and of itself. The production value of Brinckerhoff's adaptation, however, betrays the seriousness of the novel, resulting in what appears to be unintentional camp. On the other hand, Libman and Williams fare a bit better with their adaptation, injecting new utopian content into the narrative via the changes that are made, which essentially involve converting the classical dystopia of the source into a critical dystopia via some plot changes. Regardless of their successes or failures as adaptations, the cultural influence of the novel is shown by the fact that it has already been adapted twice over, not to mention the interest of director Ridley Scott, who has been involved in plans to bring another adaptation of the novel to theaters, though the project has yet to come to fruition.

Huxley's novel is a famous example of the classical dystopia, which, according to Tom Moylan, is an "epic" or "open" genre, containing a "militant pessimism" that leaves "no meaningful possibility of movement or resistance, much less radical change, embedded in any of the iconic elements of the text" (Moylan, *Scraps* 157, 162). Classical dystopias "maintain utopian hope *outside* their pages, if at all; for it is only if we consider dystopia as a warning that we as readers can hope to escape its pessimistic future" (Baccolini and Moylan, *Dark Horizons* 7). Moreover, Naomi Jacobs says of the classical dystopia that its "repulsive force . . . comes from its portrayal of a world drained of agency—of an individual's capacity to choose and to act, or a group's capacity to influence and intervene in social formations" (Jacobs, "Posthuman Bodies" 92). The endings of novels like Yevgeny Zamyatin's *We*, Orwell's *Nineteen Eighty-Four*, and Huxley's *Brave New World*, then, situate them as classical dystopias because no hope for the resistant protagonists of their plots exists within the pages of the narratives, in part because of the lack of agency that Jacobs mentions, as well as the influence and/or intervention of the systems portrayed in the works. *Brave New World* presents a world that has been socially engineered via eugenics (and dysgenics), as well as conditioning, so that society will run according to the way the system wants. Bernard Marx is exiled when he is found to have resisted the social order, and it is said that this "punishment is really a reward" because:

> [H]e'll meet the most interesting set of men and women to be found anywhere in the world. All the people who, for one reason or another, have got too self-consciously individual to fit into community-life. All the people who aren't satisfied with orthodoxy, who've got independent ideas of their own. Every one, in a word, who's any one" (Huxley, *Brave New World* 227).

For some readers, the enclave to which Marx is being sent represents some hope within the pages of the novel, undermining its status as a classical dystopia, but this enclave remains under the control of the novel's imagined system, so there will be little room for agency or resistance, even if pleasures abound. In this way, Bernard is re-subjugated by the system (as is his friend Helmholtz, another resistant character). John Savage, on the other hand, continues to resist the system, only to be frustrated to the point of suicide by the novel's end—after, in a rage, he has beaten Lenina to death. Lenina is another character who resists the system by, in her case, falling in love with John Savage. With all of these resistant characters either being re-subjugated by the system or killed, it is clear the novel is an example of the classical dystopia.

Brave New World opens somewhat like a film itself, although neither of the films discussed in this analysis make use of the novel's script-like exposition, easy as it would be to do so. Huxley's filmic prose style comes as no surprise, considering Huxley's work in Hollywood from the 1940s until his death, and *Brave New World* seems to anticipate this turn to the movies; Huxley's first paragraph reads like a screenplay direction for a Hollywood establishing shot: "A squat grey building of only thirty-four stories. Over the main entrance the words, Central London Hatchery and Conditioning Centre, and, in a shield, the World State's motto, Community, Identity, Stability" (1). Everything, in fact, before the reader joins the Director of Hatcheries and Conditioning's tour, and intercut with it throughout, provides description of what could be the *mise en scène* of a film. This description includes the direction the ground level room of the hatchery faced, the winter scene visible through the windows, the description of the light in the laboratory, the workers' white overalls and rubber gloves, the yellow-barreled microscopes, the interior of the fertilizing room, and more. Further, the Director of Hatcheries and Conditioning's dialogue throughout the tour (joined, at different points, by Mustapha Mond and Henry Foster) functions much like the dialogue in a screenplay, familiarizing the reader with Huxley's fictional world and providing the necessary knowledge of that world to contextualize the coming plot. One example of this contextualization is Henry Foster's description of the goings-on in the Embryo Store, where embryos are stored while they mature into babies ready to be "decanted." While in the Bottling Room, the embryo feeds on "blood surrogate" (10–11), which, via a centrifugal pump, is "kept . . . moving over the placenta" (11). This information contextualizes the oft-repeated rumor of Bernard's embryo having accidentally had alcohol in the blood-surrogate, which is brought up in the text by Lenina's friend Fanny—"They say somebody made a mistake when he was still in the bottle—thought he was a Gamma and put alcohol into his blood surrogate. That's why he's so stunted" (46)—and again by Benito Hoover, who asserts that the alcohol "touched his brain, I suppose" (60). This filmic contextualization of the plot pervades the first three chapters of Huxley's text, along with other pseudo-filmic devices, such as the flashback to the discovery of sleep-teaching, parenthetical cues for the child respondents to the Director of Hatcheries and Conditioning (D.H.C.) on the tour, and the corresponding intercuts of the novel's characters with Mustapha Mond's explanation of the development of history to the civilization depicted in the novel. In spite of the ways that the novel could act as a blueprint for a film adaptation, however, both of the film adaptations to date have largely ignored these cues, even as their adherence to the plot details varies.

Brinckerhoff's *Brave New World*

Burt Brinckerhoff's 1980 film version of *Brave New World* ignores the film-like structure of the novel, choosing instead to provide much of the back story contained in the novel through dramatization. Rather than presenting a tour headed up by the D.H.C. and joined at various points by other characters, as in the novel, Brinckerhoff opens his film with Mustapha Mond (Ron O'Neal) lecturing a group of young Alphas. In Mond's lecture, much of the information provided through the whole of the novel's first section is delivered, including the set-up of sexual behavior, worship of Henry Ford, and an overview of the Fordian society. Before Brinckerhoff's opening credits roll, Mond concludes that the "perfection" of Fordian civilization is that "everyone is adjusted. Everyone has been conditioned to want to do the work he has to do. And thus everyone is perfectly happy, perfectly content" (*Brave New World*, 1980). Mond's short lecture encapsulates Huxley's three-chapter exposition in a minute or so, but without the character development that Huxley gets across, in part because the lecture takes place before Bernard Marx or Lenina

Crowne have been decanted—the film actually aims to dramatize the love affair of the future D.H.C. (Keir Dullea) with Linda (Julie Cobb), who will become mother to John Savage (later Kristoffer Tabori) when the pair visit the savage reservation.

Brinckerhoff's overall approach to the adaptation seems to be to remain true to the novel, thereby disseminating the utopian content of the source to the film's audience, but the film's production value may undermine the attempt. Made for Universal Television, the film was aired on NBC in a miniseries format. Characters clad in nylon jumpsuits indicating their social strata—alphas, betas, etc.—contribute to the overall camp of the film, as do the blank-stared performances of the actors, though this aspect of the film might be rationalized as reflecting the naïveté of the characters. In spite of its low production value and the dramatization of the D.H.C.'s relationship with Linda, however, the film's content actually does stay fairly close to that of the source.

The relationship between these characters reinforces the parallelism that is suggested in the novel between Bernard and the D.H.C. as well as Linda and Lenina. In addition, dramatizing the backstory creates an opportunity to delve even more deeply into details of the World State, such as the birth control used, which foreshadows Linda's pregnancy. Even more parallelism is achieved by juxtaposing John's delivery with Bernard's embryonic trip down the production line, the former featuring an ashamed, viviparous mother and the latter an emotionless occurrence that reinforces the mechanization of human birth premised by the source text. At this point, however, the film does take one liberty: the D.H.C., because he has no emotional tie to Linda, is back in the bottling room flirting with a woman, who mistakenly adds alcohol to Bernard's bottle, undoing the novel's ambiguity of whether Bernard actually has been stunted by such a possibility. The D.H.C., learning of the error, decides to let the child be born, considering it a research possibility, and then, after some narrative elision, Bernard (Bud Cort) is shown full-grown, a proverbial cog in the machinery at "Central Hatcheries." Soon after, his trip to the savage reservation comes along, and, though the scene is heavily elided, the result is the same as the novel—John Savage and Linda return with Bernard and Lenina to the World State.

On arrival, the D.H.C. is shamed for his having fathered John, and he is transferred to Iceland to escape—the same place to which Bernard will later be transferred. Afterward, the film more or less follows the novel throughout, complete with John's celebrity status, his infatuation with Lenina and her failed attempt to seduce him, his outburst at the soma distribution after the death of Linda along with Bernard and Helmholtz (Dick Anthony Williams), and his encounter with Mustapha Mond. This encounter leads to his exile at a lighthouse in Surrey, and his discovery there by a filmmaker whose secretly gathered footage leaves John overcome with tourists.

Unlike the novel, the final scenes of the film present a situation, in which so many people have come to gawk at John in his lighthouse that he comes outside to yell at them, encountering Lenina, who is upset from having seen the film of John, which makes him look ridiculous. Although Lenina professes her love for John in this scene, officials use a thick soma vapor to disperse the crowd, and John loses Lenina in the cloud of vapor. When he finds her later, unconscious, he believes her to be dead, and he leaves her, indicating that he intends to commit suicide, but she begins to wake as he walks away. Still, it is too late; the scene cuts to a hanged John in the lighthouse. This approach to the film's ending, though not entirely derived from the novel as is much of the rest of the film, does pay homage to the role of Shakespeare in the text, given its obvious parallel to the end of the Bard's *Romeo and Juliet*. Lenina, meanwhile, is actually taken to a "moral reconditioning center," where she will forget all about John and her transgressions against the World State, which signifies her own re-subjugation and keeps the film consistent with the classical dystopia.

There is a utopian maneuver inherent in trying to keep in line with the novel that equals what might be referred to as a utopian function of dissemination. In disseminating the utopian content of the source that comes in the form of a warning against its imagined reality with little interference, that utopian content is proffered to a potentially new audience—i.e., the film's audience—and kept alive within the larger culture. Nearly fifty years after the novel's publication, then, its utopian content is presented in a new medium for what could be a wider audience, and this dissemination is utopian through and through.

Libman's and Williams' *Brave New World*

The differences between the endings of Huxley's novel and Libman's and Williams' film reveal the way the latter utilizes the novel to frame its own new utopian content. The utopian content that is present in Libman's and Williams' adaptation comes from several key changes in the conversion from novel to film, including the fact that Bernard and Lenina actually conceive their own child and escape the World State, presumably to live happily ever after. This aspect of the film, among others, produces a kind of hope within the work itself, which converts Huxley's *classical* dystopia into a *critical* dystopia. A change as significant as that of the fate of Bernard and Lenina, moreover, in addition to a variety of other changes, significantly reframes the narrative so as to allow for the inclusion of new utopian content.

Libman's and Williams' adaptation of Huxley's novel is a decidedly modernized production that portrays the World State as a society organized around a kind of fashionable decadence. Lenina Crowne (Rya Kihlstedt) is a schoolteacher in the World State who is romantically involved with Bernard Marx (Peter Gallagher), an emotional engineer that specializes in conditioning. The relationship between Lenina and Bernard is looked down upon, given that promiscuity is encouraged by the World State, so they remain just promiscuous enough to keep the reproach of others at bay. Meanwhile, emotional engineering has been failing, as workers in the lower strata of the World State are resisting their conditioning and acting out. Maintaining the frame of the source, Lenina and Bernard head to the savage reservation, and, when their helicopter crashes there, they are rescued from hostile locals by John Cooper (Tim Guinee), who takes them to his mother's house, a mobile home on the reservation. After learning that John is the son of a man from the World State, and that he has been raised on the savage reservation by a woman—

his natural mother—from the World State, Bernard decides to bring John and his mother, Linda (Sally Kirkland), back with him because of "the research possibilities." John's presence in the World State is met with some resistance, but the World Controller, Mustapha Mond (Leonard Nimoy), approves the experiment nonetheless. When the Director of Hatcheries and Conditioning (Miguel Ferrer) realizes that he is the father of John, however, he destroys the evidence and reconditions a disgruntled Delta (through a reconditioning process reminiscent of what we see in Kubrick's *A Clockwork Orange*) to "Kill Bernard Marx." The plan fails when the Delta cannot bring himself to carry out the task, and the Director is revealed as John's father anyway, when Bernard is able to recover the evidence that was thought to have been destroyed. All the while, since the arrival of John in the World State, he has become a celebrity, along with Bernard, for having been responsible for bringing him back from the reservation. During this time, John and Lenina develop feelings for one another, but John has reservations about acting on them because his Shakespeare-derived morals cause him to question the promiscuity of the World State. As in the novel, he is driven to incite a riot amongst workers receiving a soma ration outside the hospital where his mother has just died from a soma overdose, and he is brought before Mustapha Mond to explain himself. Unsatisfied with the exchange he has with Mond, John ventures off on his own to be alone, but is soon discovered by the media, who unintentionally force him off a cliff, where he falls to his death. Bernard, who has taken over as D.H.C., is then presented with the information that Lenina has become pregnant with his child, and he is faced with the choice of either reporting the pregnancy or escaping the World State. He chooses the latter. The film ends with the couple and their child together on a beach, just as Mond, laughing, realizes what has happened.

Although Libman's and Williams' adaptation reactivates Huxley's novel in some ways, the significance of the ending having been changed from that of its source takes the adaptation a step further, completely reframing the source. Nevertheless, some aspects of the adaptation demonstrate a reactivation—within the cultural and/or historical context of its production—of the source. First, in Huxley's novel, the savage becomes something of a celebrity in the World State: "All uppercaste London was wild to see this delicious creature" (153), but in Libman's and Williams' film, the savage becomes not only a celebrity, but a media sensation, demonstrating a direct critique of contemporary culture's obsession with fame. A newscast early in the film, shortly after John arrives in the World State, reports that "there's something new in town, and he's *savagely* attractive." The newscasts continue throughout the film, establishing the impact John has on the World State as the narrative develops. John's level of celebrity, however, begins to weigh on him, and this is compounded by his struggle to adjust to the World State and what he sees as its immorality, as well as his mother's death. After he is pardoned for inciting the riot during soma distribution outside the hospital where his mother has died, he is reported by the news as saying, "I want to be alone" before wandering to the countryside and camping out atop an "abandoned microwave tower." After he is discovered by the media—who appear as paparazzi might in the viewer's empirical world—and overwhelmed by the numbers that assemble, he attempts to escape the tower and the media, but they are upon him as soon as he reaches the ground, and his attempt to run away from them is foiled when he comes to the edge of a cliff, is left with no escape, and falls to his death. The role the media plays in John's death is not unlike the real-life story of the death of Diana, Princess of Wales, which took place not even one year before the film's appearance on television in April 1998. Although the official reports regarding Diana's death were that her driver, Henri Paul, had been driving drunk, the car was being pursued by paparazzi, which may have been partly responsible for Paul's loss of control of the car as he attempted to lose the pursuers. In this way, Diana's fame may have contributed to her death, just as John Cooper's fame contributes to his death in Libman's and Williams' *Brave New World*. Given this (admittedly quasi-) parallel, the film seems to reactivate the novel's indictment of media sensationalism within the historical context of its production.

In the novel, as in Libman's and Williams' film, Bernard Marx also becomes a celebrity. In bringing John back to the World State from the Savage Reservation, Huxley's Marx suddenly finds himself no longer an outcast, instead becoming just the kind of social butterfly he abhors as the narrative begins. Because "it was only through Bernard, his accredited guardian, that John could be seen, Bernard now found himself, for the first time in his life, treated not normally, but as a person of outstanding importance" (Huxley, *Brave New World* 156). This importance earns him the favor of much of the upper-caste people of the World State, as well as the affection of women, who, prior to his guardianship of the savage, would have thought him "ugly," "small," and even "stunted" (46). After returning to the World State with John, however, it is said that "[a]s for the women, Bernard had only to hint at the possibility of an invitation, and he could have whichever of them he liked" (156). Nevertheless, Bernard's newfound popularity earns him the disapproval of the one person who had been his friend previously, Helmholtz Watson, but it is no matter because he is so happy that he tells himself "never would he speak to Helmholtz again" (157). In this way, Bernard relinquishes his resistant protagonist status, being re-subjugated by the system and replaced as a resistant protagonist entirely at this point by John and, to a lesser extent, Helmholtz. This might serve as further evidence of the novel's classification as a classical dystopia, since Bernard is the initial resistor as the narrative gets underway.

Peter Gallagher's Bernard Marx in Libman's and Williams' *Brave New World* comes off as an innocent, scholarly-type character, and he brings John back from the reservation solely because he wants to study him as a genetic World State subject untainted by conditioning, not because he figures out early on that the D.H.C. is John's biological father. Furthermore, Bernard does not himself become that much of a celebrity. Instead, only his career seems to be affected positively; as the D.H.C. says, "You're moving up in the world, Marx. Congratulations." Bernard also becomes friendly with Mustapha Mond as a result of his research and from having brought John back to the World State. He also seeks out John's father, revealing that it is the D.H.C. only after an attempt on his life orchestrated by the D.H.C. As a result of all this, Bernard is positioned to take over as the new D.H.C., suggesting his possible complicity in the World State system. When Lenina comes to Bernard to tell him that she is pregnant with his child, however, he is faced with the decision of whether to attempt to explain the pregnancy away publicly, risking death or worse, or banishing Lenina from the World State, choosing the latter. Initially, this decision positions Bernard as an insensitive character, who chooses status and career over family; in effect, he is re-subjugated by the system, albeit in a different way than in the novel. However, in the end, Bernard is revealed as having joined Lenina in exile with his child after all.

Speaking of Lenina, the changes made to her specific narrative in Libman's and Williams' film also exemplify a reframing of the source. Huxley's Lenina starts out as a fairly typical World State subject, except that she has a mild scandal surrounding her near-monogamy with Henry Foster. She intends to subvert the scandal by becoming involved with Bernard Marx, and so the couple travel to the savage reservation together. Lenina is appalled by the sights and sounds she encounters there, until she lays eyes on John. Lenina's monogamy with Foster seems to signify her own resistance to the system, which comes in the form of her ability to, for all intents and purposes, fall in love, which is forbidden in the World State. Her capacity for love then centers itself on John, who rebukes her because of his morals, to the extent that she begins to represent for him his own moral weakness because he is sexually attracted to her, but the World State's conditioning has made her too willing for his renaissance-based ideas about love. Once alone at the lighthouse, John attempts to find solace, but can only think of his own desire—specifically for Lenina—so he punishes himself for these thoughts via self-flagellation. Lenina then arrives at the lighthouse herself; she cannot keep away, so intense is her love. This further demonstrates her resistance to the system. John, however, sees her and flies into a rage, beating her with the whip he had used to whip himself, ultimately killing her. In this way, no hope exists for Lenina in Huxley's text.

As an "ex-centric" subject, Libman's and Williams' Lenina comes to a different end, one that includes escape from the World State. Instead of Foster, the film presents Lenina's near-monogamous relationship as being with Bernard. As a result, John assumes they are married. Lenina does become interested in John, but it reads more like infatuation than love, and he rejects her one advance. This prompts Lenina to reach for her soma and forget the unhappiness, but she stops short, allowing herself to feel the emotion, which shows some resistance on her part. Next, she sits with John at the hospital as his mother dies, and afterward, John prompts some intimacy himself, and the viewer is led to believe that she reciprocates. At this point, she comes to accept that she may be in love with him, and that it is harming her relationship with Bernard, which may well have been love also. Lenina again turns to soma to dull the pain she is experiencing, and, during this "soma holiday," John escapes to the abandoned microwave tower. When Lenina sees John on television later, she goes to try and see him, but he dies, and she leaves with Bernard, whom she sees there, and they have sex that night, professing their love for one another. Bernard next becomes the new D.H.C., appointed by Mustapha Mond himself, and Lenina is shown teaching her class, but she goes off script, inspired by her internal struggle with the system, of which she is a subject. Next, she visits Bernard to report her pregnancy and is sent into exile. Lenina, then, resists the system herself in the film, but to a much greater extent than she does in the novel.

Another manifestation of hope in Libman's and Williams' film that contributes to its abandonment of the source's narrative frame is the character Gabriel (Jacob Chase), who appears to question the ideology of the World State on a couple of different occasions throughout the film. Gabriel is one of Lenina's students, and he is established, early in the film, as a kind of resistant subject himself. The character's likely analogue in Huxley's text is the little boy in the garden, who "seems rather reluctant to join in the ordinary erotic play" (32). The child's reluctance to participate in the "sexual game" (31) may exemplify his resistance to the World State system, but he is merely taken "in to see the Assistant Superintendent of

Psychology. Just to see if anything is at all abnormal" (32). With that, the child disappears, never to be seen in the novel again, and the reader can assume that he will be reconditioned until he has what the World State would see as a healthy appetite for the sexual games.

The reader, meanwhile, might well respond with abhorrence at the suggestion that children be encouraged to participate in such games, and any hope that the little boy's resistance will make an impact falls by the wayside when he is taken away. The film's character Gabriel is first encountered early in the film, as Lenina explains how the World State society came into existence (the film's analogue to the D.H.C.'s tour at the beginning of Huxley's novel). Gabriel, stone-faced, explains, as taught via conditioning, "today we have no crime, no disease, no war, no aging, no suffering. Each of us is genetically designed to fit perfectly into our place in society. So everyone is happy." In the next scene, Gabriel is shown in bed, seemingly uncomfortable as he sleeps and the "hypnopædia" voice drones on. It is as if he is resistant, in this moment, to hypnopædia itself, and Lenina responds by drugging him with soma. When the viewer next sees Gabriel, John is visiting his school to recite Shakespeare's *Romeo and Juliet* for the students. Most of the class thinks the play is irrelevant and outdated, but Gabriel seems intrigued, looking ashamed of his classmates for their inability to appreciate the play. Although Gabriel's resistance is mostly only manifested up to now by facial expressions, it is clear he is a resistant character himself—he seems to want to reject the system of which he is a subject in spite of his indoctrination. When Gabriel is next shown, it is in Lenina's class, watching intently as she abandons *The World Concensus Textbook*, saying, "heroes change things. We're not supposed to want anything to change. Heroes mean that one person can make a difference." While another student chides Lenina for going outside the textbook, Gabriel watches, seemingly hopeful that she will stand behind what she has said, but, when she backs down, he shows disappointment and despair. In spite of his seeming loss of hope, Gabriel remains a manifestation of hope within the narrative that leaves the viewer with hope, even more evidence that Huxley's novel has been transformed into a critical dystopia from its original classically dystopian frame. As the film comes to a close, Gabriel is once again shown in bed, but this time, he does not let the hypnopædia voices disturb him; instead, he reaches beneath his pillow, retrieving cotton swabs, which he places in his ears to block out the voices. This moment is so important to the film's reinvigoration as a critical dystopia that it is the last scene before the credits roll, and the importance that is placed on this moment solidifies the reframing of the source, as it leaves hope within the narrative itself. This in turn provides the viewer with the hope that even if such a future did come to pass, we would still be able to overcome it. That is, we would be able to "escape [such a] pessimistic future."

In their adaptation of *Brave New World*, then, Libman and Williams convert the classical dystopia of the novel into a critical dystopia, as hope is present within the proverbial "pages" of the narrative. This hope comes in several forms throughout the film, but not without still critiquing some aspects of its cultural/historical context. This conversion of the source to a critical dystopia might be indicative of what could be called the utopian function of framing within adaptation studies. Contributing to the source's utopian content by injecting new manifestations of such content into the source equals another utopian function of adaptation, and Libman and Williams achieve this end through their adaptation of Huxley's novel.

In spite of the deviations from the source text, both of the adaptations discussed here show different utopian functions of adaptation. Brinckerhoff's 1980 adaptation—though it is by no means a fidelity critic's darling—stays fairly close to its source and demonstrates what might be termed adaptation's utopian function of dissemination. While this adaptation does not exact any new critique or present much in the way of utopian content not already contained in the source, the approach to the adaptation is characterized more by fidelity than anything else, and this results in a dissemination of the utopian content of the source to a potentially wider audience, while keeping that content culturally alive. Libman and Williams, meanwhile, introduce new utopian content into Huxley's narrative, and this is a manifestation not only of the utopian function of framing, but also of the utopian impulse in general. This shows how cultural production can be an outlet for filmmakers to exercise the utopian imagination. *Brave New World* provided Libman and Williams with such an outlet, and they introduced utopian content by reframing the narrative. The conversion of a classical dystopia into a critical dystopia, moreover, might more generally demonstrate the need for hope under late capitalism, and this is yet another utopian aspect of the adaptation. In any case, these *Brave New World* adaptations call attention to Huxley's text, which, in our own brave new world, keeps hope alive.

Works Cited

Baccolini, Raffaella and Tom Moylan. "Introduction: Dystopia and Histories." *Dark Horizons: Science Fiction and the Dystopian Imagination*. Eds. Raffaella Baccolini & Tom Moylan. New York: Routledge, 2003. 1–12.

Brave New World. Dir. Leslie Libman and Larry Williams. Perf. Peter Gallagher, Tim Guinee, Rya Kihlstedt, Leonard Nimoy. Universal TV, 1998.

Brave New World. Dir. Burt Brinckerhoff. Perf. Bud Cort, Kristoffer Tabori, Marcia Strassman, Ron O'Neal. Universal TV, 1980.

Huxley, Aldous. *Brave New World*. New York: Harper & Row, 1932.

Jacobs, Naomi. "Posthuman Bodies and Agency in Octavia Butler's *Xenogenesis*." *Dark Horizons: Science Fiction and the Dystopian Imagination*. Eds. Raffaella Baccolini and Tom Moylan. New York: Routledge, 2003. 91–112.

Moylan, Tom. *Scraps of the Untainted Sky: Science Fiction, Utopia, Dystopia*. Boulder, CO: Westview Press, 2000.

Awakening 'from the Nightmare of Swarming Indistinguishable Sameness': Globalization and Marginality in *Brave New World*___

Robert Wilson

Globalization, by tying distant and irreconcilable places and cultures together, has resulted in the progressive elimination of earth's marginal areas and people. The logic is simple: if one can find a McDonald's in Prague's Museum of Communism, Paris's Rue Saint Lazare (in an historic building, no less), and in the middle of Israel's Negev Desert, then all the walls are down and *there* might as well be *here*. However, globalization's closing of all frontiers hides a secondary phenomenon: the closing of the mind, or, to be more accurate, the elimination of authenticity and agency. As the distinctiveness of once disparate societies is planed down to the finest of tolerances, so too do human choices and behaviors flatten out, themselves products of the shrinking environments. Aldous Huxley saw this trend earlier than most, and consequently, *Brave New World*, with its World State, offers a rare and prescient understanding of industrial modernity and, by extension, the misleadingly labeled "post" modern phenomenon of globalization as a *spatial* phenomenon, one that requires transgressive acts of marginalization, both accidental and self-motivated, to escape.

In Huxley's World State, each region of the planet marches to the same "bokanovskified" (4) process, sewn tight by efficient transportation (personal helicopters) and communications (ubiquitous telephones), with climate as the only notable difference. The regions of Huxley's dystopia are as distinct as the mass-produced babies that populate them. To call these regions homogeneous spaces is potentially misleading, as *spaces*, at least in the geographic sense, speaks of distances, boundaries, and little else. Spaces, however, are also *places*, "spaces which people have made meaningful" (Cresswell, *Place* 7) by coding in deeper layers of social meaning. Geographer Tim Cresswell explains that places are "how we make the world meaningful and the way we experience the world" (7), a crucial distinction, for homogeneous *places*, like fast food restaurants, often impose unexamined burdens of meaning. Cresswell observes that many "bemoan a loss of a sense of place as the forces of globalization ... [produce] homogenized global spaces" (8), though perhaps it would be more accurate to say people bemoan a *changing* sense of place, as homogenized places *do* have attached meanings: beliefs and behaviors expected by owning entities. Examination of Huxley's world-building begins here, for it is the expectations and behaviors coded into the spaces that threaten agency and authentic engagement, and consequently, it is through transgressing these place's boundaries that agency and authenticity might be regained. Two developments of modernity conspire in Huxley's vision to eliminate agency and authentic experience: the homogenization of place and the standardization of individuals.

The first marker of places coded to abrogate authenticity is the "total space," or hyperspace. Popularized by Baudrillard in *Simulacra and Simulation*, hyperspace embodies the totalized, imploded worlds currently in vogue. Fredric Jameson, speaking of L.A.'s Westin Bonaventure Hotel, describes a hyperspace as "a total space, a complete world, a kind of miniature city" (39), citing the hotel's unique architectural design, such as corridors that "seem to have been imposed by some new category of closure governing the [hotel's] inner space" (38–39). While indicative of the spatial strategies of late capitalism, hyperspaces are also indicative of the problems of travel in a globalized world: hyperspaces are without boundaries, entrances and exits recessed and masked, and, like the globalizing world, they offer a möbius strip of familiar locations and people.

Huxley's World State is built from hyperspaces; in fact, a primary science fictional technology used by Huxley—personal helicopters—clearly highlights the hyperspatial nature of London. Chapter four sees Henry and Lenina ride an elevator to the roof of the Central London Hatchery and Conditioning Centre to take Henry's personal helicopter over London to play Obstacle Golf, offering readers a helpful totalizing gaze of the city. The reader receives descriptions of several "huge table-topped buildings" (40) the size of "small town[s]" (42), the roofs of which operate as helicopter parking garages. Clearly, the distinction between locations is all but obliterated when one can simply step onto the roof of one building and fly to another, avoiding the tedious boundaries between.

Moreover, the buildings are themselves hyperspatial, resembling casinos, malls, and other loci of hybrid consumption. George Ritzer identifies not only hotels but also casinos and cruise lines—all standard(ized) tourist attractions—as hyperspaces, spaces "so vast ... one has little need or desire to go anywhere else" (*Thesis* 144). Containing everything from gymnasiums to gambling tables, cruise lines are micro-societies so complete that tourists have little reason to disembark, exotic ports of call be damned (144). Malls are no different: SF theorist Scott Bukatman observes that malls possess "a monadic self-sufficiency in which the outside world is denied" (126), labeling them "total space[s]" similar to Jameson's Bonaventure. Huxley's description of Bernard and Lenina's pre-Reservation hotel is cruise-worthy: the hotel boasts "[l]iquid air, television, vibro-vacuum massage, radio, boiling caffeine solution, hot contraceptives, and eight different kinds of scent" (67) in each bedroom, a "synthetic music plant" (67) to enhance unavoidable walking, and no less than "sixty Escalator-Squash-Racket Courts" (67). Not only have boundaries between spaces melted away, the remaining spaces offer little reason to leave, satisfying all needs.

The problem inherent in spatial homogeneity is that mobility, once a liberatory force, is rendered meaningless when there are no real borders left to transgress. Like place, mobility "carries with it the burden of meaning" (Cresswell, *Place* 6). In the Middle Ages, "to be mobile ... was to be without place, both socially and geographically" (11), a demonized, yet liberating position, as individuals were freed from burdensome obligations to lord and land by existing "on the margins ... outside of the obligations of place" (11). Without mobility, the "rigid, hierarchical system [permitting] ... little horizontal movement in space" (Huxley, "Revisited" 15) defined one's identity, and Huxley concludes that the development of industrial societies is "pushing us in the direction of a new medieval system" (15), or, in other words, towards the paradoxically *immobile* society on display in *Brave New World*.

While Huxley's dystopia seems highly mobile, the very *nature* of the mobility available ironically strips the one remaining border of meaning. Cresswell, separating the "brute fact" (3) of movement from its cultural representations and its "irreducibly embodied experience" (4), notes that one must ask "[h]ow is mobility embodied?" ("Towards" 163), for not all mobilities are equal: *in-place* mobility is made pleasant and efficient, while *transgressive* mobility is demonized and made difficult. Migrant workers, for example, once rode the rails from job to job, brutalized by railroad enforcers and labeled tramps, victims of a culture that associated wholesomeness with rootedness. The embodied experience of Lenina and Bernard's Savage Reservation excursion is marked by similar physical difficulties, as the pair, though brought to the border in comfort, are expected to hoof it through the relative squalor of the Reservation. Lenina quickly wishes they "could have brought the plane" (72) as she hates "walking ... [which makes] you feel so small" (104). The physically and psychologically debilitating mobility hardly argues for the experience's value: easy travel is denied solely to demonize both transgressive mobility and the place with which it is associated.

Cresswell identifies a "major distinction ... between being compelled to move or choosing to move" ("Towards" 163), and in McSocieties like "orderly Brave New World where perfect efficiency ... [leaves] no room for freedom" ("Revisited" 3), mobility is so scripted as to be stripped of meaning. Bryman explains that Disney controls mobility by "channel[ing] the movement of visitors in certain directions" (134) and restricting direction through the use of "lures, which Walt called 'weenies'" (134), such as kiosks and shops placed "strategically ... to maximize consumption" (134). Indeed, Disney's "weenie" strategy is a practical application of the unpleasantly embodied mobility, for socially-approved *consumptive* mobility is attached to incentives, while unprofitable mobility comes with cost: tired feet due to deficient public transportation, etc. A single bad experience dissuades deviation; presciently, Huxley implants

Disney's "weenie" strategy directly into the cortices of the World State citizenry. The Director of Hatcheries and Conditioning explains that children are reprogrammed via electrical shocks to "hate the country ... [yet] love all country sports" (15), resulting in calculable and profitable mobility (purchasing equipment, transportation, etc.). With self-directed mobility made unpleasant and meaningless, little remains but a forced march to the gift shop. Ninjalicious (a.k.a. Jeff Chapman), the late popularizer of urban exploration, offers a critique of contemporary city life not far removed from Huxley's: "urban living consists of mindless travel between work, shopping and home ... It's no wonder people feel unfulfilled and uninvolved" (3). Authentic (read: self-directed) engagement is all but impossible in environments where standardized experiences ensure standardized minds and controlled mobility prevents encountering alternative perspectives.

Not only are the spaces forming both Huxley's World State and our own stately world homogenized, but so too are the people. Though attached to clear material benefits, "our" Ford's approach creates standardized, incurious, pliant workers lacking the critical intellect antithetical to bureaucracy and willing to accept exploitation without complaint. Ritzer explains that Ford "sought to hire people who resembled animals" (*McDonaldization* 110). Huxley's debased Gammas and Epsilons are hardly unexpected extrapolations; the designers of rational management techniques coded dehumanization into the process from the beginning. Huxley cleverly introduces the reader to both the standardization process and its "products" simultaneously: the Director, discussing the mysteries of the "Bokanovsky Process" (3), is attended by a gaggle of students, each carrying "a notebook, in which, whenever the great man spoke, he desperately scribbled" (1). The students, products of Bokanovsky's method, are described in terms of mass-production—identical behaviors, identical responses, etc. Moreover, the Bokanovsky Process defamiliarizes factory workers by equating them with any product measurable by McDonaldization's holy metric of calculability. Such products can be further customized to fit whatever purpose is required: a bit of alcohol in the blood-surrogate, and all capacity for dissatisfaction dies with the relevant neural tissue. Finally, much like Ford's ideal worker base, individuals customized to fit a role can't stray far from it: being conditioned to need both work and consumer comforts ensures a strong attachment to place.

Standardizing spaces and people ultimately results in a singular, shared worldview: in short, a homogenized inner self. Psychologist Kenneth Gergen argues that extreme heterogeneity, "a plurality of voices vying for the right to reality" (7), marks postmodernity's boundary, as multiplying communications technology has replaced a mere handful of voices dictating what ideas were thought true and what choices were considered meaningful, with a chorus of thousands making unique and potentially contradictory demands. These competing voices provide "a multiplicity of incoherent and unrelated languages of the self" (6), a condition threatening to "stable" selves provided by one's religion, tribe, or World Controller. Gergen believes that this "populating of the self" (49) leads to a "multiphrenic condition … [marked by] the vertigo of unlimited multiplicity" (49), a condition some fear "debilitates any distinctive self-identity" (Sherrill 90) via inner *over*population. Even so, Huxley's citizenry, despite enjoying postmodernity's ubiquitous communications technology, are quite *de*populated, as contradictory voices are nowhere to be found. The true threat to identity is not the presence of multiple perspectives; rather, the problem lies in the quality of the perspectives present.

The World State's prenatal conditioning process, which predisposes citizens to "like their unescapable social destiny" (10), is less the populating and more ethnic cleansing, eliminating potentially dissenting outlooks. Crucially, this monophrenia is expressed via inner voices, expressed perfectly by the subliminal learning process: citizens are given, through sleep-teaching, a "moral education" (17) requiring no thought at all save the repetition of comforting axioms. It is hard to see this form of education as anything but the insertion of an unquestionable monophrenic chorus inside one's head, dictating how one must interpret experience: "I'm so glad I'm a Beta" (18). Combined with a "campaign against the

Past" (34), which eliminated alternative perspectives from the eras Before Ford, conditioning ensures that the self is "made up of ... our suggestions! (19).

Huxley addresses the danger of increasing monophrenia when he notes that by 1958 America's "great number of small journals and local newspapers ... [expressing] thousands of independent opinions" ("Revisited" 18) had all but disappeared, and with them, the plurality of voices once available. Huxley's focus on the newspaper is significant: Benedict Anderson explains in *Imagined Communities* that, in any nationalism project, newspapers create the sense of unified culture that binds nations together. Anderson concludes that the shared ceremony of reading "at daily or half-daily intervals" (35), not unlike prayer, allows the newspaper to create a "confidence of community in anonymity" (35), implicating newspapers in both grand narrative construction and McSociety's obsession with quantifiable behavior. Of course, this outcome is only possible when newspapers speak in the same voice; Huxley's numerous "small journals and local newspapers" hardly created a sense of shared identity. When newspapers all manage to tell the same story, however, the outcome is certain: monophrenia.

Because of their conditioning, citizens of the World State (excepting a few Alphas) are incapable of authentic engagement with others, despite the facts that they are so standardized and that "every one belongs to every one else" (29). Lenina, for example, is entirely unable to engage authentically with Bernard, offering canned lines rather than conversation. Bernard confesses that he'd "rather be myself ... and nasty. Not somebody else, however jolly" (59), and to this Lenina offers only "a bright treasure of sleep-taught wisdom" (59). Each of Bernard's observations is met with preprogrammed aphorisms; Lenina can only interpret her world through her radically limited monophrenic chorus. This weakness is even noticed by Bernard; his response to her "thoughts" is to identify their source: "Two hundred repetitions, twice a week" (62). To suggest that Lenina leads an authentic life is laughable: her motivations have all been scripted by an external authority. Charles Lindholm taps Rousseau as "the earliest ... spokesman for the predominant modern belief that the cultural/social surface represses the expression of the authentic natural self" (8), and, though the idea of a "natural self" is problematic, if one is made a proxy extension of a foreign agency then authentic, self-directed engagement clearly becomes impossible.

If monophrenia is attached to place, then its solution is mobility. Mobility, however, does not automatically mean agency; World State citizens are very mobile, yet nonetheless lead scripted lives. A placial violation must occur for mobility to be significant, one either placing an individual at odds with or outside of monophrenic identity spaces and leading competing voices and perspectives. By doing so, mobility can result in *positive* multiphrenia, in which one's exposure to competing voices can, if not exorcise the dominant voice outright, then at least offer the deracinating voices of Others to offset negative effect (and inoculate the individual against future exposures, pre-armed with a peanut gallery ready to heckle into irrelevance any voice with monolithic aspirations). In order to regain authenticity and agency, individuals must become marginalized, necessitating certain tactics of marginalization.

Place, Cresswell explains, is built around a simple binary: certain behaviors become normalized and "natural" (like home ownership); consequently, anything "out of place" (homelessness) becomes unnatural and suspect. "Outsiders" aren't simply foreign; they are "existentially removed from the milieu of 'our' place – someone who doesn't know the rules" (*In Place* 154). This spatial formula hints at the tactics of marginalization: individuals can make use of society's ideologically-driven placial strategies, reversing them into tactics that allow individuals to carve out niches or make full exits. Thus, for one to self-marginalize, one must become out-of-place via tactics that bring the individual into conflict with a place's "natural" rules. Tagging, for example, becomes a marginalizing "tactic of the dispossessed" by allowing for the insertion of "a mobile and temporary set of meanings … [into a city's] formal spatial structures" (47), breaking social scripting and making the graffiti artist abnormal and unnatural. Tactics of marginalization thus foreground the scripted nature of social space by redefining the transgressor as outsider and the place itself as something different from its socially-approved meaning/use.

An obvious tactic involves violating those subtle visual cues that mark a person as in-place. One can self-marginalize by consciously violating normal standards of appearance, but one can also benefit from society's strategic attempts to demonize those who inadvertently violate a place's norms. It is the latter approach that pertains to *Brave New World*, as the first tactic of marginalization seen in the novel is one of circumstance: the principal characters are made marginal by accidents of birth. Helmholtz, Bernard, and even John all benefit from unique conditions rendering them out-of-place. John, Reservation-born child of two World State citizens, is obviously out-of-place: his confession that his fellows "disliked me for my complexion" (78) is hardly shocking, nor are the various beatings he receives as a result. Of more interest might be the alienating effect of having one's mother regularly "visited" by various tribesmen, but even that is subsumed beneath the original transgression of out-of-place birth. Helmholtz is simply far smarter than his contemporaries, beneficiary of a "mental excess" (44) that leaves him, due to excessive ability, "uncomfortably aware of being himself and all alone" (44), though, unlike John, his awareness of difference only develops later in life.

Far more interesting is Bernard, whose initial marginality derives not from mental excesses (though he is intelligent, if neurotic), but rather from physical insufficiency. Born to a caste of perfect physical specimens, Bernard "stood eight centimetres short of the standard Alpha height" (43), rendering him "hardly better than that of the average Gamma" (43). While a three-inch difference hardly seems significant, in a society finely tuned to physical markers of status, three inches might as well be an extra leg. Other characters perceive Bernard as having a "small thin body" and "melancholy face" (38), and Fanny, Lenina's friend, bluntly states, "He's so ugly!" (31). Indeed, even the hypno-teaching Bernard and others receive incorporates "a faint ... prejudice in favour of size" (43); however, this mockery, combined with Bernard's awareness that he doesn't belong, grants him a powerful marginal position. As Huxley observes, "mockery made him feel an outsider; and feeling an outsider he behaved like one (43). In fact, speculations about the cause of Bernard's "deformity" further marginalize him. Rumor holds that Bernard's shortcomings result from "alcohol having been put into the poor chap's blood-surrogate" (40), implying that Bernard is a diseased or damaged specimen. Diseases and dirt, Cresswell notes, have be used historically to imply "disturbing social characteristics that combine to suggest a radical out-of-placeness" (*Tramp* 122): Lenina's mantra "cleanliness is next to fordliness" (73), when confronted with the squalor of the Reservation, is ideologically motivated.

Once a person becomes marginal, increasingly obvious impediments to authenticity fuel further efforts to escape. While mobility is crucial, it need not be *physical*; in a hyperspatial society, in which physical boundaries are meaningless, the most obvious form of transgression is social. Bryman recounts a Disney phenomenon, in which disgruntled guests "wear merchandise associated with Disney villains" (*Disneyization* 150), effectively de-moralizing an overly-moralized space. This tactic of marginalization is surprisingly effective, as the villainous attire marks the wearer as abnormal, liking what one should "naturally" hate. Bernard utilizes a similar version of this tactic, violating placial meanings by hating what he should like: rumors abound that "he doesn't like Obstacle Golf" (30) and that "he spends most of his time by himself—alone" (30). He even creates a minor scandal at Solidarity Service when asked what version of golf he had been playing prior to arrival, and he admits that he hadn't been playing any sports at all (53). In a place defined by consumption of entertainment and community, Bernard's behavior marginalizes him as effectively as a "Golf sucks" t-shirt at the Masters.

Bernard's out-of-place mobility might successfully create non-rationalized niches; however, as a tactic, it offers an incomplete solution to monophrenia. Physical mobility is necessary to offer a proper challenge. If urban space is defined by "natural" patterns of movement (sidewalks for waking, etc.), then tactics of marginalization must involve intentional violations of expected patterns through "unnatural" movement. Walker Percy argues in *The Message in the*

Bottle that, for tourists to "recover the Grand Canyon" (48) from the all-pervasive voices of authority that strip the experience of authenticity, they must get off "the beaten track" (48) and escape "the approved confrontation of the tour" (48). Simple advice, and Bernard does exactly this when, while flying with Lenina, he stops and hovers "on his helicopter screws within a hundred feet of the waves" amidst a sudden squall (60). Such a pause may seem trivial, but in McSocieties, efficiency is gospel and transportation exists to bridge consumption opportunities, thus making stopping extremely out-of-place. Cresswell labels such mobility "superdeviance ... [which] disturbs the whole notion that the world can be segmented into clearly defined places" (*In Place* 87), and while Bernard engages in a tactical act of *im*mobility, the result is the same: by going off-track, he carves a hole in an otherwise unified place, creating an authentic, recovered view of the ocean that allows him to "feel as though ... I were more me" (60), a far more challenging marginality that hints of possible alternative perspectives.

If McSocieties are defined by scripted interactions, then another tactic of marginalization must involve violating social scripts. Bernard, violating his own internal scripting, halts his helicopter simply "to look at the sea" free of "that beastly noise" (60), referring both to Lenina's attempt to flood the cockpit with radio gaga and, indirectly, to the World State's monophrenic chorus. Lenina, however, is traumatized by this transgression: crying, she repeats "it's horrible" (60) and is reduced to canned aphorisms. Percy suggests that individuals are losing the capacity for *authentic* engagement due to the colonization of the mind by expert voices and cultural packaging: sightseers measure "satisfaction by the degree to which the [Grand] [C]anyon conforms to the preformed complex" (47) provided by tourism brochures, adventure films, or, say, hypnotically-planted "moral" instruction. Lenina is like a tourist colonized and condemned to judge "present experience ... by a prototype" (53), accessing not, for example, the Canyon itself, but rather a simulacrum created by the media chorus. Bernard might escape his own packaging, but his efforts to violate Lenina's scripting must fail, as Lenina can only experience the ocean (or Bernard) in the same way a tourist must experience the Grand Canyon: through mediated meanings. Though ending in defeated irony, Bernard's effort to force Lenina off-script is nonetheless indicative of his recognition that alternatives are possible.

Ultimately, more drastic tactics are required to escape a fully homogenized society. In the past, distance might be achieved by simply heading west; in a globalized world, where such clean breaks are no longer possible, another form of potentially transgressive travel plays substitute – tourism. Once a matter of distance plus Otherness equaling adventure, tourism has become "increasingly McDonaldized" (Ritzer, *Thesis* 135), lacking opportunities for encountering Otherness. Homogeneity abounds as tourists join people of similar backgrounds (*McDonaldization* 96) for package tours and consume scripted "adventures" designed "to ensure predictability" (79). These "adventures" take place in standardized locations that offer "what they experience in their day-to-day lives" (*Thesis* 137), all of which effectively strips tourism of any challenge. Indeed, Lenina's pleasure upon learning that the hotel in Santa Fe has all the consumer comforts of home captures this scripting perfectly. Tourists ensconced even in substandard hotels, like the Aurora, are unlikely to "experience something new and different" (139), making tourism a vector for monophrenia.

Fortunately, an alternative form of "urban tourism" seeks to recapture some of tourism's lost authenticity via transgressive mobility. Practiced famously by Romantic poets mooning around old ruins, "urban exploration … [is] interior tourism that allows the curious-minded to discover a world of behind-the-scenes sights like … abandoned factories and other places not designed for public usage" (Ninjalicious 3); importantly, those who "recreationally trespass" (Garrett 1) do it partly to defy what constitutes "public use" (read: in-place behavior). By creating "alternative placial narratives … that undermine dominant capitalist narratives through playfully unproductive, pointless, or at the least largely uncommodifiable action" (Garrett 14), depthless McDonaldized places can be resisted and enriched with voices and perspectives hidden in the margins.

Bernard's need to perform uncommodifiable actions drives him to tour the Savage Reservation, a series of places easily regarded as the World State's ruins, worthless and fenced off, like any abandoned building. The Reservation is itself off the beaten path, as no "more than half a dozen people in the whole Centre had ever been" (58), and, as Bernard's status makes him "one of the few ... entitled to a permit" (58), few citizens likely ever visit. Bernard's motivations for his trip are made clear after he explains his intentions; he receives a severe dressing down from the Director (who, ironically, had taken the same trip under far more scandalous circumstances), but walks away "with a swagger, exulting ... in the thought that he stood alone, embattled against the order of things" (66). Bernard's pleasure at being out-of-place is pleasure at performing an unproductive action that does not benefit the World State.

Bernard's trip also provides much-needed authenticity, as the Savage Reservation is an out-of-place space, one of hardships to which the Director presumably lost a girlfriend who "must have ... been eaten by a mountain lion" (64–65). As the World State engineers away emotional perturbations, a place in which something traumatic enough to provoke nightmares decades later (as the Director confesses) is truly marginal. Indeed, Bernard and Lenina find emotional perturbation in their first experience of the aging process. Since the World State has conquered the aging process (though not death) for the purposes of consistent happy consumption, Bernard and Lenina's encounter with an old Indian, whose face is "profoundly wrinkled" and "body ... bent and emaciated" (73), is a powerfully affective and authentic engagement. Bernard even frames the experience in terms of authenticity, noting that the reason he and Lenina have never witnessed naked age is because the State doesn't "allow them to be like that" (73). Words like *allow* foreground the World State's instrumental control over one's fundamental human experience.

A "cure" for monophrenia's instrumental control can be found in multiphrenia, or multiple encounters with the Other that interrupt the godlike voice of authority. Gergen explains that communications technology multiplies "voices daring to question the old and institutionalized truths" (86), thus threatening unified notions of self, like those embraced by the World State. The Reservation *itself* is not multiphrenic, however; it also is a monophrenic space, where Lenina can lose herself to tribal drumming that beat "out just the same rhythms" (75) as the Solidarity Services, equating the World State's monophrenia with the Reservation's religious monophrenia. Rather, it is the *addition* of the Reservation's revelations that creates what Gergen terms a pastiche personality, a personality "constantly borrowing bits and pieces of identity from whatever sources are available and constructing them as useful or desirable in a given situation" (150). A pastiche personality offers a hedge against inauthenticity, for if "the selves we acquire from others can contribute to inner dialogues" (71), no authoritative voice is likely to usurp the rest unquestioned. This partially explains Bernard's seemingly innate resistance to the Fordist religion, for when one becomes even partially multiphrenic, losing oneself to a consensual hallucination, such as Ford's Solidarity Service, is all but impossible.

John is both the novel's best illustration of multiphrenia and its vector. Given a ragged copy of "The Complete Works of William Shakespeare" (88), John gains an alternative inner voice that opens out-of-place ways of thinking about himself and his experiences. John lacked a sufficient way of conceiving of the depth of his hate for his mother's lover, Popé, until Shakespeare provided words like "treacherous, lecherous, kindless villain" (89) that "made his hatred more real" (89). Prior to internalizing Shakespeare, John had "never been able to say how much he hated him" (89), but once "populated" by Shakespeare's distinct chorus, John becomes armed with the tools needed to think sophisticated, out-of-place thoughts. John even frames his reaction to Lenina's inauthenticity via a mash-up of Shakespeare: "O thou weed, who are so lovely and fair and smell'st so sweet that the senses ache at thee. Was this most goodly book made to write 'whore' upon?" (133). John's reliance on an inner playwright whose "magic explained and gave orders" (89) highlights the significance of access to out-of-place voices.

Helmholtz also employs Shakespeare's voice to access an inner world out-of-place in the World State: at "sole Arabian tree" he started ... but at "defunctive music" he turned pale and trembled with an unprecedented emotion" (123). In a sense, Shakespeare's voice carves a non-rationalized niche out of the undifferentiated social fabric. Helmholtz attributes Shakespeare's talent for propaganda to his "many insane, excruciating things to get excited about" (125), reasoning that one must suffer hardship to be creative; inadvertently, Helmholtz describes marginalizing experiences that set one apart and allow unique angles for authentic engagement.

Inauthenticity and compromised agency cannot long be tolerated by marginalized persons: tactics of resistance against civilization's "beastly noise" (60) always develop. These tactics might be harmless, like Bernard's transgressive mobility, or disruptive, like Helmholtz's culture jamming/riffing: dissatisfied with the inauthentic emotions expressed by state propaganda, he replaces his "Advanced Emotional Engineering" (170) class's State-approved rhymes with his own compositions just "to see what their reactions would be" (122). Harmless or disruptive, these tactics violate placial norms and thus draw fire. John's final act of resistance can be viewed as a doomed attempt to carve out a non-rationalized space. Staggered by Linda's meaningless death from soma overdose, John realizes that she "had been a slave ... [but] others should live in freedom" (143) and decides he must restore authenticity to the people. Recognizing that soma represents the World State's war on authenticity, John attempts to destroy the soma stock at a hospital. This out-of-place behavior predictably ends in a riot, though Helmholtz and (in a sense) Bernard's involvement in the resultant melee makes clear that they, too, are fully outsiders looking in.

The in-place immune system must react to the presence of foreign bodies, of course, and Bernard and Helmholtz are "punished" by exile to places where they will meet other people "too self-consciously individual" (154). John, however, is not granted exile: unlike Helmholtz and Bernard, he is *strategically* out-of-place, co-opted by the State and made a walking advertisement for the folly of crossing borders. Denied marginality, John's lighthouse retreat and self-mortification rituals can be seen as attempts to transform a thoroughly rationalized, scrutinized space into a non-rationalized one via whatever tactics remain. Sadly, his attempt to redefine space is pointless: John becomes the subject of constant media coverage, his body commodified and drained of authenticity, subject of a feely titled "The Savage of Surrey" (173). With his remaining agency co-opted by crowds of fans chanting "We-want-the whip" (175), his suicide becomes entirely reasonable, as it is his last remaining out-of-place behavior.

Less than a century after Huxley wrote *Brave New World* (let alone the six centuries separating us from the World State), every waking moment of a contemporary individual's life is bombarded by television shows selling lifestyles, advertisements selling belonging, and political talk shows selling critical thinking by proxy, each an extension of the same voice. A scripted identity bought at a mall or caught like an STD from television is hardly different from an identity injected into one's blood-surrogate: both depend upon a person's failure to recognize the violence done to them. As our world grows more homogenized, more like the World State, it is increasingly important to recognize the dangers of monophrenia and to develop tactics capable of granting the marginality necessary to escape the noise.

Works Cited

Anderson, Benedict. *Imagined Communities: Reflections on the Origin and Spread of Nationalism*. London: Verso, 2006.

Bryman, Alan. *The Disneyization of Society*. London: SAGE Publications, 2004.

Cresswell, Tim. *In Place/Out of Place: Geography, Ideology, and Transgression*. Minneapolis: U of Minnesota P, 1996.

―――. *On the Move: Mobility in the Modern Western World*. New York: Routledge, 2006.

―――. *Place: A Short Introduction*. Oxford, UK: Blackwell, 2004.

―――. *The Tramp in America*. London: Reaktion, 2001.

―――. "Towards a Politics of Mobility." *African Cities Reader II: Mobilities and Fixtures*.

African Cities Reader. Eds. Ntone Edjabe and Edgar Pieterse. 2011. Web. 20 Aug. 2013. <http://www.africancitiesreader.org.za/reader/chapters/026_TowardsaPoliticsofMobility.pdf>.

Huxley, Aldous. *Brave New World*. New York: Harper, 1969.

———. "Brave New World Revisited." 1958. n.d. Web. 1 Oct. 2013. <http://www.huxley.net/bnw-revisited>.

Garrett, Bradley. *Place Hacking: Tales of Urban Exploration*. Diss. Royal Holloway, University of London, Egham, 2012.

Gergen, Kenneth. *The Saturated Self: Dilemmas of Identity in Contemporary Life*. New York: HarperCollins, 1991.

Jameson, Fredric. *Postmodernism, or, The Cultural Logic of Late Capitalism*. Durham: Duke UP, 2003.

Lindholm, Charles. *Culture and Authenticity*. Oxford: Blackwell, 2008.

Ninjalicious. *Access All Areas: A User's Guide to the Art of Urban Exploration*. 3rd ed. Toronto: Infilpress, 2005.

Percy, Walker. *The Message in the Bottle: How Queer Man Is, How Queer Language Is, and What the One Has to Do with the Other*. New York: Picador, 2000.

Ritzer, George. *The McDonaldization of Society*. Revised ed. Thousand Oaks, CA: Pine Forge Press, 1996.

———. *The McDonaldization Thesis: Explorations and Extensions*. London: SAGE Publications, 1998.

Sherrill, Rowland A. *Road-Book America: Contemporary Culture and the New Picaresque*. Chicago: U of Illinois P, 2000.

"'Observe,' said the Director": *Brave New World*, Surveillance Studies, and the Dystopian Tradition

Sean A. Witters

Mass-scale and intimate surveillance is a signature theme of dystopian fiction and might stand as the most consistently used trope for describing the genre. From Zamyatin's *We* to *Nineteen Eighty-Four* (the text that gave the surveillance state a name), to recent popular fiction, such as *The Hunger Games*, the dystopian state is consistently presented as "a place where there is no darkness" and, thus, with (almost) no escape from the gaze of power. Considering its importance within the genre, *Brave New World* seems to be a striking outlier. The "World State" Huxley depicts has little recourse to what Louis Althusser's classic study of ideology codifies as the "Repressive State Apparatus" (i.e., the agents of state violence and punishment: police, army, etc.), relying instead on the more subtle kinds of psychological manipulation that Althusser associates with the "Ideological State Apparatus." The power of the World State also seems to require little surveillance of its subjects because it is sustained through conditioned and channeled desires, which reproduce both the material and ideological order. To be a good citizen is to desire properly, which means participating in the state's sexual and consumer rituals. The singsong rhyme, *"Orgy porgy, Ford and fun/Kiss the girls and make the One"* (84), aptly sums up the way the state uses pleasure to organize and sustain power instead of violence. *Brave New World*, in this way, marks the emergence of a vital sub-theme or counter-narrative within the genre: the critique of consumerist society and its ability to secure and sustain consent. Huxley's text, hence, does vital cultural work right on the event horizon of the massive socio-economic changes that have shaped postmodernity. In this context, the absence of a relationship between consumption and surveillance in his novel may tell us a good deal about the dystopian tradition in modernity, its evolution, and, finally, its historical blind spots, which we may, in turn, understand by looking at Suzanne Collins' *The Hunger Games* (2008)—a work that comprises both Huxley and Orwell's competing models of the dystopian and which is the product of a culture transformed by surveillance.

The distinction between the dystopian visions of Orwell and Huxley is well rehearsed and now embedded in the project of describing the genre and also of analyzing modernity and its modalities of power. Orwell gives us a world of privation, repressive violence, and collective terror. Huxley imagines a world, in which such crude technologies of discipline have been rendered obsolete by conditioning and consumption. The former replicates the totalitarian model associated with Stalinism, while the latter is more readily linked to the work of imagining the "one dimensional society," in which the necessity of the Repressive State Apparatus has been obviated by the perfection of an Ideological State Apparatus (embodied by social orders and institutions—schools, church, work—that communicate and reinforce the "story" of the social order).

In the retrospective lens of *Brave New World Revisited*, Huxley treats this point of distinction as having its central concerns in regard to the state's use of violence, writing, "In *1984* the lust for power is satisfied by inflicting pain; in *Brave New World*, by inflicting a hardly less humiliating pleasure" (26). Reflecting on the context of 1948, when totalitarian threats, on-going rationing (in Britain and across Europe), and another potential global war marked the horizon, Huxley admits that Orwell's vision seemed "dreadfully convincing." In the context of 1958, now deeply immersed in the "age of affluence," however, Huxley writes, "Assuming for the moment that the Great Powers can somehow refrain from destroying us, we can say that it now looks as though the odds were more in favor of something like *Brave New World* than of something like *1984*" (3). Huxley's comments reflect the realities of late twentieth-century life in the West, wherein the "logic of late capitalism" had made apparent the essential link between culture, consumption, and mass power.

More fundamentally, Huxley's reasoning regarding the historical progression of modes of power and their utility shares a logic with the key historical insight behind Michel Foucault's foundational study of power and surveillance, *Discipline and Punish; The Birth of the Prison.* In Foucault's assessment, the public use of extreme and arbitrary state violence, such as the ritualized 1757 execution of regicide Robert-François Damiens, actually undermined state power. The "spectacle of the scaffold" shifted attention, and possibly sympathies, from the monarchy to the "body of the condemned." Foucault observes that, "In these executions which ought to show only the terrorizing power of the prince, there was a whole aspect of the carnival, in which rules were inverted, authority mocked and criminals transformed into heroes" (61). While the ritual of the execution served its purposes for a time, it was not useful in the modern bureaucratic state, which must constantly reproduce the spectacle of its reasoning and, thus, its stability. In short order, juridical state violence was moved out of sight and replaced by regimes and rituals of reform based on the panoptic model, which constantly affirms the presence and centrality of power, even in its material absence and diffusion.

Eighteenth-century British utilitarian philosopher Jeremy Bentham conceived of the "panopticon" as a model for a more efficient and rational prison. It is based on the supposition that a "visible yet unverifiable" presence of a guard in a central observation post would automatically cause the prisoners, housed in a concentric ring, to watch themselves (201). Foucault seizes on the idea that this arrangement of the observer and the observed is a diagram for the multiplication of power that shapes modern social orders. "Panopticism," Foucault observes, "is the general principle of a new 'political anatomy' whose object and end are not the relations of sovereignty but the relations of discipline" (208). When the old model of power became "unconvincing" in the context of this new historical condition, a more flexible model that redistributed power's effects and expressions replaced it. In the complicated but shared genealogy of ideas with Foucault, Althusser reminds us that the most basic question of state power is the ability of the state to reproduce itself, both materially and ideologically. While Orwell's Big Brother state is ideologically powerful, it is, as the "Principles of Newspeak" afterword suggests, doomed. It cannot reproduce itself indefinitely because of its reliance on violence—i.e. its overemphasis on the use of the Repressive State Apparatus.

The history of the World State in *Brave New World* shows an evolution akin to the one described by Foucault. In the third chapter's fragmented narration of the history of state violence against anti-consumer, "Simple lifers," Mustapha Mond explains, "In the end… the controllers realized that force was no good" (51). In this context, the absence of a Repressive State Apparatus in Huxley's novel is understandable and important. Conditioning and *soma* make active state violence unnecessary. The only overt instance of repressive state violence in the novel (though, as the books and roses scene suggests, there is some violence involved in the state's ideological conditioning of individuals) occurs when John the Savage visits the Park Lane Hospital for the Dying and causes a riot.

After John the Savage disrupts soma distribution, exhorting the patients to be free, he, Bernard Marx, Helmholtz Watson, and rioting, *soma*-deprived patients are met by anesthetic- and *soma*-spraying police. The upheaval is resolved with a Synthetic Music Box playing "Synesthetic Anti-Riot Speech Number Two (Medium Strength)" beseeching the rioters, in tones so pathetic they even make the policemen cry, to be at peace and to be happy (214–215). As the message and trope of the policeman's tears show, even repressive action from the state is tied to ideological reinforcement. When intervention is necessary, the subjects are spared significant contact with coercive power and its exercise is entirely aimed at re-asserting the work of the Ideological State Apparatus, which is presented in this scene as an actual machine. The World State, as echoed in Mond's judgment, recognizes that violence for the sake of power, *rather than for the sake of ideology*, would disrupt the links between, "Community, Identity, [and] Stability."

The scene above is the only significant police action depicted in the novel, and the most direct encounter with the Repressive State Apparatus. So effective is the regime of conditioning, ideological inoculation, consumption, and medication that repressive violence is basically obsolete. Furthermore, violence threatens the state's primary utilitarian principle: *stability*. The World State is, as such, a utilitarian utopia. In the utilitarian state, via panopticism, discipline is delegated to subjects who conform themselves to its ideological condition, which they experience as a space of free will. A "visible yet unverifiable" surveillance system is essential to this operation. What is striking about Huxley's novel is that, while the absence of state violence is readily explainable (in contrast with Orwell), the lack of attention to surveillance that sustains, disseminates, and coordinates power is not. We are left to wonder: *"How does this key disciplinary function operate in Brave New World, or is it completely absent?"*

This pair of questions is essential to our contemporary readings of the dystopian genre and its necessary interaction with popular concerns about privacy and surveillance, as well as within the emergent field of "surveillance studies." We are, thus, obliged to read *Brave New World* (and its implied model of discipline) in conjunction with our present historical condition, in which surveillance has become an integral feature of infrastructure. As it is now configured, consumption *necessitates* surveillance in order to identify, re-configure, and sustain consumer desires, while commerce and state power work in mutually reinforcing ways to ensure and produce "total information awareness."

In his important work on surveillance studies, David Lyon describes the essential, but ambivalent, relationship the field has to Foucault and, particularly, *Discipline and Punish*. He notes that Foucault focuses on two dimensions of power: the panopticon, that "crucial 'diagram' of Foucault's work on surveillance" and the "classificatory schemes by which sovereign power would locate and differentiate treatment of the variety of prisoners" (*Theorizing Surveillance* 3). Lyon asks whether these two subjects are in fact co-extensive, noting the skepticism of contemporary scholars, including Giorgio Agamben. Lyon finds himself, and the field of surveillance studies as a whole, constantly returning to these two dimensions of thought. In this sense, *Brave New World*, as a "critical dystopia" marked by the ambiguities of the links between power, identity, and surveillance, offers a space for describing the relationship between panopticism and discipline that shapes surveillance studies, while, at the same time, providing another critical lens for describing the configurations of power in the dystopian literary tradition.

The Syntax of Stability

In their 2008 study for the MIT/University of Southampton Web Science Research Initiative, *The Spy in the Coffee Machine: The End of Privacy as We Know It,* Kieron O'Hara and Nigel Shadbolt observe that technology has produced a paradoxical change in the configuration of privacy. While material encounters between people are more "present," they leave little or no record. We are afforded more physical privacy by technology; yet the digital activities of this "disappearing body" leave a "trace" via the protocols of interaction, including audio, video, emails, text messages, keywords, financial transactions, "cookies," browser histories, and IP addresses (O'Hara and Shadbolt 1–3). O'Hara and Shadbolt remind us that postmodern surveillance is *textual* and is, at least in part, incidental to the necessary production of a "text of the self" within the protocols of consumer interactions and other activities that bridge the historical public/private divide.

In *Brave New World,* there is no apparent surveillance mechanism through which consumer activities create a text. There is also no feedback circuit involved in the consumption/production cycle. To whatever extent surveillance is imagined through the World State, it is different from postmodern surveillance because of this; hence, the assertion that *Brave New World* describes or anticipates the re-configuration of power in postmodernity may itself be becoming a historical thesis. As a periodizing term, "postmodern" is useful to this extent. It is, however, worth acknowledging David Lyon's effort to revise the historical classification of modes of surveillance. In *Surveillance Studies: An Overview,* Lyon describes three primary modes of surveillance "face to face," "filebased," and "interface surveillance" (75). These modes have been used to describe the evolution of surveillance: pre-modern surveillance was "face to face," modern surveillance was "filebased," and postmodern surveillance operates through interface systems that facilitate textual surveillance. He notes, however, that these periodizing classifications are "artificial and analytical distinctions" and that these three modes "may overlap and be found in the same context at the same time" (Lyon 75).

To whatever extent surveillance is employed by the World State, it is primarily face to face or filebased. In the case of Bernard Marx, the "de-canting" rumors that surround him have the dual function of ensuring "face to face" social scrutiny and producing panoptic self-scrutiny. We see the effects in his rooftop discussion with Helmholtz Watson. When Helmholtz begins to question the value of writing about "a Community Sing, or the latest improvement in scent organs" (69), Bernard hushes him, imagining someone is listening behind the door. When this proves not to be the case, he explains to Helmholtz, "I suppose I've got things on my nerves a bit. When people are suspicious with you, you start being suspicious with them" (70). In this declaration, Bernard affirms that he is a subject of the panoptic gaze, and that it shapes his behavior, even his "being."

The primary mode of Bernard's surveillance is "face to face"— as is exemplified by his anxiety in this scene. The social surveillance of gossip may also have resulted in "filebased" surveillance by the state, as is suggested by the link between the early scene, in which Bernard submits his reservation trip permit to the Director, and the later "trial" with Mond. More generally, we may infer from the decanting factory tour that the World State must have mechanisms for monitoring the effectiveness of conditioning, but unlike much of the dystopian genre, those mechanisms receive no attention in the novel. Furthermore, in terms of distinguishing between modes of surveillance and their effects, neither Helmholtz's dissent nor Bernard's self-implicating paranoia register any record except in the text of the novel (a point to which I will return) precisely because their relationship is entirely face to face. They do not use any communication medium that would leave a trace or text of their meetings, patterns or rates of interaction, or ideas. The consumers in *Brave New World* receive, but do not create, technological communication events—reflecting the unidirectional configuration of power that defines the state.

Though postmodern surveillance is shaped by a range of practices and technologies, from biodata analysis to CCTV, consumer data and its integration with social media have emerged as essential coordinating functions. In the context of dystopian imagining, this function compounds the already ominous implications of consumer culture. Interface surveillance (and the "metadata" it seeks and also generates), relies upon voluntary or passively generated user feedback. In *Brave New World,* the metadata the characters volunteer in their consumer activities (whether attending "feelies," selecting Malthusian belts, or choosing between Electromagnetic or Obstacle Golf), may result in "face to face" surveillance, as is the case with Bernard ("they say he doesn't like Obstacle golf"), but the state appears to be unconcerned about the information that might be gleaned from these activities.

This is unsurprising, since the Fordist state model is based on a hierarchical orientation of desire and consumption. This hierarchy is exemplified in the design and operations of its conditioning system: desires and identities conform to the methods and means of production and there is no reciprocity. A Beta, for instance, is a total model of body, thought, and desire, and this model dictates his or her consumer identity. Since identity has been lifted out of history, there is no revision or evolution in its production of consumer desires other than to offer novelties concocted, without feedback, by the state. This reflects the thinking of the state's namesake. Henry Ford, who famously declared, "Any customer can have a car painted any color that he wants so long as it is black" (71). This declaration, as he explains, was part of his program to "build a motor car for the multitude"; hence, the designs of his utilitarian capitalist scheme and the material issues it faced left no room for customization. Desires would conform to the product, rather than the other way around. The multitude in *Brave New World* is treated as having no autonomous or unconditioned desires; hence, surveillance of its subjects, as consumers, is not an issue. The text of the self that a subject would generate and which might be discovered through consumer metadata would merely affirm a conditioned identity model. In this regard, it is important to note David Lyon's assertion that surveillance of identities has the curious effect of affirming the consequent. His insight reflects a broader consensus in studies of the relationship between identity and the "drive to know"—from Foucault to Sedgwick. Once a category of identity has been created, it may be reproduced by being "discovered" again and again through surveillance oriented toward that category. Huxley's novel seems to affirm this point. For the World State and its Fordist vision of identity, there is no point in collating endless portraits of Alpha, Beta, Epsilon, Delta and Gamma desires. Furthermore, the state's emphasis on stability means that its configuration of the relationship between consumer desire and production is distinct from postmodern configurations of marketing and manufacturing.

When discussing the state's vision of the relationship between work and consumption with John the Savage, Mond explains, "Every change is a menace to stability. That's another reason we are so chary of applying new inventions. Every discovery in pure science is potentially subversive: even science must be treated as a possible enemy" (225). This presents an irony in regard to the state's effort to use consumer novelties to control its subjects. Though it insists, "ending is better than mending" (50), the state is not interested in variations in desire and consumption precisely because they must constantly assert "identity" as the link between "community" and "stability."

As the state motto suggests, "identity" is conceived by the World State in terms of its function in the syntax of state order (i.e., as the term that coordinates "community" and "identity") rather than as a reflection of the relationship between individuals and social roles. In their notable study, *The Watchman in Pieces: Surveillance, Literature, and Liberal Personhood*, David Rosen and Aaron Santesso use this relationship between individuals, surveillance, and social roles to re-think the curiously narrow work of surveillance studies. They focus on the relationship between literature and the "habits of mind" necessitated by surveillance societies. Rosen and Santesso observe,

> Surveillance, *the monitoring of human activities for the purposes of anticipating or influencing future events,* is not the same thing as literature. It does, however, share some of literature's interests—most notably discovery of the truth about other people—and is susceptible to some of the same temptations of literature (Rosen and Santesso 10).

Surveillance and literature, they argue, are "kindred practices" and key developments in surveillance theory have been worked out in literature. They make particular note of the way that surveillance necessitates narrative interpretation of otherwise disparate data points. Rosen and Santesso use this alignment of practices to challenge one of the key assumptions of Foucauldian panopticism: that "in a surveillance situation power flows outward from the observer to the (utterly abject) observed" (13). Rather, they argue that control of narrative may be in the hands of the observed or that the relationship may produce a "clash of narratives." This observation is vital to their study of the formation of liberal personhood and the increasing attention both literary and surveillance practices place on the effort to align allegories of character with social identities.

This leads Rosen and Santesso to revise the classic Orwell and Huxley debate by embedding their novels in the project of re-imagining the modern self through liberalism and the social forums it created. Writing on *Brave New World* as a satire of liberal personhood, they observe, "Largely unconcerned with the jackbooted modes of surveillance that interested Orwell, Huxley is nevertheless deeply invested in the more pleasurable and participatory forms of social watching" (Rosen and Santesso 183). This insight offers a vital means for reading the function of the public spectacle in *Brave New World* and the ways in which the characters accept and even revel in being the subject of the public gaze. I would like, however, to return to their foundational argument in order to re-read *Brave New World* as a surveillance text and to subsequently describe the recent evolution of the relationship between dystopian fiction and surveillance studies.

Rosen and Santesso contend that, "If surveillance is, on some level, all about reading and authorship, so literature has been deeply engaged with, and transformed by, changing ideas of observation and control" (13). Their project implies the possibility for re-thinking my original questions regarding the function of surveillance in *Brave New World*. While Huxley's novel is not particularly concerned with *depicting* the operations of surveillance in the same way Zamyatin and Orwell's dystopian novels are, *Brave New World*, nevertheless, enacts and imagines the work of surveillance via its narrative structure. Chapter three is especially important in this context. It is the novel's most formally daring chapter and echoes the high modernist experiments of Joyce, Eliot, and Dos Passos, particularly their sweeping and fragmented depictions of social space. In the second section of the chapter, the narration skips between Mond's history lesson at the hatchery, Lenina's dressing routine, and Bernard's conversation with Henry Foster. With each new section in the chapter, the fragmentation increases and paragraphs become single sentences, until we are reading snippets of conversation, isolated phrases, and mottos:

"The introduction of Our Ford's first T-Model..."

"I've had it nearly three months."

"Chosen as the opening date of the new era."

"Ending is better than mending; ending is better..." (52).

The work of the reader in this chapter is to re-construct narrative by attributing the statements and thoughts to specific characters or to the official voices that fill the minds of the characters. At the same time, the reader is tasked with constructing a meta-narrative that explains the formal variation in the text and situates these disparate thoughts and speech acts within the form and plot. In this way, Huxley's novel asks the reader to use the habits of mind that Rosen and Santesso argue are essential to the workings of surveillance. The logic of meta-data is anticipated by the logic of meta-narrative. As modernist text, however, this deterritorialization of narrative and form is ultimately reterritorialized within the logic of file-based surveillance, Linnaean classification, and allegories of identity. As with the violent pre-history of the World State, the novel produces disruptions in narration, but seeks clear and stable resolution.

In the concluding chapter, Mond disappears from the text and the reader continues observing his otherwise unexplained experiment with John the Savage. Though John attempts to elude surveillance and take control of narrative, telling Bernard, "I'm damned if I'll go on being experimented with" (243), in the end, his identity determines his function in narrative. After the climactic orgy of violence, the name, "John," disappears from narration and dialogue and he becomes only "the Savage" and, finally, "Mr. Savage"—a formal name that is also his identity in the surveillance narrative. The last image of the novel is a kind of surveillance log that triangulates his body in space and time. "Slowly, very slowly, like two unhurried compass needles, the feet turned towards the right; north, north-east, east, south-east, south, south-south-west; then paused, and, a few seconds later, turned as unhurriedly back towards the left" (259). The Savage is finally located, identified, and stabilized. He is, in this moment, resolved to the narrative role he had already been assigned. As the "savage" always is in the story of modernity, he was doomed. That is his essence and his identity. This conclusion re-asserts the role of the reader as the central figure of surveillance and the character as the object.

Observing and Consuming Identities

Re-reading *Brave New World* as a text that enacts surveillance demands a return to David Lyon's questions about the relationship between panopticism and the "classificatory schemes" of discipline (3) and suggests a program for re-thinking the genealogy of dystopian narratives established by Huxley. Across major dystopian fictions of the late twentieth century by Bradbury, Burroughs, Vonnegut, Burgess, and Dick, we can trace coalescing attention within the genre to the problematic relationship between consumer desires, categorization, and state surveillance. All of these authors, in one way or another, tangle with the implications of the questions uttered by Philip K. Dick's protagonist in *A Scanner Darkly*: "What does a scanner see? I mean, really see? Into the head? Down into the heart? Does a passive infrared scanner like they used to use or a cube-type holo-scanner like they use these days, the latest thing, see into me—into us—clearly or darkly?" (192). In this moment, the split character, Bob Arctor, gives voice to a quintessential modernist anxiety: the Yeatsian fear that the "center cannot hold." With this anxiety, we approach, but do not attain, the inversion of the observer/observed relationship that structures contemporary re-thinking of the flow of power in Foucault's panoptic model. We find an important instance of that relationship in *The Hunger Games*—which stands as a representative dystopian fiction of postmodern surveillance society.

The Hunger Games continues and extends dystopian fiction's exploration of the relationship between observer and observed and enacts a vital synthesis within the genre by pairing Orwell's model with Huxley's. At first glance, Suzanne Collins' *The Hunger Games* seems to have a lineage that runs directly back through Shirley Jackson's "The Lottery" to *Nineteen Eighty-Four*; yet, the major work of the novel and its film adaptation is to perform key aspects of the work *Brave New World* initiates and which Rosen and Santesso see as characteristic of the "kindered" relationship between literature and surveillance. Panem's repressive state model is Big Brother-esque, using privation, isolation, and terror to sustain the Capitol's control of the Districts. It is important, however, that the novel is not restricted to the space of the Districts alone. The two spaces of the novel, District 12 and the Capitol, respectively embody the dystopian traditions of Orwell and Huxley. As in *Brave New World,* the Capitol is a space of consumer excess and banality—one in which social control is maintained through public spectacles of consumption. Through Katniss Everdeen's blinkered eyes, we see the contrast, which hints at the gilded containment of Capitol resident. As a subject of that Orwellian space, she wonders, "What do they do all day, these people in the Capitol, besides decorating their bodies and waiting around for a new shipment of tributes to roll in and die for their entertainment?" (65). The entertainment the Capitol residents experience as the central ritual of culture and a space of pleasure is, however, compulsory for the Districts. Ironically, that distinction between pleasure and compulsion is blurred or inverted as Katniss converts the games from a spectacle of domination to a forum for staging a revolt.

The story of *The Hunger Games* is shaped by the lessons Katniss learns as a subject of surveillance. Gradually, from her fiery debut to her kiss with Peeta, she learns to perform an identity that, while affirming the desires of the Capitol audience and the Gamemakers, also subverts their power. She learns a tactic so essential to both feminist and postcolonial challenges to power: *mimicry*. As imagined by Luce Irigaray, subversive mimicry of the style of power is a tactic for, "jamming the theoretical machinery of power, of suspending its pretension to the production of a truth and of a meaning that are excessively univocal" (78). In this manner, Katniss inverts her role from being the object of consumer activities to observer and manipulator of consumer desires. The very feature of the game that is meant to control her as a consumer, the sponsors, becomes a feedback mechanism for her counter-surveillance of her observers. Via Haymitch and her own experimentation, she learns to manipulate, mimic, and re-direct the desires of the audience, and thus the narrative of the games.

Through this experience, Katniss becomes a canny observer of the complex relationship between her public persona and her private desires. Contemplating the real meaning of her relationship with Peeta, Katniss observes, "These are questions to be unraveled back home, in the peace and quiet of the woods, when no one is watching. Not here with every eye upon me" (359). *The Hunger Games* thus marks another refinement in the relationship between literature and surveillance. Katniss, at once a surveilled consumer and a celebrity "brand," enacts the dilemma of the subject in postmodern surveillance culture, re-thinking configurations of privacy and learning to *perform* her public image. As a novel of post-televisual and digital culture,

The Hunger Games is conceived within the context of interface systems that are both mechanisms of surveillance and potential tools of subversion. The question for the subject in this condition is the very dilemma posed by surveillance studies for the dystopian literary tradition. *The Hunger Games* tries to work out the cultural problems the postmodern surveillance subject faces, much in the way *Brave New World* did for modernity. In this regard, we may take the central icon of the book, the mockingjay, as the key trope that embodies the function of the novel in culture and that expresses the power and problems of mimicry in a surveillance society. Katniss explains that the birds, "lost the ability to enunciate words but could still mimic a range of human vocal sounds, from a child's high pitched warble to a man's deep tones" (43). The mockingjay song and icon become a way for Katniss to communicate solidarity since the song and image resonate through public space. While she uses it to express her "branded" and observed self, it speaks in other registers, without creating a wholly knowable and legible text of the private self. It does not clearly enunciate its function, but it mimics the fused operations of surveillance and consumption that structure the game, creating a mechanism for the spectators to begin to observer the observers.

Works Cited

Althusser, Louis. "Ideology and Ideological State Apparatuses." *Lenin and Philosophy and Other Essays.* Trans. Ben Webster. New York: Monthly Review Press, 2001.

Baker, Robert S. *The Dark Historic Page: Social Satire and Historicism in the Novels of Aldous Huxley.* Madison, WI: U of Wisconsin P, 1982.

Dick, Philip K. *A Scanner Darkly.* New York: First Mariner Books, 2011.

Ford, Henry. *My Life and Work.* New York: Double Day, 1922.

Foucault, Michel. *Discipline and Punish: The Birth of the Prison.* Trans. Alan Sheridan. New York: Vintage Books, 1995.

Huxley, Aldous. *Brave New World.* New York: Harper Perennial, 2006.

_____. *Brave New World Revisited.* New York: Rosetta Books, 2010.

Irigaray, Luce. *This Sex Which Is Not One.* Trans. Catherine Porter. Ithaca, NY: Cornell UP, 1985.

Lyon, David. *Surveillance Studies: An Overview.* Cambridge: Polity, 2007.

_____. *Theorizing Surveillance: The Panopticon and Beyond.* Portland, OR: Willan Publishing, 2006.

Monaghan, Peter. "Watching the Watchers." *Chronicle of Higher Education.* 17 Mar. 2006. Web. 14 Jan. 2014. <http://chronicle.com/article/Watching-the-Watchers/19633>.

Montag, Warren. *Althusser and his Contemporaries.* Durham NC: Duke UP, 2013.

Moylan, Tom. *Scraps of the Untainted Sky: Science Fiction, Utopia, Dystopia.* Boulder, CO: Westview Press, 2000.

O'Hara, Kieron and Nigel Shadbolt. *The Spy in the Coffee Machine: The End of Privacy as We Know It.* Oxford, UK: One World, 2008.

Orwell, George. *Nineteen Eighty-Four.* New York: Plume, 2003.

Rose, David and Aaron Santesso. *The Watchman in Pieces: Surveillance, Literature, and Liberal Personhood.* New Haven, CT: Yale UP, 2012.

Postmodernism and the Cultural Logic of Dystopian Fiction: *Brave New World* and M. T. Anderson's *Feed*

M. Keith Booker

Aldous Huxley's *Brave New World* (1932) is one of the founding texts of modern dystopian fiction, projecting a chilling satirical account of a dehumanized future world that represents the fulfillment all the worst tendencies he saw in the interwar world around him. For narrative purposes, Huxley stipulates that the excesses of his future world society are a reaction to an apocalyptic biological war at the beginning of the twenty-first century, designed to prevent such a phenomenon from ever occurring again, largely by removing from human experience the kind of strong passions that might lead to such an event. M. T. Anderson's *Feed* (2002), published exactly seventy years later, appeared precisely in that early twenty-first century, brilliantly projecting (but only slightly, alas) from its own postmodern world to a society that is spiraling out of control on a path toward hedonistic, consumerist self-destruction, metaphorically fiddling away, while the world around it decays into economic and environmental ruin. Anderson's future society is hurtling toward apocalypse, rather than looking back on it, though the society continues to march forward on the path of capitalist self-indulgence, while doing little or nothing to combat the collapse of the natural world, a collapse that is, in fact, largely the result of that same capitalist self-indulgence. Given that Huxley's post-apocalyptic world is the result of overreaction to crisis, while Anderson's possibly pre-apocalyptic world is the result of ignoring a crisis, it is truly striking how similar those worlds really are. This essay will examine some of those similarities, while seeking to explain why, in fact, these similarities are not surprising after all, but are built into the logic of late consumer capitalism, which is, in fact, the prevailing logic behind both of these dystopian worlds. Indeed, both Huxley and Anderson describe future dystopian worlds that

214

Critical Insights

are quintessentially postmodern as described in the work of cultural theorist Fredric Jameson, who has described postmodernism as the "cultural logic of late capitalism," or as the cultural product of capitalism in its late, post-imperial, global phase.

For Jameson, postmodernism is the cultural manifestation of a world, in which global capitalist modernization is complete, all earlier forms of cultural organization have been swept aside, and nature itself has been replaced by a thoroughly commodified version of culture. This historical process leads to a number of specific phenomena, all of which are evident in both *Brave New World* and *Feed*. These include a loss of genuine individualism, as individual subjects become merely interchangeable elements of the capitalist economic system, functioning more as consumers in a sea of consumerism than as thinking citizens, hardly able even to experience genuine feelings in the traditional sense; unable to experience any genuine sense of historical continuity, these fragmented postmodern subjects are, most of all, unable to imagine any genuine historical change brought about by concerted political action.

This sense of living in an era of complete modernization is particularly clear in *Brave New World*. As Robert Combs notes, the citizens of Huxley's dystopia have been carefully taught to think of themselves as living in an age after historical change has been completed: "What they take to be the objective facts of their lives are post-revolutionary, post-historical, post-individual 'solutions' to all the problems of life" (163). With all change having already occurred in the past, no further change is needed. Further, there is no need to know about the past, a time of upset and upheaval because the tranquility and stability of the present have rendered irrelevant any lessons that might have been learned from the past. Everything in this world is completely modern, all vestiges of the past having been banished to the Savage Reservations.

Granted, most of what Combs describes here has to do with the status of the world state of *Brave New World* as a post-apocalyptic society, established in the wake of the destructive Nine Years' War (2004–2013) and dedicated to assuring that such a war can never happen again. This war (we learn from the hypnopaedic conditioning that that passes for education in this society, pumping advertising-style slogans into the minds of the sleeping) was followed by "the great Economic Collapse," creating a crisis condition, in which "there was a choice between World Control and destruction. Between Stability and ..." (36). While the ellipsis here is in the text, so that the alternative to stability is not identified, it is clear from the context (and the bulk of the text) that the alternative is not simply instability, but possibly socialism. The New World society that grows out of this crisis is certainly devoted to stability, designed to eradicate all possible sources of disruption in the placid status quo. But it is a particularly capitalist form of stability that places a strong emphasis on the new—as long as "new" means new consumer goods and not new ideas or possibly new forms of social and political organization. Later in the text, World Controller Mustapha Mond attributes the conditions that led to the war to an unrestrained quest for new knowledge in science and new expressions of truth and beauty in art and literature, leading to an ongoing quest for the more and the better that made stability impossible. But Mond goes on, "What's the point of truth or beauty or knowledge when the anthrax bombs are popping around you? That was when science first began to be controlled—after the Nine Years' War. People were ready to have even their appetites controlled for them. Anything for a quiet life" (175).

Control and stability, then, are the chief values of the world society of *Brave New World*, and virtually every aspect of this society has been designed in the interest of supporting these values. Perhaps the most obvious way this society seeks to ensure stability is to prevent any sort of emotional upsets in individual citizens, largely by suppressing their ability or opportunity to experience strong emotions at all. The citizens are, in fact, kept pacified through an early version of what, in the 1960s, would become a mantra of the counterculture: "sex, drugs, and rock and roll." Citizens are encouraged to engage in complete sexual promiscuity, pursuing superficial, recreational sex with anyone and everyone who is interested in joining them, no emotional commitments required, or even allowed. Meanwhile, the entire populace is kept stupefied via the drug "soma," which apparently has "all the advantages of Christianity and alcohol; none of their defects" (42). In short, soma provides some of the same function once provided by religion, so that, in this society, the opiate of the masses is, well, an opiate. And, finally, high art and literature, such as Shakespeare, have been banned altogether because they might tend to trigger strong emotions; the citizens of this society are instead bombarded with a constant barrage of mindless, thoroughly commodified works of popular culture, even in their sleep. As Mond puts it, "You've got to choose between happiness and what people used to call high art. We've sacrificed the high art. We have the feelies and the scent organ instead" (169). Indeed, the citizens of this society apparently have access to a whole range of entertainment media, including radio and television, in addition to high-tech multimedia presentations, such as the "feelies," or "feeling pictures," which add touch, taste, and smell to the sight and sound of normal movies. Major organs of the world government (the various Bureaux of Propaganda, employing techniques developed in the College of Emotional Engineering) are devoted entirely to producing an endless stream of mindless popular culture for these various media, ensuring that there will never be a shortage of new material, though of course the "new" material will be pretty much the same as the old material.

The world of *Feed* is also dominated by pervasive media. While it includes classic science fiction motifs, such as domed cities, flying cars, and recreational trips to the moon, its principal "novum," or technological innovation that sets the world of the text apart from our own real world, is the "feed" of the title, which is essentially little more than a high-tech internet that operates via implants in the brains of individual citizens, allowing them to be directly on-line at all times. The feed is particularly popular with the young, like the teenage narrator/protagonist Titus, who have grown up with it, having known no world in which they were not continually in the feed.

In short, the characters of *Feed* have virtually no experience of reality that is not mediated through the feed, living in the state that Jean Baudrillard described as hyperreality, a key aspect of the postmodern condition, in which "reality" has dissolved altogether, replaced by simulations that are representations, for which there is no original in reality. Thus, ensconced in their domed neighborhoods, the book's young characters observe fabricated elements of nature, such as simulated clouds and simulated sunsets. In one scene, Titus and his girlfriend Violet visit a farm, but this classic back-to-nature outing is anything but: the farm they visit is a "filet mignon" farm, where the "fields" are covered with truly grotesque vast waves of artificially-grown filet mignon (beneath a sky of artificial clouds), in which errors in genetic coding occasionally lead to the anomalous (and grotesque) growth of actual organs, like eyes or hearts, sprouting from the meat (144).

The official popular culture of Huxley's dystopian society is produced by a massive "Culture Industry" of the kind described by Horkheimer and Adorno as a key element of modern capitalist societies. But the disposable and interchangeable nature of the artifacts produced by the Culture Industry of *Brave New World* actually goes beyond what is described by Horkheimer and Adorno, extending into the realm of the postmodern as described by Jameson, who notes that "what has happened today is that aesthetic production today has become integrated into commodity production generally" (4). For Jameson, postmodern art represents the complete triumph of commodification in the aesthetic realm, reducing works of art to the status of pure commodity. Meanwhile, the emphasis on suppression of feeling that informs not only the productions of the Culture Industry, but also social attitudes toward sex and drugs in this society, corresponds quite closely to the notion of the "waning of affect" that Jameson sees as a central consequence of life in the postmodern world, where a general flattening of experience and a fragmentation of the subject make deep feelings of any kind more and more difficult (10).

The oppressive future America of *Feed* also depends heavily, for its functioning, on a continual stream of popular culture, this time supplied by the feed. Actually, the feed, like our own internet, seems to have four basic functions. First (and the way it most resembles the popular culture of Huxley's World Society), it pumps a never-ending stream of entertainment alternatives into the brains of consumers, helping to distract them from the overwhelming economic and environmental crisis that surrounds them. This mindless entertainment works, like the products of Horkheimer and Adorno's Culture Industry, essentially to pacify and stupefy individual consumers—though it should also be noted that it is extended into a drug-like experience analogous to Huxley's soma, in which specialized sites are designed to disrupt normal brain functioning, sending the user into a state of "mal." Second, the feed provides an unprecedented consumer experience, providing consumers with an endless array of advertisements, customized just for them, that help to direct them to various shopping sites where they can make purchases with the flick of a brainwave, as it were. Third, the feed does have educational applications and is heavily used in the privatized schools that pass for an educational system in this future world, though these applications operate more in a mode of indoctrination than true education, much like the hypnopaedic instruction in *Brave New World*. Finally, perhaps the most forward-looking aspect of the feed in Anderson's text is its advanced use of social networking (in a book published two years before the founding of Facebook). Indeed, Titus, the book's teenage narrator/protagonist, is constantly on-line with his friends, "chatting each other" and sharing virtually all of their experiences in real time. Unfortunately, this experience seems, rather than furthering a genuine sense of community, to act more as a suppression of individualism, making all of the book's teenage characters tend to look and act alike, which, of course, furthers the purposes of consumer capitalism, for which marketing is greatly simplified if individual tastes are highly standardized.

This networking of the very brains of individuals in Anderson's future America in many ways recalls the repeated mantra in *Brave New World* that "everybody belongs to every one else," though the particularly possessive wording in Huxley's case makes it clear that this interconnection among individuals constitutes not so much a genuine community of mutually-committed subject as it does a thorough commodification, in which each individual has been reduced to the status of an object, interchangeable not in the sense that each is equally valuable and has equal rights, but in the way that all commodities are interchangeable. Consumerism, of course, is as crucial to the world society of *Brave New World* as it is to the future America of *Feed*. The economy of Huxley's desire-driven society is dependent upon the constant urge of individuals to consume, not only soma, songs, and each other, but a whole variety of manufactured consumer goods. For example, all recreational activities in this society are designed to require elaborate equipment that must be frequently replaced, thus increasing consumption. Thus, "the Controllers won't approve of any new game unless it can be shown that it requires at least as much apparatus as the most complicated of existing games" (21). Moreover, one of the many advertising-style slogans that govern this society is "ending is better than mending" (37). When an item breaks or becomes worn, consumers are urged to throw it away and buy a (presumably fancier and more expensive) replacement, thus stimulating consumption. However, the rulers of this society have learned a great deal from the mistakes of the past, realizing that they must encourage consumption through subtle means because the "conscription of consumption" by which "every man, woman and child [would be] compelled to consume so much a year" would lead to nothing but "conscientious objection on an enormous scale. Anything not to consume. Back to nature" (37). Thus, rather than being forced to buy, say, new clothes, individuals are treated to a nightly dose of hypnopaedic conditioning that simply encourages them to *want* to buy new clothes, including such repeated phrases as "I love new clothes, I love new clothes" (40).

Thanks to the technological resources of the feed, the society of Anderson's book has taken this sort of stimulation to consume to a whole new level, as Titus and his friends experience a world, in which their very brains are filled with advertisements at all times. Thus, in one telling scene, Titus, in a bout of teenage angst, rebels against the world around him in the only way he can imagine— not by refusing the imperative to consumer, but by consuming even more. Distraught over the impending death of Violet (essentially at the hands of the feed) he undergoes a seeming moment of rebellion, when he frantically strips off all his clothes, as if to rid himself of the trappings of consumerism. But, with nothing else left to do, he then engages in an on-line shopping binge by excessive shopping for *more* clothes. When the feed points him toward a sale at an on-line site called "Multitude," he orders a pair of "draft pants." Finding little satisfaction in the purchase, he orders another pair, then another, all in the same nondescript "slate" color. Then he tracks them through the system via the feed, feeling them moving toward him, as if this is the only way he can gain a sense of agency and control, a sense that, for once the feed is doing his bidding, rather than the reverse (292–93).

As Clare Bradford has noted, in this society "the young are offered consumerism as a substitute for participation in citizenship" (129), so Titus here, frustrated with the status quo, can think of no action to take but to buy things. Titus knows only what the feed tells him to know, so it is no surprise that, in his moment of impotent rage against the feed, he turns simply into more use of the feed, buying pants he doesn't need until his on-line bank account is entirely depleted.

This mode of excess is typical of his generation. The closest they can come to conceiving a teenage prank against the system, for example, occurs when the Coca-Cola company (still thriving in this future world) offers a promotion in which free Cokes are awarded to consumers who mention the product in their everyday conversations, thus making the consumers themselves part of Coke's far-reaching web of advertising. In response, Titus and his friends decide to mention Coke constantly, even if it makes no real sense in their conversations, so they "decided to take them for some meg ride by all getting together and being, like, *Coke, Coke, Coke, Coke* for about three hours so we'd get a year's supply. It was a chance to rip off the corporations, which we all thought was a funny idea" (158). In short, Titus and his friends maintain enough teenage rebelliousness to want to undermine the corporations that they know dominate their world, but they have insufficient imagination to be able to conceive of any rebellion beyond doing in excess what the corporations actually want them to do.

Of course, points in this Coke-mentioning program are also deducted if the product is mentioned in a negative way or if the consumer says anything positive about Pepsi, apparently still the main rival to Coke, making it clear that the feed works both ways: not only does it virtually direct every thought of its individual participants, but it detects their thoughts and behavior as well, knowing their every move and their every utterance, keeping them under total surveillance at all times. Implanted in the very brains of individual subjects, it is ultimate in panoptic observation and subtle psychological control.

From this point of view, it is significant that Violet, the one member of Titus's circle who actually has some experience of reality that is unmediated by the feed, is the only one who is able to mount even the semblance of a resistance to the feed. After all, she had the feed installed at a relatively late age due to her parents' suspicions of its possible negative consequences, and she continues to have access to information from sources other than the feed because she is home schooled by her professor father, who prefers books to the feed and who attempts to instill in Violet some genuine critical thinking abilities, while maintaining in their home a connection to the past via his collection of physical books and other now-obsolete artifacts of a world gone by. Violet, for example, has even been taught to write with a physical paper and pen, an ability that Titus finds both quaint and amazing.

Neither Violet nor her father, though, is unable to conceive of any genuinely subversive mode of resistance to the feed, just as Bernard Marx, her rough equivalent in Huxley's text, is unable to mount any significant challenge to the powers-that-be in his society. Violet's reluctant parents, for example, realized how disadvantaged she would be by not having a feed implant, and so had one belatedly installed when she was six years old. Subsequently, she does seem more resistant to the feed than her friends, but the best she can come up with as a mode of subversion is to try to confuse the feed's ad-targeting software by visiting sites in which she actually has no interest, so that it cannot accurately calculate what her true interests are. Meanwhile, her parents' delay in having her fitted with a feed implant proves her undoing; after an anti-feed activist hacks the feeds of the teenagers while they are vacationing on the moon, the others eventually recover, but she contracts a fatal disease, apparently because her implant is less integrated with her brain due to the late installation.

If Titus "rebels" against the feed though the excessive purchase of pants, and his friends rebel through excessive promulgation of the advertising of the Coca Cola company, it is also the case that excess in general is the characteristic mode of this consumerist society. Thus, if excessive exploitation of the natural environment has essentially destroyed that environment, driving the characters to live inside protected domes, the society reacts with still more exploitation of nature, as even environmental destruction is turned into a corporate resource. Whales, for example, are nearly extinct, but that just makes them more valuable: a few of them are kept alive in the heavily polluted oceans by supplying them with a "non-organic covering," just so they can be hunted down and killed as an activity designed to promote bonding among members of corporate management teams, as when Titus's father goes on one such "corporate adventure" late in the text, much in the way that the Savage Reservations of *Brave New World* is regarded as an exotic vacation destination, available only to the most privileged citizens of the "civilized world" (280–83).

The father, of course, like other members of the management team, remains blissfully aloof to the obvious allegorical implications of this whale-hunt, in which the wanton destruction of a beautiful and valuable natural resource is carried out purely in the interest of the goals of the corporation, with no attention paid to the larger costs of the enterprise. Nature is there to be used and manipulated for profit, just as the feed-driven education system teaches children that information is there to be used in an instrumental way, without any true understanding or appreciation.

The citizens of the dystopian society of *Brave New World* do not have devices implanted in their brains, but their "education" similarly consists largely of conditioning that is designed not to teach them to think critically, but in fact to teach them not to think at all, instead blindly drifting through their lives as consuming machines, meanwhile working jobs they have literally been designed and manufactured to perform. And these manufactured infants are produced like branded products, given Greek-letter labels to indicate the level of the role they are intended to play in society, from the Alpha + individuals, who are intended to be the society's movers and shakers, to the lowly Epsilons, who are intended to be its lowliest manual laborers. Everybody may "belong to every one else," but clearly, some people belong more than others. Indeed, via the zygote-splitting Bokanovksy process, new citizens can be produced in large batches of absolutely identical infants, but Alphas, produced in lower quantities, stand starkly apart from the mass-produced lower rankings.

The society of *Feed* does not have quite this level of technology for engineering individuals as "hardware," but then it doesn't need such technology because it is so good at manipulating individuals' "software" through the feed. On the other hand, it does seem headed in the direction of *Brave New World*–like genetic manipulation. There is, for example, a considerable amount of research into genetic engineering going on in this society, and individuals can even be produced as clones of famous historical personages, as when one of Titus's friends, Link, apparently turns out to be a clone of Abraham Lincoln, cloned, Titus tells Violet via chat, "from the bloodstains found on Lucy Todd Lincoln's opera cloak" as part of a government experiment, to which his family had access because they are "really old and mega rich" (186).

Violet quickly corrects Titus's identification of "*Mary* Todd Lincoln," but he has little interest in the detail, his education having taught him that such things are not important for individuals to know or remember because it can always be looked up on the feed. Titus recalls a time when his grandparents were kids when the schools were still run largely by the government, but by the time of his generation, these public schools are a thing of the past, replaced by a vast for-profit corporate enterprise that runs the entire educational system as one large School. Moreover, whereas the earlier public schools were concerned with imparting what Titus regards as useless facts, like "*this happened in fourteen ninety-two, da da da da*" (109, Anderson's italics), this new corporate school system "teaches us how the world can be used, like mainly how to use our feeds" (109–10).

This emphasis makes clear both the tendency of this society to see the world as an object to be used (especially by Americans, despite the fact that the inhabitants of the rest of the world seem to be getting increasingly fed up with being used by Americans) and the belief that the main thing that needs to be learned in schools is how to use the feed, because the feed itself will take care of everything else, ensuring that the knowledge individuals have of the world will all be mediated through the feed, giving them virtually no direct unmediated access to reality.

The lack of interest in historical facts expressed here by Titus may seem little different from the attitudes of many teenagers in our own contemporary world—just as the impact of the feed seems to grow out of the projected fears of many parents in our own world that the internet will make their children lazy and stupid, more adept at Googling than at genuine understanding or critical thought. Thus, Titus tells us that parents were initially excited by the prospect that the feed would place a virtually unlimited fund of information literally within the brains of their children. As he notes, "Everyone is supersmart now. You can look things up automatic, like science and history, like if you want to know which battles of the Civil War George Washington fought in and shit" (47).

It is clear from this passage, of course, that, even with easy and constant access to the feed, Titus knows virtually nothing about history—nor does he want to know anything because he prefers to rely on information from the feed, while he, meanwhile, concentrates on its more entertaining aspects. This lack of any real interest in history clearly relates to the loss of historical sense that Jameson sees as a key symptom of the postmodern condition.

Titus and his friends know that the world is collapsing around them, and they themselves even experience lesions and a variety of physical ailments that indicate their reaction to the toxic environment in which they live. But their only way of dealing with this fact is to distract themselves via the feed, keeping themselves entertained, or even drugged, so that they do not have to deal with, or even think about the reality that faces them. The lesions themselves even become fashion statements: this society can turn anything and everything into a marketing opportunity. The one thing Titus and his friends are utterly incapable of doing is conceiving of a project of political action that might lead to genuine historical change. They have, in short, no ability to view their present-day situation as something that will one day be the historical past of a new and different world, displaying precisely the lack of a "perception of the present as history" that Jameson sees as crucial to the postmodern inability to think historically (284). In this sense, they again directly resemble the citizens of Huxley's future world, who have been taught in an even more calculated way that the lessons of the past are useless, that "history is bunk," as Henry Ford, worshipped in this hyper-capitalist society almost as a deity himself, notoriously claimed. Yet Ford epitomized the very attitudes that led the world of *Brave New World* to ruin in the first place, so it is little wonder that relying on his wisdom has produced a post-apocalyptic world that is dystopian, rather than utopian.

Of course, as we all know, those who forget the past are doomed to repeat its mistakes, so it is no surprise that the official vision in *Brave New World* that all problems have been solved is delusional. Huxley's text, if anything, is even more dire as a warning of our possible future than is Anderson's, despite the sense of approaching apocalypse that informs the latter, as opposed to the long-past apocalypse of the former. In any case, both *Brave New World* and *Feed* end on predictably somber notes, as the deaths of John the Savage and of Violet bring no promise of redemption. John, having hanged himself in despair, twists back and forth in the wind, his repeated movement echoing the entrapment of Huxley's new world in a perpetual present. Titus similarly sinks into despair at the side of Violet's deathbed, trying to conceive of a vision of resistance to the feed "set against the backdrop of America in its final days" (297). But then the feed itself kicks in and has the last, apocalyptic word, repeating one of advertising's best-known mantras in a context that makes its message particularly chilling, suggesting little hope for this society: "Everything must go! Everything must go. Everything must go."

Works Cited

Adorno, Theodor W. *The Culture Industry: Selected Essays on Mass Culture*. Ed. J. M. Bernstein. 2nd. ed. London: Routledge, 2001.

Anderson, M. T. *Feed*. Somerville, MA: Candlewick P, 2002.

Baudrillard, Jean. *Simulacra and Simulation*. 1981. Trans. Sheila Faria Glaser. Ann Arbor, MI: U of Michigan P, 1995.

Bradford, Clare. "'Everything must go!': Consumerism and Reader Positioning in M. T. Anderson's *Feed*." *Jeunesse: Young People, Texts, Cultures* 2.2 (2010): 128–37.

Combs, Robert. "The Eternal Now of *Brave New World*: Huxley, Joseph Campbell, and *The Perennial Philosophy*." *Huxley's* Brave New World: *Essays*. Jefferson, NC: McFarland, 2008.

Huxley, Thomas. *Brave New World*. 1932. *Brave New World & Brave New World Revisited*. New York: Harper Perennial, 1965.

Jameson, Fredric. *Postmodernism, or, the Cultural Logic of Late Capitalism*. Durham, NC: Duke UP, 1991.

RESOURCES

Chronology of the Life of Aldous Huxley_____

1894	Aldous Leonard Huxley is born in Godalming, Surrey, England, on July 26.
1911	Huxley completes his first (unpublished) novel. An illness (keratitis punctata) leaves him virtually blind for the next two to three years.
1914	Huxley's brother, Noel Trevelyan Huxley, commits suicide while suffering from clinical depression.
1915	Working as a farm laborer at Garsington Manor, home of Lady Ottoline Morrell, Huxley meets a number of important personages, including Maria Nys (a war refugee from Belgium), who would ultimately become his first wife. Huxley also meets the English writer D. H. Lawrence, who would become a long-time friend. Huxley becomes a regular visitor to the estate over the next several years, meeting many prominent individuals there.
1916	While a student at Balliol College, Oxford, Huxley edits *Oxford Poetry*; he graduates with a BA in English literature. He publishes a volume of his own poetry.
1917	Huxley is briefly employed in a clerical position, acquiring provisions for the British Air Ministry in London. In September, he begins a period teaching French at Eton College (a subject he taught because English literature, for which he was better qualified, was not included in the curriculum there).
1919	At the urging of Middleton Murry, who was reorganizing the venerable literary journal, Huxley

joins the staff of *Athenaeum*. Huxley marries Maria Nys.

1920	Huxley's son, Matthew, is born.
1921	Huxley leaves his position at *Athenaeum*. His first published novel, *Crome Yellow*, appears to a positive critical response.
1923	Huxley's second published novel, *Antic Hay*, is also a success. Aldous and his family move to the villa Castel Montici, in Florence Italy, where they will reside for much of the next two years.
1925	*Those Barren Leaves* is published. The Huxleys embark on an Asian tour that will take them to India and China.
1928	*Point Counter Point* is published. The book will become Huxley's first big financial success as a writer.
1929	Huxley sees his first talking picture in Paris. He is not impressed by this example of "standardized amusement."
1930	*This Way to Paradise*, a stage adaptation of *Point Counter Point*, is performed in London. D. H. Lawrence dies, with the Huxleys present. The Huxleys buy a farmhouse in Sanary-sur-Mer, in southeastern France, where Aldous will write *Brave New World*.
1931	Huxley's play, *The World of Light*, opens in London on March 30, but closes after a short run, despite glowing reviews.
1932	*Brave New World* is published. Huxley edits the published edition of *The Letters of D. H. Lawrence*.

| 1933 | In January, Adolf Hitler becomes chancellor of Germany. The Huxleys take a five-month trip to the Americas, visiting the West Indies, Guatemala, and Mexico. Sanary begins to be flooded with German exiles, many of them artists and writers, making Huxley more aware of conditions in Germany. |

| 1934 | Huxley's American tour results in a travel book, *Beyond the Mexique Bay*. |

| 1936 | *Eyeless in Gaza* published after a long struggle. It was the book Huxley had the most difficulty writing. Tensions worsen in Europe as the Spanish Civil War begins, signaling Nazi/Fascist expansionism. |

| 1937 | With conditions continuing to worsen in Europe, the Huxleys relocate to the US, where Huxley soon began to try his hand at screenwriting, despite his frequently expressed antagonism toward the film industry. His first script, *Success*, is a satire of the advertising industry, but would never be produced. |

| 1938 | The Huxleys settle in Hollywood. The Marx Brothers soon become among their closest acquaintances there. Under the influence of another acquaintance, Gerald Heard, Huxley begins to develop a serious interest in Eastern philosophy, especially Vedanta and the Indian-born mystic philosopher Jiddu Krishnamurti. Huxley is engaged to write the screenplay for a high-profile biopic of Marie Curie; the film would be made, though Huxley's script was discarded. |

| 1939 | Huxley meets Margaret Corbett, who introduces him to the work of Dr. W. H. Bates, the developer of a controversial method of vision improvement. Huxley would eventually try the method and write a book (*The Art of Seeing*) about his success with it. Huxley's forty- |

fifth birthday party is attended by such luminaries as Charlie Chaplin, Orson Welles, Helen Hayes, and English writer Christopher Isherwood, who would become a close associate. *After Many a Summer* is published, marking a successful return to novel-writing for Huxley. World War II begins in Europe.

1940	A screen adaptation of Jane Austen's *Pride and Prejudice*, starring Greer Garson and Laurence Olivier, is released with a screenplay co-written by Huxley. Huxley and Heard become acquainted with the Swami Prabhavananda, leader of the Vedanta Society of Southern California.
1941	Huxley writes the first of his forty-eight articles for *Vedanta and the West*, the journal of the Vedanta Society. The U.S. enters World War II at the end of the year.
1942	*The Art of Seeing* is published.
1944	A novel, *Time Must Have a Stop*, is published. Huxley gets his second screenwriting credit for a film adaptation of *Jane Eyre*. Huxley writes the introduction to the Vedanta Society's edition of *Bhagavad Gita*, co-edited by Isherwood.
1945	Huxley publishes *The Perennial Philosophy*, intended to introduce the public to the spiritualist ideas he had been studying for the past several years. Huxley is engaged by Disney to work on the script for the film adaptation of *Alice in Wonderland*. The film would not be released until 1951, with Huxley not among more than a dozen writers who got screen credit. World War II ends.
1946	Huxley publishes a book entitled *Science, Liberty and Peace*, expressing concern that the advancement of

science has had the unintended social consequence of concentrating power in the hands of the few. Many find his attacks on universal free public education in a book a bit disturbing. Huxley begins work on a screen adaptation of his short story "The Gioconda Smile." It would eventually be released in 1948 as *A Woman's Vengeance.*

Huxley drives with Maria from California to New York, leaving California for the first time since 1938. Concerned that the progress of the world was making his original warnings more relevant than ever, Huxley writes a new foreword for a re-issue of *Brave New World.*

1948	*Ape and Essence* becomes Huxley's second dystopian novel. The Huxleys sail to Europe in mid-June, their first trip there since leaving in 1937. Huxley's adaptation of "The Gioconda Smile" is a success on the London stage. *A Woman's Vengeance* is Huxley's third (and last) screenplay credit.
1949	Orwell's *Nineteen Eighty-Four* is published.
1950	Huxley travels to Italy to gather material for a historical novel with which he was struggling and which he would never complete. Huxley begins to dabble with L. Ron Hubbard's Dianetics at the end of the year.
1952	Maria is diagnosed with a malignant tumor. Huxley publishes *The Devils of Loudun*, a non-fiction novel about witchcraft and demonic possession in seventeenth-century France. Some felt that the story of the persecution of a priest accused of witchcraft was an allegory of the persecution of communist sympathizers in the contemporary U.S., casting suspicion on Huxley amid the anticommunist hysteria that was sweeping America.

1953	An FBI investigation of Huxley concludes that he is not a communist sympathizer. Huxley begins to experiment with mescaline, an event he would document the next year in *The Doors of Perception*, which would become a popular text of the 1960s drug culture. Huxley's pacifism continues to cause him to be denied American citizenship. The Huxleys go on another European trip, which also takes them to Cairo and Beirut.
1955	*The Genius and the Goddess* is published. Maria Huxley dies of breast cancer. Long troubled by an inability to retrieve certain childhood memories, Huxley first experiments with LSD, in the hope that it will help with the memory retrieval.
1956	Huxley marries the former Laura Archera, an Italian-born violinist and psychologist.
1957	A Broadway adaptation of *The Genius and the Goddess* closes after five nights.
1958	Huxley appears on American television in an interview with television journalist Mike Wallace. Huxley publishes *Brave New World Revisited*, examining the progress of the world in the years since the publication of *Brave New World*.
1960	Huxley is diagnosed with cancer of the tongue, which soon spreads. Huxley spends nine weeks as a visiting professor at the Massachusetts Institute of Technology, lecturing on the topic of "human nature."
1961	A fire destroys the Huxley home and many of his personal papers, including his personal library with his own book margin annotations. The unfinished manuscript of *Island*, however, is saved. During a trip

to England, Huxley is again interviewed for television, this time by John Chandos of the BBC.

1962	Huxley's last novel, *Island*, is published. Huxley spends the first months of the year as a visiting Ford Professor at the University of California at Berkeley. Much of the year is dominated by cancer treatments and by work on Huxley's last book, *Literature and Science*, published in 1963.
1963	A television adaptation of "The Gioconda Smile" is broadcast in Australia. Huxley dies on November 22, the day U.S. President John F. Kennedy is assassinated.
1965	Harper's popular paperback omnibus edition of *Brave New World & Brave New World Revisited* is published. It will become the single most widely read and referenced edition of Huxley's best-known novel.
1967	A British television adaptation of *After Many a Summer* is broadcast on BBC.
1968	Laura Huxley's memoir of life with Huxley, *This Timeless Moment: A Personal View of Aldous Huxley*, is published. A BBC mini-series adaptation of *Point Counter Point* is broadcast.
1971	Ken Russel's *The Devils*, a film adaptation of *The Devils of Loudun*, is released.
1980	An American television adaptation of *Brave New World* is broadcast on NBC on March 7, written by Doran William Cannon and directed by Bert Brinckerhoff.
1998	A particularly loose television adaptation of *Brave New World* is broadcast on NBC, notably featuring Leonard Nimoy as Mustapha Mond. The editorial board of the Modern Library names *Brave New World* as number

five on its list of the greatest novels of the twentieth century; their readers' poll names it number eighteen. The board poll names *Point Counter Point* number forty-four.

Works by Aldous Huxley

Novels

Crome Yellow, 1921

Antic Hay, 1923

Those Barren Leaves, 1925

Point Counter Point, 1928

Brave New World, 1932

Eyeless in Gaza, 1936

After Many a Summer, 1939

Time Must Have a Stop, 1944

Ape and Essence, 1948

The Genius and the Goddess, 1955

Island, 1962

Short Story Collections

Limbo, 1920

Mortal Coils, 1922

Little Mexican [U.S. title: *Young Archimedes*], 1924

Two or Three Graces, 1926

Brief Candles, 1930

Jacob's Hands: A Fable, discovered in 1997 [co-written with Christopher Isherwood]

Collected Short Stories, 1944

Poetry Collections

Oxford Poetry (editor), 1916

The Burning Wheel, 1916

Jonah, 1917

The Defeat of Youth and Other Poems, 1918

Leda, 1920

Selected Poems, 1925

Arabia Infelix and Other Poems, 1929

The Cicadas and Other Poems, 1931

Collected Poems 1971, posthumous

Essay Collections and Nonfiction

On the Margin, 1923

Along the Road, 1925

Essays New and Old, 1926

Proper Studies, 1927

Do What You Will, 1929

Vulgarity in Literature, 1930

Music at Night, 1931

Texts and Pretexts, 1932

The Olive Tree and Other Essays, 1936

Ends and Means, 1937

Words and Their Meanings, 1940

The Art of Seeing, 1942

The Perennial Philosophy, 1945

Science, Liberty and Peace, 1946

Themes and Variations, 1950

The Doors of Perception, 1954

Heaven and Hell, 1956

Adonis and the Alphabet [in U.S. *Tomorrow and Tomorrow and Tomorrow*], 1956

Collected Essays, 1958

Brave New World Revisited, 1958

Literature and Science, 1963

Moksha: Writings on Psychedelics and the Visionary Experience 1931–63, 1977

The Human Situation: Lectures at Santa Barbara, 1959, 1977

Travel Books

Along The Road: Notes and Essays of a Tourist, 1925

Jesting Pilate: The Diary of a Journey, 1926

Beyond the Mexique Bay: A Traveller's Journey, 1934

Other

Pacifism and Philosophy, 1936

An Encyclopedia of Pacifism (editor), 1937

Grey Eminence, 1941

The Devils of Loudun, 1953

The Politics of Ecology, 1962

Selected Letters, 2007

Bibliography

Adorno, Theodor W. "Aldous Huxley and Utopia." *Prisms*. 1967. Trans. Samuel and Shierry Weber. Cambridge, MA: MIT Press, 1983.

Baker, Robert S. *Brave New World: History, Science, and Dystopia*. Boston: Twayne, 1990.

Bedford, Sybille. *Aldous Huxley*. New York: Harper & Row, 1974.

Bloom, Harold, ed. *Aldous Huxley's* Brave New World. New York: Chelsea House, 1996.

Booker, M. Keith. *The Dystopian Impulse in Modern Literature: Fiction as Social Criticism*. Westport, CT: Greenwood, 1994.

Bryfonski, Dedria. *Bioethics in Aldous Huxley's* Brave New World. Farmington Hills, MI: Greenhaven Press, 2010.

Buchanan, Bradley W. "Oedipus in Dystopia: Freud and Lawrence in Aldous Huxley's *Brave New World*." *Journal of Modern Literature* 25.3–4 (Summer 2002): 75–89.

Claeys, Gregory. "The Origins of Utopia: Wells, Huxley and Orwell." *The Cambridge Companion to Utopian Literature*. Ed. Gregory Claeys. Cambridge, UK: Cambridge UP, 2010. 107–31.

Clark, Walter H. "Drugs and Utopia/Dystopia." *Utopia/Dystopia?* Ed. Peyton Richter. Cambridge, MA: Schenkman, 1975. 109–23.

Congdon, Brad. "'Community, Identity, Stability': The Scientific Society and the Future of Religion in Aldous Huxley's *Brave New World*." *English Studies in Canada* 37.3–4 (Sept.–Dec. 2011): 83–105.

De Koster, Katie, ed. *Readings on* Brave New World. San Diego, CA: Greenhaven Press, Inc., 1999.

Dasgupta, Sanjukta. "Geographies and Gender: Ideological Shifts in *Brave New World* and *Island*." *Aldous Huxley Annual* 8 (2008): 207–219.

Deery, June. "Technology and Gender in Aldous Huxley's Alternative (?) Worlds." *Extrapolation: a Journal of Science Fiction and Fantasy* 33.3 (1992): 258–273.

Diken, Bulent. "Huxley's Brave New World—And Ours." *Journal for Cultural Research* 15.2 (Apr. 2011): 153–72.

Dunaway, David King. *Huxley in Hollywood*. New York: Harper & Row, 1989.

Fietz, Lothar. "Myth, History, and Utopianism: Ideology and Ideology Criticism in Aldous Huxley's Work." *Aldous Huxley Annual: A Journal of Twentieth-Century Thought and Beyond* 6 (2006): 135–47.

Firchow, Peter. *Aldous Huxley: Satirist and Novelist*. Minneapolis: U of Minnesota P, 1972.

———. *The End of Utopia: A Study of Aldous Huxley's* Brave New World. Lewisburg, PA: Bucknell UP, 1984.

———. Science and Conscience in Huxley's *Brave New World. Contemporary Literature*. 16.3 (Summer 1975): 301–16.

———. "Wells and Lawrence in Huxley's *Brave New World.*" *Journal of Modern Literature* 5.2 (April 1976): 260–78.

Frost, Laura. "Huxley's Feelies: The Cinema of Sensation in *Brave New World.*" *Twentieth-Century Literature* 52.4 (Winter 2006): 443–473.

Hickman, John. "When Science Fiction Writers Used Fictional Drugs: Rise and Fall of the Twentieth-Century Drug Dystopia." *Utopian Studies: Journal of the Society for Utopian Studies* 20.1 (2009): 141–70.

Horan, Thomas. "Revolutions from the Waist Downwards: Desire as Rebellion in Yevgeny Zamyatin's *We*, George Orwell's *1984*, and Aldous Huxley's *Brave New World.*" *Extrapolation: A Journal of Science Fiction and Fantasy* 48.2 (Summer 2007): 314–39.

Huxley, Aldous. *Brave New World Revisited*. New York: Harper & Row, 1965.

Huxley, Laura Archera. *This Timeless Moment*. New York: Farrar, Straus & Giroux, 1968.

Izzo, David Garrett and Kim Kirkpatrick, eds. *Huxley's* Brave New World: *Essays*. Jefferson, NC: McFarland, 2008.

Klein, Michael. "Modern Myths: Science Fiction in the Age of Technology." *Frontiers of Cyberspace*. Ed. Daniel Riha. Amsterdam, Netherlands: Rodopi; 2012. 255–79.

Kumar, Krishan. *Utopia and Anti-Utopia in Modern Times*. Oxford, UK: Blackwell, 1987.

March, Christie. "A Dystopic View of Gender in Aldous Huxley's Brave New World (1932)." *Women in Literature: Reading through the Lens of Gender*. Ed. Jerilyn Fisher & Ellen S. Silber. Westport, CT: Greenwood Press, 2003. 53–55.

Matter, William. "On *Brave New World*." *No Place Else: Explorations in Utopian and Dystopian Fiction.* Ed. Eric S. Rabkin, Martin H. Greenberg, and Joseph D. Olander. Carbondale, IL: Southern Illinois UP, 1983. 94–109.

McQuillan, Gene. "The Politics of Allusion: *Brave New World* and the Debates About Biotechnologies." *Studies in the Humanities* 33.1 (June 2006): 79–100.

Meckier, Jerome. *Aldous Huxley: Satire and Structure.* London: Chatto & Windus, 1969.

———. "Huxley's Americanization of the *Brave New World* Typescript." *Twentieth-Century Literature* 48.4 (Winter 2002): 427–460.

———. "Onomastic Satire: Names and Naming in *Brave New World*." *Aldous Huxley Annual.* 3 (2003): 155–198.

Moylan, Tom. *Demand the Impossible: Science Fiction and the Utopian Imagination.* London: Methuen, 1986.

———. *Scraps of the Untainted Sky: Science Fiction, Utopia, Dystopia.* Boulder, CO: Westview Press, 2000.

Moylan, Tom and Raffaella Baccolini, eds. *Dark Horizons: Science Fiction and the Dystopian Imagination.* London: Routledge, 2003.

Pintér, Károly. *The Anatomy of Utopia: Narration, Estrangement and Ambiguity in More, Wells, Huxley and Clarke.* Jefferson, NC: McFarland, 2010.

Posner, Richard A. "Orwell versus Huxley: Economics, Technology, Privacy, and Satire." *On* Nineteen Eighty-Four*: Orwell and Our Future.* Eds. Abbott Gleason, Jack Goldsmith, and Martha C. Nussbaum. Princeton, NJ: Princeton UP, 2005. 183–211.

Rabinovitch, Valery. "The Critical Dialogue between *Brave New World* and *Island*." *Aldous Huxley Annual: A Journal of Twentieth-Century Thought and Beyond,* 9 (2009): 183–90.

Sawyer, Dana. "Brave New World-View: Aldous Huxley, Environmental Prophet." *Aldous Huxley Annual: A Journal of Twentieth-Century Thought and Beyond* 8 (2008): 221–38.

Sawyer, Dana. *Aldous Huxley: A Biography.* New York: Crossroad Publishing, 2002.

Seed, David. "Aldous Huxley: *Brave New World*." *A Companion to Science Fiction* Ed. David Seed. Malden, MA: Blackwell, 2005. 477–88.

Smith, Brian. "Beyond Totalitarianism: Hannah Arendt and Aldous Huxley's *Brave New World*." *Aldous Huxley Annual: A Journal of Twentieth-Century Thought and Beyond* 6 (2006): 77–104.

―――. "Haec Fabula Docet: Anti-Essentialism and Freedom in Aldous Huxley's *Brave New World*." *Philosophy and Literature* 35.2 (October 2011): 348–59.

―――. "Jeffersonian Reminders: Aldous Huxley on Property, Happiness, and Freedom." *Aldous Huxley Annual: A Journal of Twentieth-Century Thought and Beyond* 9 (2009): 205–27.

Smith, Grover, ed. *The Letters of Aldous Huxley*. New York: Harper & Row, 1969.

Texter, Douglas. "All the World a School: The School as Metaphor for Oppression in *Brave New World* and *Nineteen Eighty-Four*." *Foundation: The International Review of Science Fiction* 37 (103) (Summer 2008): 73–95.

Wiener, Diane. "Mentalism, Disability Rights, and Modern Eugenics in a 'Brave New World.'" *Disability & Society* 24.5 (2009): 599–610.

Woodcock, George. *Dawn and the Darkest Hour: A Study of Aldous Huxley*. Montreal, New York, London: Black Rose Books, 2007.

About the Editor

M. Keith Booker is professor of English and director of the comparative literature and cultural studies program at the University of Arkansas in Fayetteville. He has written or edited numerous articles and more than forty books on literature, literary theory, and modern culture. His publications include *The Dystopian Impulse in Modern Literature: Fiction as Social Criticism* (1994); *Dystopian Literature: A Theory and Research Guide* (1994); *Monsters, Mushroom Clouds, and the Cold War: American Science Fiction and the Roots of Postmodernism, 1946–1964* (2001), and *The Science Fiction Handbook* (2009, co-written with Anne-Marie Thomas). He is the editor of the volumes *Dystopia* (2013) and *Contemporary Speculative Fiction* (2013) in Salem Press' "Critical Insights" book series.

Contributors ⎯⎯⎯⎯⎯⎯⎯⎯⎯⎯⎯⎯⎯⎯⎯⎯⎯⎯⎯⎯

Jackson Ayres is assistant professor of English at Texas A&M University—San Antonio, where he teaches modern and contemporary British literature. He has published articles on twentieth-century British drama, contemporary British fiction, and the films of Orson Welles. His current book project explores post-1945 British fiction in light of the era's political and cultural anxieties over totalitarianism and totalization.

M. Keith Booker is professor of English and director of the comparative literature and cultural studies program at the University of Arkansas in Fayetteville. He has written or edited numerous articles and more than forty books on literature, literary theory, and modern culture. His publications include *The Dystopian Impulse in Modern Literature: Fiction as Social Criticism* (1994); *Dystopian Literature: A Theory and Research Guide* (1994); *Monsters, Mushroom Clouds, and the Cold War: American Science Fiction and the Roots of Postmodernism, 1946–1964* (2001); and *The Science Fiction Handbook* (2009, co-written with Anne-Marie Thomas). He is the editor of the volumes *Dystopia* (2013) and *Contemporary Speculative Fiction* (2013) in Salem Press' "Critical Insights" book series.

Richard Carr is a lecturer in history at Anglia Ruskin University, UK, and has served as a By-Fellow at Churchill College, University of Cambridge. He has published widely on twentieth-century British politics, including the monograph, *Veteran MPs and Conservative Politics in the Aftermath of the Great War* (2013), and the co-edited volume, *The Foundations of the British Conservative Party* (2013). His articles range from eugenics in the 1920s to diplomacy in the 1930s. He will publish a book on One Nation politics in 2014 and is currently researching a book on Charlie Chaplin.

Gregory Claeys is professor of history of political thought at Royal Holloway, University of London. He is the author of *Machinery, Money and the Millennium: From Moral Economy to Socialism* (Princeton University Press, 1987), *Citizens and Saints: Politics and Anti-Politics in Early British Socialism* (Cambridge University Press, 1989), *The French Revolution Debate in Britain (*Palgrave Macmillan, 2007), *Imperial*

Sceptics: British Critics of Empire, 1850–1920 (Cambridge University Press, 2010), *Searching for Utopia: The History of an Idea* (Thames & Hudson, 2011; German, Spanish, Portuguese, Japanese editions), and *Mill and Paternalism* (Cambridge University Press, 2013). He has edited *The Cambridge Companion to Utopian Literature* (Cambridge University Press, 2010) and co-edited, with Gareth Stedman Jones, *The Cambridge History of Nineteenth-Century Political Thought* (Cambridge University Press, 2011), as well as some fifty volumes of primary sources. His current research is on the concept and historical manifestations of dystopia.

Gerardo Del Guercio has taught at the Royal Military College of Canada (St-Jean) and Collège Jean-de-Brébeuf. *His books include The Fugitive Slave Law in The Life of Frederick Douglass, an American Slave and Harriet Beecher Stowe's Uncle Tom's Cabin: An American Society Transforms Its Culture* (Edwin Mellen, 2013) and *Perspectives on Edgar Allan Poe: Collected Essays* (Lehigh University Press). His essays have been published by *Southern Studies* and Oxford University Press.

Nicole Fares is an MFA student in translation at the University of Arkansas in Fayetteville.

Alexander Charles Oliver Hall is a professor of literary and cultural studies currently stationed in the department of English at Kent State University in Kent, Ohio. He has been active in the Society for Utopian Studies as the editor of its newsletter, *Utopus Discovered*, and his publications usually fall within that field, dealing particularly with dystopian literature, film, and other cultural products.

Bradley W. Hart is a lecturer at California State University, Fresno. He has written extensively on interwar Britain, the international eugenics movement, and the British far right. In 2013, he co-edited a volume entitled *Foundations of the British Conservative Party* and is currently working on a biography of an interwar British anthropologist, who cultivated extensive ties with the Third Reich.

Thomas Horan is an assistant professor in the department of English at The Citadel and specializes in twentieth-century British literature and modern drama.

Josephine A. McQuail received a PhD from the University of California at Berkeley. A professor at Tennessee Technological University, she has had work appear in journals, such as *Blake: An Illustrated Quarterly; The Blake Journal; The New Review of Children's Literature and Librarianship*; and *Modern Language Studies*; and in collections, such as *Gissing and the City* and *Bloom's Literary Themes*. Formerly executive director of the Northeast Modern Language Association (2003–2006), she currently serves in the American Association of University Professors, United Campus Workers, and the Tennessee Education Association. Her current research interests include William Blake, James Joyce, and New Zealand writer Janet Frame.

Katherine Toy Miller (pen name M. Kaat Toy) has a PhD in English (creative writing–fiction) from Florida State University and an MFA in creative writing (fiction) from the University of Arizona. She publishes and presents scholarly narratives on D. H. and Frieda Lawrence, Aldous Huxley, and Georgia O'Keeffe, all mutual friends who lived in Taos, New Mexico, Miller's own permanent residence. She has also published a prose poem chapbook, *In a Cosmic Egg* (2012), at Finishing Line Press; a flash fiction book, *Disturbed Sleep* (2013), at FutureCycle Press; novel selections; short stories; flash fiction; prose poetry; creative nonfiction; and journalism.

Robert Wilson teaches at Lindsey Wilson College in Kentucky and is currently finishing his dissertation on the picaresque in contemporary science fiction.

Sean A. Witters is lecturer in the department of English at the University of Vermont, where he teaches courses in literary and critical theory, race and ethnic literature, dystopian fiction, and American literature. He received his PhD in English and American literature from Brandeis University. His doctoral thesis explores the interaction between American authors and the "logic of the brand" in the mid-twentieth century literary marketplace. He has published and presented on Aldous Huxley, Mary McCarthy, James Baldwin, and J.D. Salinger. He is currently writing a study of the emergence of the "addict" in fiction, culture, and medicine.

Index

Dark Horizons 167, 180, 245
Darwin, Charles 17, 111, 112
Darwin, Erasmus 140, 150
Darwinian theory 114
Darwin's Bulldog 17, 112
Dasenbrock, Reed Way 76
Dasgupta, Sanjukta 61
*Dawn and the Darkest Hour: A
Study of Aldous Huxley* 151,
246
Death Comes for the Archbishop
154
*Decade of Progress in Eugenics:
Scientific Papers of
the Third International
Congress of Eugenics Held
at American Museum of
Natural History New York,
August 21–23, 1932, A* 121
Deery, June 56, 128
Defence of the Realm Act, The 27
de Koster, Katie 70
Del Guercio, Gerardo v, vii, 40,
250
Deltas 108, 109, 146
democracy 29, 31, 32, 37, 92, 94,
105
despotism 106
deterritorialization 209
*D.H. Lawrence: Dying Game,
1922–1930* 53
Dick, Philip K. 210
dictatorship 31, 36, 49, 94, 95, 99,
103, 104, 106, 119
Die Neue Rundschau 48, 53
Dilworth, Leah 156
Dionysian sacrifice 68

Director of Hatcheries and
Conditioning, The 57, 108,
123, 168, 169, 173
Director of the Hatcheries and
Conditioning Centre 144
discipline 96, 104, 123, 131, 199,
200, 202, 203, 209
Discipline and Punish 129, 136,
200, 202, 212
*Discovery of Fetal Alcohol
Syndrome, The* 151
Disneyization 190, 196
Dispossessed, The 127, 136
Disraeli, Benjamin 33
District 12 210
Doors of Perception, The 41, 236,
240
Dos Passos 208
Dostoyevsky, Fyodor 43
Downs, Elizabeth 49, 53
Drabble, Margaret 78
drugs 9, 10, 21, 96, 133, 216, 218
Duke Law Journal 136
Duke of Windsor 33
Dullea, Keir 170
Dunaway, David King 150, 243
dystopia 16, 52, 68, 70, 107, 150,
180, 213, 243, 244, 245,
247, 249
dystopian fiction vi, 214, 215,
217, 219, 221, 223, 225,
227, 245
*Dystopian Impulse in Modern
Literature, The* 16, 76, 87,
106, 136, 243, 247, 249
Dystopian Literature 247, 249
dystopian novel xi, 4, 74, 77, 235
dystopian repression 14
dystopian satire 20